Democratization in Late Twentieth-Century Africa

Recent Titles in
Contributions in Political Science

Ethnoregional Conflict in Democracies: Mostly Ballots, Rarely Bullets
Saul Newman

Neocolonialism American Style, 1960–2000
William H. Blanchard

Government Structures in the U.S.A. and the Sovereign States of the Former U.S.S.R.:
Power Allocation Among Central, Regional, and Local Governments
James E. Hickey, Jr. and Alexej Ugrinsky, editors

Roman Catholicism and Political Form
Carl Schmitt
Translated and annotated by G. L. Ulmen

International Theory: To the Brink and Beyond
Andrew P. Dunne

To Sheathe the Sword: Civil-Military Relations in the Quest for Democracy
John P. Lovell and David E. Albright, editors

President Reagan and the World
Eric J. Schmertz, Natalie Datlof, and Alexej Ugrinsky, editors

Ronald Reagan's America
Eric J. Schmertz, Natalie Datlof, and Alexej Ugrinsky, editors

Germany for the Germans? The Political Effects of International Migration
Wesley D. Chapin

Out of Russian Orbit: Hungary Gravitates to the West
Andrew Felkay

Ideas of Social Order in the Ancient World
Vilho Harle

Voting Rights and Redistricting in the United States
Mark E. Rush, editor

Democratization in Late Twentieth-Century Africa

Coping with Uncertainty

Edited by
Jean-Germain Gros

Contributions in Political Science, Number 385

Greenwood Press
Westport, Connecticut • London

Library of Congress Cataloging-in-Publication Data

Democratization in late twentieth-century Africa : coping with
   uncertainity / edited by Jean-Germain Gros.
      p.   cm.—(Contributions in political science, ISSN 0147–1066
   ; no. 385)
   Includes bibliographical references and index.
   ISBN 0–313–30793–8 (alk. paper)
   1. Democracy—Africa, Sub-Saharan.   2. Africa, Sub-Saharan—
Politics and government—1960–   3. Post-communism.   I. Gros, Jean-
Germain, 1964–   II. Series.
JQ1879.A15D466   1998
320.967′09′045—dc21   98–14231

British Library Cataloguing in Publication Data is available.

Library of Congress Catalog Card Number: 98–14231
ISBN: 0–313–30793–8
ISSN: 0147–1066

First published in 1998

Greenwood Press, 88 Post Road West, Westport, CT 06881
An imprint of Greenwood Publishing Group, Inc.

Printed in the United States of America

The paper used in this book complies with the
Permanent Paper Standard issued by the National
Information Standards Organization (Z39.48–1984).

10 9 8 7 6 5 4 3 2 1

Contents

Preface   vii

Abbreviations   ix

1. Introduction: Understanding Democratization   1
   Jean-Germain Gros

2. Democratization in Malawi: Its Roots and Prospects   21
   Sam A. Mchombo

3. Cameroon: A Flawed Transition to Democracy   41
   Tatah Mentan

4. Nigeria: Militarization and Perpetual Transition   59
   Julius O. Ihonvbere

5. Democracy, State-Building, and "Nations" in Ethiopia: 1974–95   77
   Kassahun Berhanu

6. Leadership and Democratization: The Case of Tanzania   97
   Jean-Germain Gros

7. Elections and Democratic Transition in Ghana: 1991–96   113
   Kwamina Panford

8. The Irony of Wealth: Democratization in Gabon   129
   Nelson N. Messone and Jean-Germain Gros

Bibliography   147

Index   157

About the Contributors   163

Preface

The genesis of this collaborative effort can be traced to May of 1991, when the editor happened to be in Cameroon at the apogee of popular resistance to the Biya regime. In those days of *villes mortes* (ghost towns) and *conference nationale souveraine* (sovereign national conference), the democratic vortex seemed certain to engulf anyone who dared to stand in its way. But things did not turn out as envisioned by Cameroonian democracy activists. Paul Biya "won" both the 1992 and 1997 presidential elections; he was not alone. Jerry Rawlings of Ghana, who overthrew at least one elected government in 1981 and then brazenly professed his lack of faith in the ballot box, has emerged as one of Africa's most respected "new democrats," having "won" elections in 1992 and 1996. Omar Bongo of Gabon and Daniel arap Moi of Kenya are still standing firm. Of course, the 1990s also have seen the displacement of some of Africa's most entrenched former dictators; the late Kamuzu Banda of Malawi and Mengistu Haile Mariam of Ethiopia are now political relics of a seemingly distant past.

After observing the mixed record of post-Cold War elections and politics in Cameroon and other African countries, I could not resist the temptation to assemble a group of scholars and have them compare and contrast various African cases of transition from unipartyism to multipartyism. The result is this text, which situates political events, including elections, in late twentieth-century Africa in the larger context of democratization. But what is democratization? Why do countries democratize? What factors, both internal and external to African countries, appear to be critical in explaining democratization outcomes; in other words, why success in some cases and setback and stalemate in others? What are the prospects for democracy in sub-Saharan Africa? The pursuit of answers to these questions is what this work is all about. The approach is very straightforward. Following an introductory chapter, seven transition cases are examined: Malawi, Cameroon, Nigeria, Ethiopia, Tanzania, Ghana, and Gabon respectively.

The contributors are, in the main, Africa-born scholars and prodemocracy activists. Three were intimately involved in the struggle for political change in their respective countries. The perspectives of people who know what it is like to face down authoritarianism adds strength to the study by giving it a more trenchant edge. Indeed, there is much to be found here that some might consider iconoclastic, perhaps even heretical. This is good. The pursuit of knowledge requires occasional controversies out of which new insights and wisdom may emerge. It is also salutary that the contributors come from more than one professional discipline: there are five political scientists, one linguist, and one former journalist and radio commentator, now dean of communications studies at Yaoundé University. The diverse nature of the group, combined with the fact that some of its members have been tested for battle, make the work more enjoyable to read than it might otherwise have been.

One institution and several individuals contributed mightily to this manuscript. Honorable mention of each one is necessary, although, in the end, only I the editor and the writers should be held responsible for the ideas expressed herein. The University of Missouri Research Board generously funded part of the project. The chapters on Tanzania and Gabon (written jointly) would not have been possible without financial support from the board. Furthermore, the Department of Political Science at the University of Missouri–St. Louis reduced my spring 1996 teaching load to facilitate the completion of the tedious task of editing. Professor Ho-Won Jeong, who spent 1995–96 as a Theodore Lentz post-doctoral fellow at the University of Missouri–St. Louis was always available for informal one-on-one discussions with me. Professor Ruth Iyob also provided useful advice. Above all, the Africa-based contributors are commended for their participation. Carrying out high-quality research under conditions of scarcity and uncertainty is not easy. Yet they came through, even though on numerous occasions they were on the receiving end of long-distance telephone calls at odd hours and some terse notes, which thinly disguised my impatience.

Abbreviations

ADMARC	Agricultural Development and Marketing Corporation
AFORD	Alliance for Democracy
AFRC	Armed Forces Revolutionary Council
AFRC	Armed Forces Ruling Council
AIDB	Agricultural and Industrial Development Bank
ARC-CNS	Alliance for Change in Cameroon through a Sovereign National Conference
BP	British Petroleum
CCM	*Chama Cha Mapinduzi*
CD	Campaign for Democracy
CDS	Center for Democratic Studies
CFA	*Communauté Financière Africaine*
CNC	Committee for National Consensus
COD	*Coordination de l'Opposition Démocratique*
COR	Council for Ogoni Rights
CPDM	Cameroon People's Democratic Movement
CPP	Convention People's Party
CRC	Constitutional Review Committee
CRTV	Cameroon Radio and Television
CUF	Civic United Front
DPN	Democratic Party of Nigeria
DWM	December Women's Movement
EC	European Community
ECOWAS	Economic Community of West African States
EDU	Ethiopian Democratic Union
EEC	European Economic Community
ELF	Eritrean Liberation Front
EPLF	Eritrean People's Liberation Front
EPRDF	Ethiopian Peoples' Revolutionary Democratic Front

EPRP	Ethiopian People's Revolutionary Party
EU	European Union
FAC	*Forces Alliées pour le Changement*
FUAPO	*Front Uni des Associations et Partis de l'Opposition*
GDM	Grassroots Democratic Movement
GNP	Gross National Product
GSO	*Groupe Spécial d'Opération*
ICDA	Interim Committee for Democratic Alliance
IMF	International Monetary Fund
ING	Interim National Government
IOT	International Observer Team
KANU	Kenya African National Union
LESOMA	Socialist League of Malawi
MAFREMO	Malawi Freedom Movement
MCP	Malawi Congress Party
MEISON	All-Ethiopia Socialist Movement
MFJ	Movement for Freedom and Justice
MORENA	*Mouvement de Redressement National*
MOSOP	Movement for the Survival of the Ogoni People
MPLA	Popular Movement for the Liberation of Angola
MYP	Malawi Youth Pioneers
NAC	Nyasaland African Congress
NADECO	National Democratic Coalition
NCCR	National Committee for Constitutional Reform
NCOPA	National Coordination of Opposition Parties and Associations
NCPN	National Center Party of Nigeria
NDC	National Democratic Congress
NDC	National Democratic Convention
NDI	National Democratic Institute
NEB	National Election Board
NEC	National Executive Committee
NEC	National Electoral Commission
NGO	Non-Governmental Organization
NIP	National Independence Party
NLC	Nigeria Labor Congress
NPP	National Patriotic Party
NPP	New Patriotic Party
NRC	National Redemption Council
NRC	National Republican Convention
NYCOP	National Youth Council of Ogoni People
OAU	Organization of African Unity
OLF	Oromo Liberation Front
PA	Peasant Associations
PDG	*Parti Démocratique Gabonais*
PGP	*Parti Gabonais du Progrès*
PHP	People's Heritage Party
PMAC	Provisional Military Administrative Council
PNC	People's National Convention
PNDC	Provisional National Defense Council

PNP	People's National Party
PRP	People's Revolutionary Party
RENAMO	*Resistencia Nacional Moçambicana*
RNB	*Rassemblement National des Bûcherons*
SAC	*Service d'Action Civique*
SAMACO	Save Malawi Council
SAP	Structural Adjusment Program
SATUCC	South African Trade Union Coordinating Council
SDF	Social Democratic Front
SDP	Social Democratic Party
SMC	Supreme Military Council
SSS	State Security Service
TANU	Tanganyka African National Union
TGE	Transitional Government of Ethiopia
TPLF	Tigray People's Liberation Front
UDF	United Democratic Front
UDI	Unilateral Declaration of Independence
UDP	United Democratic Party
UNCP	United Nigeria Congress Party
UNDP	National Union for Democracy and Progress
UNITA	National Union for the Total Liberation of Angola
UP	United Party
UPC	*Union des Populations du Cameroun*
UPG	*Union du Peuple Gabonais*
UPNO	Underrepresented Peoples and Nations Organization
UPS	*Union Progressiste Sénégalais*

1
Introduction: Understanding Democratization

Jean-Germain Gros

For most of its history as an independent state, Malawi was so thoroughly dominated by the late Hastings Kamuzu Banda that it acquired the unofficial distinction of being a one-man state, "Bandastan." The obituary of Banda-style, autocratic rule was pronounced in May of 1994, when the people of Malawi voted the former dictator out of office and ushered in one of the most successful transitions to democratic rule in sub-Saharan Africa. Unfortunately, Malawi's example has not been the norm on the subcontinent. More common is the tendency for long-time incumbents—such as Paul Biya of Cameroon and Omar Bongo of Gabon—to try to hold on to power at all costs, for newly elected leaders to exhibit behavior patterns similar to those of their nonelected predecessors, or for the military to return to power after flirtations with democracy "fail" to materialize into full-blown romance (e.g., Nigeria under Sani Abacha).

This collection of essays is literally about seven sub-Saharan African countries, including those just mentioned, but mere storytelling, however amusing from time to time, is not its real aim. Instead, this text attempts to come to grips with the dialectic of regime change, or democratization, under conditions of uncertainty. The country study approach is used because it is unavoidable in cross-national political analyses. Indeed, how can the enigma of democratization, or for that matter politics in general, be studied in the abstract, devoid, as it were, of geographic space or locale, time frame and people—in others words, without nation-states and the actors who help to shape how they are governed? Furthermore, sound social science research requires that generalizations be made only after the evidence is examined; theories should always follow investigations, not the other way around. This *geist*, or spirit, underpins each of the chapters. This chapter does two things: it introduces democratization as a concept and political reality in late twentieth-century Africa, and provides a roadmap for what is to come in the book.

THE CONCEPT OF DEMOCRATIZATION

Democratization is a transitional phenomenon involving a gradual, mainly elite-driven transformation of the formal rules that govern a political system.[1] Thus democratization is not an end-game; rather, it is a means to an end, which is democracy.[2] Countries democratize so that they may, one day, become democratic. A democratizing country can be distinguished from a democratic one mainly by differences in political culture. Put another way, democratization might be described as a stage in the evolution of country where the rules governing power alternation and state-society relations (discussed later), though ostensibly based on democratic ideals, have not been fully internalized. In democratizing countries some groups or powerful individuals might still find normal to come to power by force and deny certain basic rights to some of their fellow citizens. Indeed, the populace, in the name of so-called law and order, may actively support ending democratization. By contrast, democracy can be said to exist when the formal rules of the political game, based as they are on principles of popular participation and sovereignty, are overwhelmingly accepted by the polity.

The notion that there are mature and fragile democracies is hereby rejected, as is much of the literature on consolidation. A country is either democratic or it is not. What is commonly called fragile or nonconsolidated democracy is, in fact, democratization at a specific phase in its development. Because democratization is a process, it is neither unilinear nor static: it can move forward, stagnate, or be reversed. Furthermore, even though democratization is elite-imposed political reform, the impetus for it need not come from the top; indeed, in Africa and elsewhere, democratization has often come about as a result of pressure from various sources, including domestic civil society and the international community (more on these later). Democratization in late twentieth-century Africa is part of the worldwide process of political transformation that is taking place in the aftermath of the Cold War. Its origins lie not only in the fact that sub-Saharan Africa is an integral part of the world system of nation-states, and therefore not insulated from sociopolitical, cultural, and even philosophical influences from the outside, but also because African societies themselves are undergoing profound internal changes. Distinct voices are emerging in Africa, articulating the universality of principles, which the ideologues of yesteryear might have dismissed as "un-African."

Two distinct phases may be identified in a democratizing regime, although one does not necessarily guarantee the other. The first phase of democratization is sometimes called political liberalization, wherein leaders of a country open the political system to competition.[3] In Africa, where the one-party state held sway for much of the postcolonial period, this step has involved amending constitutions to permit opposition parties to operate legally and establishing timetables for multiparty elections at various levels of government. The second phase of democratization is more difficult and spans a much longer time period. It involves creating the conditions that will lead to the rule of law. In postcolonial Africa formal state-society relations were asymmetrical and favored the state. Moreover, relations between state institutions were equally unbalanced, with the executive branch, usually with the support of the military, dominating the other two branches (i.e., the legislature and judiciary). African executives enjoyed extraordinary powers until 1990; they were heads of state, heads of government, and heads of their ruling parties; they could appoint at least some members of the legislature and they appointed all judges and top civil servants. The lack of limits on executive prerogatives encouraged arbitrary behavior; citizens were treated as appendages to the national leader's extended household (as in Malawi), which led some scholars to dub Africa's postcolonial regimes "neopatrimonialist."[4]

In the second phase of democratization the goal is to make intrastate and state-society relations more balanced. Separation of power (especially judicial independence), checks and balances, administrative decentralization and accountability, freedoms of speech, press, assembly, and, less frequently mentioned, civilian hegemony over the military are some of the components of the second phase of democratization. A truly democratizing country must not only officially embrace multipartyism and the principle of free and fair elections, it must also show that it is committed to the establishment of what the French call an *état de droits* (literally meaning a state of rights), which guarantees a broad range of civil liberties to its citizens. For purposes of simplification, in the remainder of this chapter political liberalization is referred to as phase one of democratization and movement toward a state of rights as phase two.

Technically a majority of African countries are in phase one of democratization; most have legalized multipartyism and have held at least one multiparty election since the end of the Cold War. African countries have taken these steps under different circumstances. In some countries, democratization of the phase one type was embraced by incumbents who had long been hostile to pluralism (e.g., Malawi, Gabon, Kenya); in others, incumbents had to be swept from office—in some cases violently—before reform could be contemplated (e.g., Mali and Ethiopia); in others still, there was a constitutional emasculation of incumbent power through so-called national conferences, culminating in the first multiparty elections held in decades. However, multiparty elections have been the subjects of controversy in many countries. For example, Cameroon's transition to multipartyism, especially the presidential elections it has held since 1990, has been heavily criticized (see chapter 3). Considerably fewer African countries have made it fully to phase two, although some have made more progress toward that goal than others. Malawi, South Africa, Benin, and Mali are in phase two of the democratization process. In all four countries, elections held between 1990 and 1994 led to the coming to power of opposition forces, and institutions and practices that fundamentally strengthen society vis-à-vis the state have been put in place.

South Africa's recently adopted constitution has been dubbed one of the most liberal in the world; Malawi's newspapers have flourished with surprising speed and apparently without much government interference since the late Banda's departure. Ironically, Banda may have been the most famous beneficiary of political change in the new Malawi. His acquittal on murder charges in 1996 by a jury of his peers may have been a sign of an emerging independent judiciary. (In fairness, the lack of a conviction may have also underscored the need to reform Malawi's justice system.) In Benin, there have been not one but two consecutive multiparty presidential elections since 1990, and progress in protecting civil liberties there is apparently resented by laggard African states (e.g., Nigeria and Burkina Faso).[5]

Perhaps the most important lesson Africa has provided to the world in the late twentieth century is that virtually all of its states, including those that are on the verge of collapse or that have collapsed and recovered (e.g., Liberia), have embraced at least phase one of democratization. It is not a stretch to assert that democratization (phase one), however imperfect, has achieved ideological hegemony in sub-Saharan Africa. No one is openly calling for a return to the *status quo ante*. Even in the countries where the military has forced its way back to power (e.g., Nigeria, Burundi), soldiers have found it necessary to promise a return to elected civilian rule, although increasingly they throw themselves in the lot by shedding their uniform. The transformation is all the more remarkable in view of the fact that before 1990 all but a handful of African states were ruled by one-party, often one-man, regimes. Why democratization at this time in African history? What accounts for differences in the experiences of various countries with it? What are the prospects for democracy, which is the end-game of democratization, on the African continent? These three questions form the bases of Chapters 2 through 8. It is, therefore, appropriate at this juncture to provide guidance to readers, so they will understand the sequencing of each case study.

THE FRAMEWORK

To understand the ubiquity of democratization on the African subcontinent, and the mixed outcomes it has had, requires both macro and microanalytical perspectives. The levels of analysis approach, always a favorite among international relations theorists, is useful in this connection.[6] Three types of factors, each corresponding to a specific level of analysis, seem to have been crucial to democratization and its *dénouements* in late twentieth-century Africa: individual leadership, societal pressure, and the international community. These are not necessarily mutually exclusive; all three are likely to be present at any given time but in varying order of importance. Nor do the elements that make up each level of analysis always have salutary effects. To say, for example, that the international community shapes democratization in Africa is not to say that it always does so positively and singlehandedly. Ultimately, transition outcomes are determined by whether prodemocratization forces, regardless of the levels of analysis to which they belong, come together at the right historical juncture to overwhelm their anti-democratization counterparts.[7]

Leaders

Regimes have democratized in Africa thanks to relatively enlightened leaders. This has been the case during the latest wave of democratization as well as before. The following prototypes of African leaders may be identified in the postcolonial period. First, there were the early democratizers, who included leaders such as

Leopold Senghor of Senegal and Seretse Khama of Botswana.[8] Admittedly few and far between, prodemocratization leaders in postcolonial Africa were able to establish enduring pluralistic systems of government in an age when one-partyism dominated the African political landscape. The case of Senghor is especially interesting. Senghor led a de facto one-party state in Senegal from 1966 to 1974; however, in July of 1974, he reintroduced multipartyism, albeit in a way that left his *Union Progressiste Sénégalais* (UPS) in a very advantageous position.

In the 1990s, Julius Nyerere and Kenneth Kaunda come closest, among African leaders, to the two early democratizers just mentioned, as does Nelson Mandela. Both Nyerere and Kaunda were committed to the idea of democracy during their tenure in office but not to multiparty democracy. They presided over relatively benign one-party states, and neither has been accused of personal corruption. Zambia under Kaunda was among the first African countries to liberalize in 1990, and Tanzania's Nyerere became one of the most forceful and articulate advocates of political reform in Africa. With the possible exception of Khama, all four leaders might be said to have been philosopher-kings: people who, despite their other flaws, were imbued with basic democratic instincts.

The second prototype of African leaders are the opportunistic democratizers. This category includes those who, in 1989–90, sensed the coming of the prodemocracy juggernaut and attempted to divert (or dilute) it to their fortune. Opportunistic democratizers see democratization as just one more challenge to autocratic rule, not as an opportunity to create an entirely new governance system or regime. Consequently, they are more likely to agree to implement phase one of democratization (political liberalization) than phase two—if phase one does not threaten their rule. Omar Bongo of Gabon and the late Houphouet Boigny of Ivory Coast are opportunistic democratizers. Throughout their career both leaders have ruled by effectively combining political acumen with brutality (with Boigny resorting to the latter more sparingly than Bongo). After deriding prodemocracy activists in January of 1990, Bongo convened a national conference in April and manipulated the deliberations to his advantage. He also attempted to literally buy off members of the opposition by offering them cash and government posts. Boigny, after legalizing multipartyism in 1990, held elections so quickly that the opposition hardly had the time to make a credible showing.

Opportunistic democratizers are not necessarily incumbents; they also are found within the ranks of the political opposition. In general, such individuals may be long-time members of the ruling elite who, sensing the turning of the tide, jump ship and become opposition leaders. Their interest in democratization does not go far beyond a desire to replace their incumbent rivals and settle old scores; they see democratization (phase one) as an opportunity to come to power legitimately, before exhibiting behavioral patterns similar to those that prevailed in yesteryear. After all, opposition-produced opportunistic democratizers were socialized in the corrupt tricksterism of the single-party state. Opportunistic democratizers may even come from the bosom of civil society institutions (e.g., trade unions), but were either never committed to democracy or quickly became intoxicated by newly bestowed power. Ange Félix Patassé of the Central African Republic, Pascal Lissouba of Congo and, especially, Frederick Chiluba of Zambia are examples of opposition-produced opportunistic democratizers (or neoautocrats).

Another prototype of African leader is the born-again democratizer, who is somewhere between the first two prototypes. The born-again democratizer is usually someone who undergoes ideological epiphany to keep Western aid flowing, but the conversion may or may not be genuine. With the disintegration of the Soviet bloc, and with it the end to alternative sources of economic and military assistance available to poor countries, born-again democratizers have become legion in late twentieth-century Africa. Their preponderance reflects the continent's dependent position within the world economy. Jerry Rawlings of Ghana is an example of a born-again democratizer. The prospects for democratization in Ghana were initially very bleak. Rawlings himself had participated in the overthrow of not one, but two civilian governments. Moreover, in the months following his second coup, Rawlings's rhetoric was decidedly antidemocratic and anticapitalist. However, when aid from the Soviet Union and Libya was denied, Rawlings quickly came around to embracing democracy and capitalism, and surpassed expectations in the process. Rawlings probably accepted donor-sponsored economic and political reform for survival reasons at first, but it is too simplistic to argue that pleasing the international community is all that motivates him. Rawlings certainly did not have to go as far as he has. There was less international pressure on him to hold a second multiparty election in 1996; yet he did and the election was dubbed freer and fairer than the 1992 ballot.

Nevertheless, it is imprudent to cite Ghana as an example of a democratizing country in the same vein as Malawi, where the former incumbent held elections (or was forced to), lost, and resigned from power. It is not clear that Rawlings would be willing to leave office were he to lose in an election. His love for the trappings of power seems to supersede his interest in bringing about genuine democratization to Ghana. A telling sign as to whether Ghana is truly democratizing should come when Rawlings's tenure expires and cannot be expanded without constitutional manipulation. At the same time, Ghana in the 1990s has probably made more progress toward political modernity than either Gabon or Ivory Coast. Newspapers operate without noticeable restrictions; private radio stations have mushroomed all over Accra. For anyone who has been to Ghana in the late 1990s, the air of optimism and *glasnost* is inescapable. Born-again democratizers also include Mathieu Kerekou of Benin (who, unlike Rawlings, was ousted from power before being brought back in 1996), Meles Zenawi of Ethiopia, and Dos Santos of Angola. These individuals are, to repeat, casualties of the end of the Cold War.

Formerly associated with the Eastern bloc, the likes of Kerekou saw their "significant other" unexpectedly vanish in 1990, and, leading extremely poor and (or) war-ravaged countries, these leaders had no choice but to accept the dictates of the West and their domestic opposition. (In Ethiopia, the old regime was actually defeated on the battlefield.) When one's chosen partner cannot show up at the party, if one is smart—or otherwise desperate—one dances with any willing suitor. Mathieu Kerekou gambled and lost in Benin in 1990, only to return to power in 1996. In the waning months of the Ethiopian civil war, Zenawi abandoned his

Marxist-Leninist rhetoric, and, upon dislodging Mengistu in 1991, quickly launched an interesting political experiment in Ethiopia based on so-called ethnic federalism. Indeed, it seems that American support for the entry of the former Ethiopian rebels into Addis Ababa was conditioned on their leaving the Leninist veil at the gate of the old city. In Angola incumbent Dos Santos and his Popular Movement for the Liberation of Angola (MPLA) ran successfully against Savimbi and the National Union for the Total Liberation of Angola (UNITA) in 1992, only to see Savimbi reject the results and return to the bush.

The fourth prototype of individual leaders are the recalcitrant democratizers, who have had to be dragged into implementing reform. Generally, recalcitrant democratizers are people whose hold on power is tenuous, or so they think. They seem to believe that even a modest political opening will lead to their demise. Recalcitrant democratizers are relics of an earlier era who simply lack the imagination and inclination to adapt to an uncertain environment; consequently, they tend to rely overwhelmingly on intimidation to address democratic challenges to their rule. Recalcitrant democratizers tend to be those African leaders who came to power under violent circumstances or succeeded charismatic founding fathers. They also tend to be leaders whose country is in a state of socioeconomic disintegration, and whose personal appeal and popular base are rather limited. Finally, recalcitrant democratizers tend to be concentrated in French-speaking Africa, although they also can be found outside of France's *pré carré* (or sphere of influence).

The late Mobutu Sese Seko of the old Zaire, the late Juvénal Habyarimana of Rwanda, Ngassimbé Eyadema of Togo, Paul Biya of Cameroon, and Daniel Arap Moi of Kenya are examples of recalcitrant democratizers. Democratization carried out by recalcitrant democratizers tends to be profoundly flawed (more so than in the previous cases), simply because democratization success hinges heavily on a leadership committed to democratic ideals. Democratization undertaken by recalcitrant democratizers will either be blocked or distorted beyond recognition. The removal of recalcitrant democratizers may be a sine qua non for moving to phase two of democratization; otherwise, all that obtains is stagnation and frustration at phase one.[9] In this vein, the forced eviction of Mobutu Sese Seko from power may have been a necessary condition for democratization in the former Zaire, although, judging by the apparent excesses of Laurent Kabila, it probably was not a sufficient condition.

The foregoing was meant to introduce one very important point, which is amplified in Chapter 6: individual leaders matter in history. In an era when much of social science research has tended to focus on institutions, the individual actor has often been forgotten. Here he is brought back in, as one of the levels of analysis by which regime change or democratization has to be understood. How crucial the role of the individual leader is depends on his (or her), personal attributes, the degree of institutionalization of formal politics in the country, and the democratization phase in question. A leader who is well respected by his friends and foes, personally untainted by corruption, and blessed with communicative and negotiating skills has a very good chance for success in launching democratization (phase one). Tanzania shows that such a leader need not be formally in office; Nyerere had a far greater role in the country's democratization than former incumbent president Ali Hassan Mwinyi, who was, in fact, a reluctant convert. Individual-driven regime change has its pitfalls; unless quickly institutionalized, reforms undertaken largely at the behest of an enlightened leader may not survive his or her mortality. One more point should be made about the individual level of analysis. The enlightened individual leader does not always initiate regime change on his own cognizance; sometimes, he is a conduit through which a progressive faction of the elite expresses its preferences. In this sense, the individual level of analysis can be taken either literally or somewhat less so.

Society

Democratization in Africa has been shaped by the milieu, in other words, the socioeconomic and political compact. Institutions are therefore extremely important. By institutions we mean formal structures like the economy, the military, labor and student unions, and the church; but we also mean the norms, habits, and processes that have governed African politics since indpendence. The link between democratization in Africa and the economy is made by most of the contributors. Kamuzu Banda was unable to defy the will of the international community because Malawi's extreme poverty made it dependent on foreign aid; Paul Biya's perceived incapacity to manage the Cameroon economy, one of the most successful in Africa until the mid-1980s, became a major political issue in 1991. Other authors also have recognized that popular dissatisfaction with economic malperformance, graft, and corruption undermined neopatrimonial rule throughout Africa.[10] However, any argument rooted in economism must be made carefully and on a case-by-case basis rather than accepted at face value. Economic performance is not always a good predictor of regime change. Some African countries that have performed well economically have not necessarily been bastions of democratization. Ivory Coast, which by most measures is a success story, remains mired in autocratic rule under Henri Konan Bédié. Other countries, much better endowed in natural resources (e.g., Gabon, Cameroon, Nigeria, the former Zaire) than Ivory Coast, have fared even worse. Not only have such countries been poor economic performers, they have barely undergone political liberalization (phase one); at least one (i.e., Nigeria) has, in fact, reversed the process since 1993.

These examples would seem to contradict a major strand in political thought in the last fifty years, espoused by the esteemed Seymour Martin Lipset and the modernization theory school, which says that rich countries, since they tend to have large, educated middle classes, are more democratization-prone than poor ones.[11] The reality is that it is the poorest African countries, such as Benin, Malawi, and Mali (South Africa is excluded because of its unique experience), that have made the most significant strides toward democratization. The lesson bears repeating: natural resource endowments do not predict how well countries will perform economically and politically; nor does performance at one level predict performance at another, as good capitalists do not necessarily make good democrats.

There may, in fact, be an inverse relationship between national wealth and democratization. Relatively abundant resources may shield nonreformers from the domestic and external pressure to implement political change. In most of the African cases where long-time incumbents have lost power, they were running against a backdrop of depleted national treasuries: Kerekou in Benin, Banda in Malawi, Kaunda in Zambia, and Nguesso in Congo. The last case is illuminating; because of its oil wealth, Congo is technically not a poor country by African standards. In order to support the bureaucratic elite's consumption habits, the quasimilitary government of Nguesso had heavily mortgaged Congo's future oil revenue by accepting payments from the French oil companies Total and Elf-Aquitaine years before new oil sources were discovered and exploited. By the time average Congolese citizens discovered the racket in 1990 and began to clamor for their rightful piece of the national pie, Nguesso simply had no money to satisfy their demand. Not surprisingly, he lost the presidential election in 1992, only to return to power by force in 1997.

Incumbent autocrats with deep pockets can literally buy off their opponents with cash, cabinet posts, or lucrative positions in state-owned enterprises. Also, autocrats leading countries with resources (especially oil) that the international community needs are in a better position to remain defiant in the face of criticism, because they know that externally based prodemocratization pressure typically stops at the oil tanker's edge. In other words, the ability of autocrats to resist international pressure for change is determined, in part, by the resource endowments of their economy and the degree of foreign participation in the exploitation therein. The more resources a country has that the international community needs, the more leverage that its leaders have in manipulating domestic and international pressure to their advantage. Thus, it is quite possible that, in some cases, national wealth may be a deterrent to democratization.

By contrast, leaders in poor states may be unable to resist pressure and, noblesse oblige, more receptive to calls for democratization. Poverty is not being elevated to the level of political virtue here; it is merely being pointed out that, in Africa at least, wealth is a very imperfect predictor of political (or, for that matter, economic) progress. Where democratization is concerned, it may be advantageous for a country to be poor during phase one, since poverty has been shown to constrain intransigence by dependent elites. To maintain the momentum of democratization, that is, to convince the populace that it is something worth keeping, economic rejuvenation may be necessary. In other words, the economy has differential impacts on democratization, depending on the country and phase(s); it is also one of many societal factors, and perhaps not as crucial as the next factor.

The military is, as Chapter 4 points out, the ace in the hole in African politics. Depending on how they were treated under the previous order, soldiers may either be receptive to democratization efforts or resist them. Like all other institutions and organizations, the military is concerned, first and foremost, with safeguarding its interests. It will lend support to whichever group or regime it believes will preserve and advance those interests, which, admittedly, are not always well defined. In Malawi, the regular army was treated poorly by Kamuzu Banda; it played a subservient role vis-à-vis the former dictator's personal army. Consequently, when conditions were ripe, Malawi's regular army successfully launched Operation Bwezani against the murderous Malawi Young Pioneers, which significantly tilted the balance of forces in favor of the democratic opposition.

Presidents Biya in Cameroon and Bongo in Gabon (with help from the French) made sure that their respective armies were taken care of. In spite of opposition demands to the contrary, Cameroonian and Gabonese soldiers were given even broader powers during the period of popular protests in 1990 and 1991, and, in the end, they stayed on the side of authoritarian rule. In the current African conjuncture, whose side the military is on in the struggle between ostensibly prodemocratization forces and autocrats is crucial. If the military is not actively on the side of the former, it must, at least, remain neutral. It is important not to assume, however, that the military in Africa is an interest-specific institution that is always obedient to hierarchical norms. Quite often, it is neither.

The African military is saddled by the same kinds of cleavages that are to be found in the rest of society; it is divided by ethnicity, region, and religion. Power-holding politicians have deliberately maintained division within the military by promoting loyal officers from particular regions and ethnic groups and putting them in charge of strategic barracks (usually those with tanks, ammunition depots, and fuel supply). In Chapter 3, Professor Tatah Mentan shows the connection between ethnicity and rank in the Cameroon army. There are more generals from Biya's Center-South provinces than there are from the rest of the country; this policy was first put in place by Biya's predecessor (former President Ahidjo), during whose tenure Fulani northerners occupied prominent positions in the military. Military officers also may have a free reign to engage in illegal and extra-legal activities to supplement their officially meager income; rank-and-file soldiers and police officers often do the same on a smaller scale. Because the African military is often politicized and steeped in corruption, the institutional threat it poses to democratization is enormous. At the same time, military action against entrenched autocrats has been known to facilitate regime change, at least up to a point; Malawi and Ethiopia are evidence of this.

In addition to the economy and the military, civil society has had a significant impact on democratization in Africa. "Civil society," as used here and throughout the book, refers to the sum total of voluntary formal associations and informal institutional arrangements that straddle the state—i.e., the government in power and its coercive armor—and the primary units of society—individuals, families, clans, and so on.[12] Among its institutions civil society can count the church, labor unions, parallel savings associations, boys and girls clubs, charity organizations, and secret orders. Civil society provides opportunities for individuals and groups to engage in activities that do not encroach on those better performed by the state. The importance of these activities, as Alexis de Tocqueville remarked, emanates from the need of the citizenry for self-government in matters not directly concerning *res republica*.[13] Civil society is the realm of voluntary cooperation, self-government, and sympathy (which Adam Smith called "fellow feeling").[14] Civil society can also be an important tool for political transformation, as Poland demonstrated in the 1980s.

What types of civil society institutions have been most visible in Africa's democratization drive? Among the most influential institutions, but also perhaps the least noted by scholars, are religious institutions. In Malawi, it was the Catholic Church's belated activism that initially provided the forum for organized opposition to Banda. Even the church had to move carefully; Banda's thuggish MYP did not draw a firm distinction between the laity and the clergy. The Malawi case is interesting because it shows that the influence of institutions, like that of individual actors, varies, according to the phase of the struggle against authoritarianism. The Catholic Church provided the initial outlet for opposition to Banda; the secular opposition then became emboldened and formed political parties; the international community muscled in by threatening to cut off aid; the regular army, rising up against Banda's personal army, propelled the movement toward victory. The church acted more as a catalyst, but by itself it probably would not have been able to overthrow Banda. In Gabon, not only was the Catholic Church an integral part of the opposition to Bongoism, it also supplied the most serious opposition candidate, Father M'Ba. The Mourides in Senegal have played an important role in cementing support for Abdou Diouf's regime, and, in parts of Somalia, Islamic law has replaced secular law in the wake of the collapse of the Somali state.

Other civil society institutions that have proven consequential for democratization in Africa are professional associations. As a respected member of the Cameroon Bar Association, Yondo Black's arrest in 1990 sparked opposition to continued one-party rule in that country.[15] Black was able to combine his courage with his knowledge of the law to challenge political monopoly by the Cameroon People's Democratic Movement (CPDM). In Kenya, members of the bar acted similarly toward Moi. In Nigeria, both lawyers' and journalists' associations have fought for civic freedoms, despite considerable dangers to fellow members (there is also a nascent, politico-environmental movement in Nigeria, especially in Ogoniland). The one weakness with African professional and civic associations is that, because they tend to be small in number, urban based and interest specific, their efficacy tends to be spatially and politically limited. Farmers' associations are notorious for their absence in the debate on democratization, and where they have participated, they have done so in support of questionable democrats. Jerry Rawlings of Ghana probably got much of his support during the 1992 and 1996 elections from cash-crop up-country farmers, rather than from school teachers and other professionals in Accra, Kumasi, and Cape Coast.

Unless urban-based professional groups link up with their rural counterparts, democratization in Africa could remain an urban elite affair, utterly unconnected to the lives of the vast majority of Africans. Nevertheless, the advent of professional associations as a political force in African politics is a potentially significant development; it suggests that African society may be becoming less divided by ascriptive norms such as gender, age sets, and ethnicity, and more by those of professional and individual achievements. The multiplication of cross-cutting civil society institutions also may be a reflection of greater specialization and a more differentiated division of labor than has hitherto been the case. These were, in part, the social transformations that facilitated liberal democracy in the West, and there is no reason why they could not play a similar role in late twentieth-century Africa. On the other hand, given what was said earlier about religion, Africa runs the risk of being pulled in opposite directions by the ascriptive and nonsecular institutions of religion and the secular professional associations. Societal pressure has been largely responsible for the drive by African elites to democratize, but there is one remaining factor.

The International Community

The fall of the Berlin Wall in 1989 echoed throughout Africa. Many of the region's autocrats had long-standing ties with Eastern European leaders. Mobutu was said to have been particularly shaken by the death of Ceaucescu in Romania; former East Germany's secret service organization provided training to Ethiopian intelligence officers. The West, once the end of the Cold War made it safe to give human rights primacy over security issues, began to push former African client regimes toward reform. Where Francophone Africa was concerned, former President François Mitterrand's declaration at the 1990 La Baule summit that France would link economic aid to democratization efforts has been hailed as the beginning of political reform in the former French colonies.[16] The World Bank, Africa's largest institutional financier, also played a role.

There is no question that an international environment that was receptive to democratization in the early 1990s made a difference, particularly in Africa's poorest states. In Benin, Congo, Niger, and Malawi, the need to remain eligible for external financial aid, made all the more paramount by depleted national treasuries, forced incumbents in these countries to succumb to demands for change. The international community has also been useful in helping African countries to handle what might be called the mechanics of phase one of democratization better. International organizations such as the National Democratic Institute and the Carter Center have provided much needed expertise in voter education and registration, election observation and monitoring (there is a difference between the two), and even electoral conflict resolution. However, the role of external actors and events as catalysts for democratization in Africa should not be overblown. Indeed, external actors do not always have a salutary influence.

By and large, the international community has been effective in pressing for democratization in Africa during phase one, that is to say, external pressure has been most consequential in forcing countries to legalize multipartyism and hold multiparty elections. It has been less successful in getting African countries to move toward phase two. The reason is not hard to see. Besieged leaders who are afraid that genuine democratization will usurp their power, but are nevertheless under pressure to initiate change, may see the limited reforms embedded in phase one (liberalization) as a way to get the proverbial monkey off their back, not necessarily as a prelude to something larger. They may, for example, hold minimally free and fair elections that are mainly intended to mollify critics, but accomplish little else (e.g., respecting civil liberties). They may agree to an opposition press but set the rules so arbitrarily that private news sources are routinely silenced. Initially, besieged elites may not even agree to liberalize, preferring instead to rely on traditional methods of cooptation and coercion to deal with their opposition. One cannot help but recall the vitriol with which Moi reacted when calls for political reform in Kenya were first uttered in 1990. Although Moi, after much tergiversation, did agree to hold elections in 1992, he has since gradually reverted to old habits.[17] Countries can, indeed, become stuck in particular reform modes.

The international community itself has been less than united. The division has been used very effectively by leaders such as Omar Bongo to pit one international interest against the other. While the end of the Cold War may have made the West less willing to tolerate autocracy, it also may have inaugurated an era of conflicts not between East and West, or North and South, but between North and North over Africa. Specifically, there has been diplomatic wrangling between former colonial powers such as France and the remaining superpower, the United States. France has been very skeptical of outside (read: American) "interference" in its former colonies. The Gaullist government of Jacques Chirac appears to be more concerned about maintaining French influence in the *pré carré* than democratization. Elsewhere in the subregion, the international community, especially the United States, uncertain about inserting itself too deeply into African affairs (in part because of the Somalia experience), appears to limit its interest to the symbolic and visible aspects of democratization. Elections are treated as though they are sui generis evidence of democratic rule.

The international community, when it has managed to be united, has been timid in pushing for serious political reform in Africa. Incumbents like Paul Biya, Omar Bongo, and Daniel Arap Moi know too well that, when faced with external pressure, all they have to do is wait it out. Sooner or later, the international community does come around. In Kenya, prodemocracy activists, with encouragement from the international community (especially the U.S. embassy in Nairobi), went head-to-head with the Moi regime in the early 1990s, but once the 1992 presidential election was concluded (and deemed "free and fair"), they were very much left on their own. Many were subsequently picked up and mistreated (e.g., Richard Leaky) by Moi's army and Kenya African National Union (KANU) toughs, with barely a word of protest from outsiders. The fickleness of external political support for democratization in Africa is dangerous in so far as it exposes activists to reprisals as soon as the spotlight is turned off. The power of autocratic African incumbents is so overwhelming that sustained and coordinated external pressure for democratization is needed as a counterweight. Alas, this is seldom the case.

Finally, Western encouragement of democratization in Africa has not been matched by greater financial commitment to those countries that have advanced the furthest in the process. The ability of countries to attract external funding continues to be based more on their willingness to implement market reform measures—which are often not popular—than on their democratization credentials. Genuinely democratizing African countries such as Benin, Mali, and Malawi, have not received the kind of financial support from the West that would facilitate the deepening of democratization. Worse, states with less than impressive records, such as Cameroon and Kenya, continue to receive aid, its occasional suspension notwithstanding. Even where foreign aid and democratization appear to be linked, other considerations often tilt the balance in favor of some states. South Africa is poised to receive the lion's share of U.S. development assistance in the coming years, which, however well deserved, is needed even more in poorer states. Sub-Saharan Africa, as a region, simply has not reached the level of importance to the "powers-that-be" in the world that would make it a prime target for far-reaching external intervention (i.e., foreign aid, capital investment, trade) that promotes democratization. Democracy or not, the poorest states in Africa, with small consumer markets and precious few natural resources, are unlikely to become magnets of international investment and assistance, even though some of them have made the greatest strides toward democratization.

THE DIALECTIC OF DEMOCRATIZATION

What explains differences in the experience of countries with democratization? The outcomes of democratization efforts in sub-Saharan Africa stem from the dialectical, or contradictory, nature of the processes that lead to social change. The forces that create pressure for democratization may also subvert it; moreover, the forces whose positive influence on democratization is beyond question may be either completely absent in some countries or lacking in the critical mass necessary to counter authoritarian tendencies. For example, to succeed democratization requires leadership, but many of Africa's leaders, especially its longtime incumbents, are questionable democrats of the recalcitrant and born-again types. Party pluralism may be indispensable to modern democracies, but parties in young nation-states may also revive primordial sentiments, as leaders attempt to shore up their "natural" base by playing the ethnicity card. In this connection, it should always be kept in mind that Africa's democratization efforts are taking place against the backdrop of incomplete—some would say yet-to-begin—nation-building. Many of Africa's poorest states were the first to initiate political reform in the early 1990s, because their dependence made them vulnerable to domestic and international pressure. Some have, until now, surpassed expectations (e.g., Benin, Malawi, even Ghana). But how does one build democracy in countries with a large reservoir of poor people whose chances at improving their lot are, to say the least, modest? In other words, how does one keep popular support for democratization and thus protect it from reactionary forces, if democratization is not expected to result in a marked amelioration in people's living standards? On the other hand, well-endowed or robust economies (the two are not the same), however necessary for sustaining democratization, may also delay its introduction by giving leaders the resources they need to buy off opponents, keep soldiers on their side, and crack down on dissidents. Civil society institutions, such as the Catholic Church in Malawi, can play an important role in galvanizing opposition against authoritarian rule, but they also can be mobilized in support of the status quo.[18] Indeed, the same the Catholic Church that initially fought for democratization in Malawi was eerily silent in the Rwanda genocide, with some of its priests accused of complicity in that sad drama.

The international community—meaning mainly the West—is a force to be reckoned with in African politics, but its influence is not always salutary. Some external powers have been downright cool to democratization on the continent when it seems to threaten their interests. Globalization, the process so romanticized by diffusionists, has helped to put authoritarianism on the defensive;[19] it has also brought to the fore economic prescriptions, such as Structural Adjustment Programs, whose implementation in a democratizing regime is very problematic. Liberal democracy and its handmaiden (i.e., capitalism) face a profound contradiction in sub-Saharan Africa. Everywhere liberal democracy's hallmark has been to extend political rights while remaining mum on economic rights. This may be fine in countries where basic needs are already largely satisfied; however, in sub-Saharan Africa, where standards of living are the lowest in the world, newly enfranchised citizens may insist on using their muscle to turn back market reform and link political rights with economic rights. It should not go unnoticed that democratization has propelled African populists (e.g., John Fru Ndi in Cameroon, Father M'Ba in Gabon, Mrema in Tanzania) to the forefront of political battles, thereby posing a "threat" to the West's expectation of an Africa that is both democratic and capitalist. The life conditions of the masses of Africans render a more radical vision of democracy almost inevitable. For the West and Africa's elite, the existence of this alternative vision necessitates limiting democracy to its bourgeois form, but the African populace may have other ideas. Thus, the interminable struggle between opposites continues. The dialectical nature of democratization, and of social change in general, is such that outcomes will be determined by the push and pull of various forces; moreover, outcomes will be reversible, thus generating uncertainty.

There is no country in sub-Saharan Africa today, including South Africa, where democratization cannot be rolled back. The ease with which elected leaders have been toppled by the military and warlords (Niger, Sierra Leone, Congo, Burundi), some even before they enter the State House (Algeria and Nigeria), confirm this. To be sure, democratization probably is safer in some countries than in others, but the corner against authoritarianism has not been turned. This is why democratization in late twentieth-century Africa must cope with uncertainty, which explains the title of this text. There is not likely to be a universally accepted one-size-fits-all theory of democratization, however laudable efforts to do so might be. The reality of democratization in late twentieth-century Africa is simply too unpredictable to permit neat theorizing. To comprehend why come countries have advanced further than others on the uncertain journey of democratization, it is necessary to examine how the various factors embedded in the levels of analysis identified in this chapter have coalesced (or failed to do so) in specific instances. The approach adopted here is multivariate, relying, as it were, on the interplay between the individual, society, and the international community.

ORGANIZATION OF THE BOOK

The chapters are organized around the forementioned levels of analysis. Chapters 2 through 5 mainly use a society-centered approach to analyze democratization in Malawi, Cameroon, Nigeria, and Ethiopia respectively. In Malawi (Chapter 2), the church played a major role in galvanizing support against Banda; its efforts were supplemented by Malawi's regular army, nascent political groupings, and external pressure. In Cameroon (Chapter 3), the Biya regime was confronted by a legitimacy crisis in the early 1990s because of its failure to arrest economic stagnation. The economy and corruption became the rallying cries against the incumbent; however, democratization was subverted because of elite intransigence and continued external support, especially from France. Thus in the Cameroon case, the international community, led by the former colonial power, may have had a negative impact on democratization.

In Nigeria (Chapter 4), it is the military that has been preeminent in formal politics; the influence of political society, as represented by parties, has tended to be weak, as has, at least until recently, civil society. The impact of external factors on democratization in Nigeria has until now been nil, although, as Professor Ihonvbere argues, international pressure may have been responsible for the belated and untested overtures of the Abacha regime. Nigeria has been able to resist democratization because of its oil wealth and its position as a regional hegemon. Nigeria has been consistent in intervening in places—Liberia and Sierra Leone—where the international community is not willing to expand resources, and this has given it an importance that "lesser" states do not have. While the military has been the primary stumbling block to democratization in Nigeria, in Ethiopia (Chapter 5) it was a military victory of former rebel forces over the Derg that made democratization, even in its infantile form, possible. Here again, it is possible to see the contradictory influence of social forces on regime change.

Chapters 6, 7, and 8 are based on the other two levels of analysis: leadership and the international community. Chapter 6 makes a strong case for examining democratization in Tanzania as the brainchild of Julius Nyerere, the country's paramount leader. Nyerere's influence in Tanzania has been so overwhelming that he can be said to be an institution himself. While democratization undertaken by committed democrats has obvious advantages—for one thing, support at the highest level insures that the process will not be undermined from within the ruling elite—it also has one danger: it may have a short life span unless institutionalization takes place quickly. Tanzanian democratization is thus beset with a profound contradiction: on the one hand, without Julius Nyerere it might not have evolved as smoothly as it has; on the other, with Nyerere always lurking in the background, institutionalization is very difficult. Chapter 7 attempts to account for democratization outcomes in Ghana by examining the role that international donor-induced economic reform has played in cementing support for Rawlings. Chapter 8 emphasizes both the individual leader approach, in this case the role of Omar Bongo, and the failure of the international community to push for democratization in Gabon. More than in the other chapters, the external dimension of democratization is emphasized in Chapters 7 and 8, although they do not ignore the leadership-society nexus.

The countries examined in this study were not chosen haphazardly. Each country had to be broadly representative of particular African regime types, the region in which they are physically located, and colonial experiences (or lack thereof). Also, the editor sought to include countries with both large and small population sizes. These criteria were deemed essential for making broad generalizations. For example,

Cameroon and Gabon, by virtue of their wealth, system of government—that is a unitary state with a strong presidency—and relation to France are fairly typical of the relatively rich Francophone African states. Their experience with democratization roughly matches that of Ivory Coast in West Africa. By examining Cameroon and Gabon in the same volume, it is possible to extrapolate lessons which might be applicable to countries with similar profiles in the subcontinent.

The same logic applies to Ghana. Relatively wealthy at independence, Ghana almost disintegrated politically and economically in the early 1980s after alternating between weak civilian regimes and military autocracies. Ghana's political history, in fact, closely matches that of Nigeria, Liberia, and Sierra Leone, although size and other differences should not be overlooked. One difference between Ghana and Nigeria stands out: Ghana is poorer than Nigeria and therefore more dependent on the international community. The differences in democratization outcomes between the two countries may be due to their differing immunity from external pressure. The inclusion of Ghana and Nigeria in this study is intended to capture the paradox of resource endowments in the African context.

Ethiopia, Tanzania, and Malawi are roughly on the eastern side of the continent, but this played only a part in the decision to include them in the study. After 1975, Ethiopia was the Afro-Marxist state par excellence. The nationalization of industries, collective farming, widespread indoctrination, an intelligence apparatus patterned after that of East Germany, a vanguard party, and, above all, excessive abuses of power became the hallmarks of the Mengistu regime. These methods were variably replicated in the other Afro-Marxist states of Angola, Mozambique, and Benin. And, with the exception of Benin, all of the states of the Afro-Marxist type were challenged by counterinsurgency groups. The one difference that sets Ethiopia apart from the other beleaguered Afro-Marxist states is that its civil war had a strong secessionist bent; in Angola and Mozambique, military confrontations were pursued to achieve power-taking (and power-preserving) objectives by elites who were manipulated by external forces in search of African clients.

Ethiopia underscores the difficulties of former Afro-Marxist states with large, fragmented polities and a lengthy history of civil wars. How to integrate former enemies into the security apparatus and build trust among civilians, who may have supported different factions, are two of the challenges facing democratizing regimes that are emerging from strife. In Ethiopia, the first task was made unnecessary because one of the protagonists (the former Ethiopian army) was vanquished on the battlefield; but, as Professor Berhanu points out, there is still a need for social healing, which is not taking place (in his view). Military success can engender overconfidence, arrogance, and self-rigteousness by the victors, making them less likely to accomodate their opponents and threatening democratization in the long run. The Ethiopian People's Revolutionary Democratic Front (EPRDF), or for that matter the Eritrean People's Liberation Front (EPLF), seems to think that military victory has conferred upon it the right to govern without opposition. In addition, the continued significance of ethnicity in African politics makes Ethiopia a good case study. Ethnic differences are enshrined in the constitution, in an effort to craft "ethnic federalism." Ethiopia may have a lot to teach Africa, good and ill, in the upcoming years.

If before 1991 Ethiopia was a textbook case of a dependent and extremely repressive Afro-Marxist state, complete with a personality cult around Mengistu, Malawi was its mirror image, with due regard for Banda's ideological orientation, which was procapitalist and Western almost to the absurd. Thus, if there is a case that is representative of the demise of the tyrannical, right-wing African regime, Malawi is probably it, as Ethiopia under Mengistu represents the tyrannical left-wing regime. Malawi's lack of resources also puts it on par with Ethiopia; in fact, both countries have had nearly identical annual per capita Gross Domestic Product (GDP). Malawi was also chosen because of its small size and population base, in contrast to Ethiopia's relatively large landmass—even after Eritrea's departure Ethiopia remains among the largest states in Africa—and population. Thus, allowance was made for similarities and differences, as well as extremes. Finally, Malawi, has been one of the political success stories in Africa. Since this book is about democratization in all of its outcomes, it would have failed in its mission if it did not include at least one successful case.

Tanzania stood mid-way, ideologically, between Ethiopia and Malawi. Under Nyerere, Tanzania was neither doctrinally Marxist nor pro-Western. While choosing the path of rural socialism for much of its postcolonial history and maintaining close ties to Eastern Europe and China, Tanzania cohabited rather well with Western capitalism, especially Scandinavian capitalism. Moreover, while Nyerere's dominant presence can be compared to Banda's and Mengistu's, his personality did much to temper the worst excesses of the neopatrimonial Tanzanian state. As Chapter 6 points out, there is no question that Nyerere, whether in or out of office, was (is) Tanzania's paramount spiritual leader, but he also went out of his way to imbue the Tanzanian one-party state with a modicum of limited democracy, and when he felt it was time, he was among the most forceful proponents of multipartyism. Tanzania's experience represents what might be called African Fabian socialism led by an enlightened political figure, and, although in some ways unique in Africa, it parallels somewhat the experience of Zambia under Kaunda and, perhaps even more so, Senegal under Senghor. In sum, Ethiopia, Malawi, and Tanzania cover a wide spectrum of ideologies during the Cold War and democratization outcomes.

CONCLUSION

The political gains recorded in Africa at the close of the twentieth century have been significant. Where the one-party, even the one-man, state used to reign supreme, multipartyism—imperfect to be sure—has sprouted. Indeed, since 1990 the overwhelming majority of African states have embraced what is perhaps the easiest aspect of democratization—that is, phase one or political liberalization—but judging by consistently high electoral turnout rates, Africans take their new citizenship responsibilities very seriously. Even though there have been relatively few instances of office turnovers, some longtime incumbents, such as Kaunda in Zambia and Banda in Malawi, have been defeated. The era of one-partyism, statistically implausible electoral margins of victory, and unaccountable life presidents is over for now. The wisdom of overcentralized state power and the "proper" role of ethnicity in political engineering are being reconsidered in countries like Ethiopia, raising fresh challenges for scholars and politicians. Simply put, this is an exciting time to be a student of African politics.

Any enthusiasm must, however, be tempered by the continued presence of longtime autocrats, such as Moi of Kenya and Biya of Cameroon, who, having been forced to subject themselves to the rigors of multiparty politics, continue to evince disdain toward the rule of law (phase two). Even neophytes whose coming to power was made possible by political liberalization have shown a tendency to use the tactics of an earlier era. Frederick Chiluba's behavior in office thus far in Zambia does not inspire much confidence in Africa's "new" democrats; neither does the performance of the government of the Central African Republic's Ange Félix Patassé, whose survival appears to depend entirely on the continued presence in Bangui of French troops. Pascal Lissouba in Congo was equally disappointing, which probably contributed to his violent overthrow. It is imprudent to predict how far and for how long democratization efforts will go (and last) in Africa. The future of democratization is, indeed, uncertain on the African continent. What this text tries to do is to capture the contradictions and uncertainty of the process in seven case studies without turning readers into Afro-pessimists.

NOTES

1. Georg Sorensen, *Democracy and Democratization* (Boulder, CO: Westview Press, 1993).

2. There is no universally accepted definition of democracy, except in the literal sense of people rule (from the Greek words *demos* for people and *kratein* for rule). What is meant by democracy here is liberal or political democracy, as defined by Robert Dahl. See Robert Dahl, *Polyarchy* (New Haven, CT: Yale University Press, 1971).

Although the democratic principles or conditions enunciated by Dahl are probably universal, we agree that conceptualizing democracy in Africa poses problems. For a brief but excellent treatment of this issue, see Fortman Bas de Gaay, "Conceptualizing Democracy in an African Context," *Quest* 8, no 1 (1994). For an African perspective, see K. A. Busia, "The Ingredients of Democracy," G. C. Mutiso and S. W. Rohi, eds., *Readings in African Political Thought* (London: Heineman Educational Books Ltd., 1986).

3. Jenifer Widener, ed., *Political Liberalization in Africa* (Baltimore, MD: Johns Hopkins University Press, 1991).

4. Goran Hyden and Michael Bratton, eds., *Governance and Politics in Africa* (Boulder, CO: Lynne Rienner Publishers, 1991).

5. Howard French, "An African Anomaly: Election Up for Grabs," *New York Times*, 2 March 1996.

6. For an eloquent synopsis of the levels of analysis approach, see Charles Kegley and Eugene Wittkopf, *World Politics: Trend and Transformation*, 6th ed., (New York: St. Martin's Press, 1997). A valiant effort to synthesize contemporary theories of democratization can be found in Pearl Robinson, "Democratization: Understanding the Relationship between Regime Change and the Culture of Politics," *African Studies Review* 37, no. 1 (April

1994). For a treatment of democratization in Africa, see Samuel Decalo, "The Process, Prospects and Constraints of Democratization in Africa," *African Affairs* 91 (1992).

7. A simple taxonomy of democratization outcomes includes the following categories: success, stagnation or blockage, and failure. Nuances in each category are allowed, such that success may be partial or complete. Complete success would clearly involve the cases where multiparty elections, deemed "free and fair" by independent observers, have been held, preferably more than once, and where clear improvements in human rights can be discerned. Malawi, South Africa, Mali and Benin are in this category. A partial success is Ghana, where two consecutive multiparty elections have been held and where there is greater freedom, especially press freedom; yet doubts remain as to what Rawlings might do when his term expires, or what he might have done if the outcomes of the 1992 and 1996 elections had been different. Cameroon, Kenya, Gabon, and probably much of Africa, are examples of stagnating democratization. The transition process in these countries has not been officially aborted, but neither does it seem to move forward. Elections continue to be deeply flawed, opposition parties operate under serious constraints, and human right violations are still common. Finally, there are failed transition cases, where an elected government is overthrown by the military (e.g., Burundi) or by an armed faction allied with a warlord (Congo-Brazzaville). A transition can also fail before an elected government is sworn in, in which case the military coup is an act of preemption, as opposed to one of reaction, against democratization. It should be stressed that democratization outcomes are never final in the sense of their being irreversible. The environment of democratization is dynamic, not static; therefore, success, depending on the correlation of forces of the moment, can become failure or stagnation.

8. For a case-by-case treatment of four "democracies" in postcolonial Africa, see John Wiseman, *Democracy in Black Africa* (New York: Paragon House Publishers, 1990). The work may seem somewhat outdated in light of setbacks in Gambia and more positive developments elsewhere.

9. Adam Przeworski, "Some Problems in the Study of the Transition to Democracy," Guillermo O'Donnell, Philippe Schmitter and Laurence Whitehead, eds., *Transitions from Authoritarian Rule: Comparative Perspectives* (Baltimore, MD: Johns Hopkins University Press, 1986).

10. Nicolas Van de Walle, "Political Liberalization and Economic Reform in Africa," *World Development* 22, no. 4 (April 1994).

11. Seymour Martin Lipset, "Some Social Requisites of Democracies," *American Political Science Review* 53 (1959).

12. Philippe Schmitter, "Society," in *The Transition to Democracy: Proceedings of a Workshop*, Commission on Behavioral and Social Sciences and Education, National Research Council (Washington, DC: National Academy Press, 1991).

13. Alexis de Tocqueville, *Democracy in America* (New York: Knopf, 1945).

14. D. D. Raphael, A. L. Macfie, eds., *The Theory of Moral Sentiments* by Adam Smith, Indianapolis, IN: Liberty Fund 1984).

15. See Jean-Germain Gros, "The Hard Lessons of Cameroon," *Journal of Democracy* 6, no. 3 (July 1995).

16. François Gaulme, "La France et les Pays du 'Champ': Le Tournant de la Baule," *Marchés Tropicaux*, 28 Décember 1990.

17. Donatella Lorch, "Is Kenya Sliding Back Toward Repression?" *New York Times*, 1 December 1995.

18. Some scholars are, in fact, pessimistic about the capacity of African civil society to play a positive role in the democratization process; they consider it a hindrance. See Robert Fatton, *The State and Civil Society in Africa* (Boulder, CO: Lynne Rienner Publishers, 1992).

19. Diffusionists, or demonstration effect theorists, generally believe that the end of the Cold War will lead to the globalization of "free" market economies and liberal democracy. See Francis Fukuyama, *The End of History and the Last Man* (New York: Free Press, 1992).

2
Democratization in Malawi: Its Roots and Prospects

Sam A. Mchombo

INTRODUCTION

An old political song in Malawi had lyrics that proclaimed: "*Zonse zimene za Kamuzu Banda.*" (Everything whatsoever belongs to Kamuzu Banda). It used to be a source of amusement to enumerate the things that could be said to belong to Kamuzu Banda, for, as the song went on to say, *misewu yonse, ya Kamuzu Banda* (all the roads belong to Kamuzu Banda), *azimayi onse, ya Kamuzu Banda* (all the women belong to Kamuzu Banda), and so on. In effect, the only line that had to be filled in was the following: All X belong to Kamuzu, where the variable X could be almost anything. The problem was not so much with the enumeration of what did or could belong to Kamuzu Banda as with determining what could not or did not so belong. Indeed, the postindependence period in Malawi was marked by the extraordinary fact that all aspects of political power came to be concentrated in the hands of one individual, the then His Excellency, Life President, Ngwazi Dr. Hastings Kamuzu Banda, to give him his full title. In its thirty years of existence as an independent sovereign state, Malawi came to attain the rare and dubious distinction of shifting from a one-party state to a one-man state.[1]

In 1994, the once all-powerful President Banda and the whole apparatus established to prop up his rule were replaced by a new democratic system of government. Indeed, Kamuzu Banda and his cohorts, specifically, his long-time female companion, Miss Cecilia Tamanda Kadzamira (formerly referred to as the official state hostess and respectfully addressed as Mama Kadzamira) together with her uncle, John Tembo, the former governor of the Reserve Bank of Malawi and later minister of state in the president's office were, for the better part of 1995, either under house arrest or in prison on suspicion of, inter alia, murder of former government ministers and other politicians. How did Malawi come to be tyrannized by a political system that has been characterized even during the best of times as a leviathan one-party state dominated by a small dictatorial clique—the triumvirate of

Banda, Tembo, and Mama Kadzamira?[2] Why did the dictatorial regime succumb to pressure in 1994? What are the prospects for democratization in Malawi?

MALAWI'S ROAD TO INDEPENDENCE

The nationalist fervor that swept Africa in the immediate post-World War II era was understandable. The costly war had not merely put a major strain on the economic resources of the European colonial masters, but it left Europe sufficiently weakened as to desist from militaristic solutions to political agitation in the colonies. This era also witnessed a shift in the centers of power, with the United States and the Soviet Union emerging as the new power brokers on the international scene. By dint of political ideology and economic policy, as well as security arrangements, Western Europe was closely allied with the United States or capitalist Washington, D.C. while Eastern Europe was aligned with the Soviet Union or communist Moscow. The other countries affiliated themselves with one of those two blocs depending on what political ideology they felt sympathetic toward, or, rather, where they sought aid.

Clearly, the human suffering and the indignities that the war had eminently made manifest, wherein the colonial masters displayed basic human frailties and engaged in atrocities that belied any pretensions to civilized conduct, tainted the moral high ground that provided the basic underpinning to colonialism. Malawians had previously made efforts to free themselves of the yoke of colonialism, such as during the John Chilembwe uprising in 1915. The postwar period provided an exceptionally opportune moment for Malawians to rid themselves of colonialism and thereby gain political and, to whatever extent possible, economic independence. It was in this climate that the first generation of African nationalist leaders emerged. Malawi, as it searched for credible leadership, came to identify Dr. Hastings Kamuzu Banda as the best candidate to lead it to independence. Since political developments in independent Malawi have been inextricably interwoven with the personal character and leadership style of Kamuzu Banda, no analysis of Malawi can be complete without examining Dr. Banda himself.

President Banda came from Kasungu in the central region of Malawi. Born, according to some accounts, in the late 1890s, he received a missionary education, beginning in Kasungu under a *Kachere* tree.[3] By all accounts Banda was a hardworking individual who took to his studies with great zest. In the tradition of the times he traveled on foot to South Africa in the early 1920s to seek employment in the mines. A brief sojourn en route in what was then southern Rhodesia, now Zimbabwe, where he worked as an orderly at a hospital, influenced his decision to study medicine. When he eventually got to South Africa, his literacy helped him get a position as a clerk. He continued to study privately and was eventually spotted by an American missionary, most likely of the African Methodist Episcopal Church, who recommended that he travel to the United States to further his education. Following this suggestion, he studied at Wilberforce Academy in Ohio, then at Meharry College in Tennessee where he studied medicine, and eventually at the University of Chicago. Because the British did not readily recognize American degrees, a fact that was bound to make it difficult for Banda to practice medicine in British-controlled Malawi, he decided to travel on to the United Kingdom to buttress his medical qualifications. He studied at the Royal College of Physicians and Surgeons in Edinburgh. He then proceeded to practice medicine in Liverpool (1939), North Shields (1940–44), and subsequently in Willesden, North London (1944–53).

It certainly took dedication to education to achieve all this, especially given the social circumstances pertaining to race and much else that prevailed during the period. To Banda's credit he used his life to show that hard work and dedication do indeed pay dividends. In London Banda networked with other African intellectuals, among whom were some of the first generation of nationalist leaders, such as Jomo Kenyatta and Kwame Nkrumah. He was also strategically placed to lobby for Malawi among British politicians. Without detracting from the contribution that Kamuzu Banda may have made to the cause for Malawi's independence, it must still be noted that he was outside the country and thus did not inspire any radical activity among the people. On the contrary, agitation for political change was given formal expression within Malawi by a number of young nationalists who, in 1944, formed the country's first national political organization, the Nyasaland African Congress (NAC), which later became the Malawi Congress Party (MCP). Banda was an active supporter of the NAC but the groundwork had been laid by others.[4]

AUTHORITARIANISM AND EARLY CAPITALISM

It did not take long for authoritarianism to surface after Banda's accession to power, because Malawi was plunged into a cabinet crisis virtually right after gaining independence in 1964. The more perspicacious elements in the government who had noticed the first signs of autocratic rule, even while negotiations over the terms of independence with the British were under way, decided to break ranks with Banda. When prominent nationalists, such as Henry Chipembere, Kanyama Chiume, Augustine Bwanausi, Orton Chirwa, Willie Chokani, and others, who sought more democratic participation in government, rose against Banda's methods, the country was thrown into political turmoil. Their departure to neighboring countries in effect created the conditions for the country's degeneration into authoritarianism. The subterfuge rested on matters of security; those dissident ministers who tried to form some kind of opposition to Banda from outside the country provided the immediate rationale for serious erosion of human rights.

The security of the country and that of its leader became intertwined and increasingly the focus of domestic affairs. Any seditious act, meaning capable of undermining the authority of the leadership and of the Malawi Congress Party, was punished with utmost severity. This took the form of detention without trial, a practice inherited from the colonial administration, usually meted out with the highest degree of arbitrariness.[5] Naturally, to achieve this degree of control Banda required watchdog institutions. These came in the form of both the regular branches and the special branch of the police force. In addition, he commandeered the more visible and downright rough League of Malawi Youth and the Malawi Young Pioneers (MYP).

Trained in part by the Israelis, the MYP was originally conceived as a means for training young people in agricultural and technical skills that would give them the expertise to become self-sufficient or, unrealistically, self-employed. The idea was to ease the pressure on a wage economy that could not absorb the entire work force. However, the MYP developed into a paramilitary force that became the armed wing of the MCP, a separate armed force with its own provisions for intelligence gathering, which was brazen in its approach to the quelling of opposition to Banda. The MYP was exempt from prosecution or arrest by the police, which conferred on its members the license to engage in physical harassment of the people with impunity. The MYP protected national security through activities such as enforcing purchase of MCP annual membership cards, attacking the property of individuals suspected of having links with dissidents, and hounding members of the Jehovah's Witnesses sect out of the country because of their unwillingness to acknowledge secular authority and their resistance to purchasing MCP cards.

Along with the MYP, the women, who Banda referred to by the Chichewa kinship term of *mbumba*, were mobilized into a Women's League whose primary function seemed to be dancing for President Banda whenever he made public appearances. The use of the term *mbumba*, the deferential use of *Mama* (the mother of the nation) for Miss Cecilia Tamanda Kadzamira, the state hostess, and Banda's frequent references to members of Parliament and government ministers as "my boys," provides some basis for claiming that Banda's rule was neopatrimonialist.[6] Banda viewed the nation as an extension of his household and ruled it as though he were ruling a family compound, as his actions and choice of words indicated.

In a matrilineal system, such as that of the Chewa, a man is responsible for the welfare of his mother(s), sisters, and their children, especially his nieces. These are collectively referred to as his *mbumba* (or family), and to them he is their *nkhoswe* (loosely translated as guarantor). *Mbumba* members are dutifully respectful of their *nkhoswe*, who is the most important person in the group. The choice of the label *mbumba* to refer to the women in Malawi, and Banda's self-appointment as their *Nkhoswe number one* underscores the neopatrimonialist nature of his regime. The subsequent incorporation of the women into the elaborate security apparatus, besides being expedient, exploited the psychology of kinship, especially in regard to the loyalty that a *nkhoswe* can expect to get from his *mbumba*.[7]

A major clampdown on the opposition and basic freedoms provided for by the constitution became necessary because Banda's policies, both domestic and, especially, foreign, were unpopular. On the domestic front Malawi adopted a capitalist free-market ideology. Malawi had started off as an "economic slum" lacking exploitable minerals, and its economic salvation lay in the exploitation of the land and labor. The land became the most important source of economic progress. However, in the creation of a middle class, which would be a buffer between the rich few and the poor masses, the land apportionment was extremely skewed. The

Banda-Kadzamira-Tembo triumvirate became the major land owners, with most of the top politicians and civil servants securing estates as well, while the largely dispossessed majority engaged in subsistence agriculture.[8]

The estates required labor, and once again the masses provided it very cheaply. In addition, the foreign markets were not accessible to the ordinary farmer. The produce, primarily rice, corn, cotton, groundnuts or peanuts, and tobacco had to be sold to a parastatal body, the Agricultural Development and Marketing Corporation (ADMARC), at low prices fixed by that body, and was exported at open market prices. This strategy probably contributed to the elimination of the deficit on the recurrent budget in the late 1970s. Tea farming, already monopolized by white farmers with plantations in the Mulanje-Thyolo area in the southern region, was largely inaccessible to the Malawian peasantry, who merely provided cheap labor. The "economic progress" did not translate into anything meaningful for the masses, who saw themselves working more for less, while the rich few got richer.

The skewed land distribution went in tandem with inequalities in the availability of other necessities. While Banda engaged in grandiose schemes, such as building personal palaces and an inordinately expensive high school called the Kamuzu Academy, where no black person was good enough to teach, medical and educational facilities in the country declined.[9] The majority merely eked out an existence. The policies that accounted for such "capitalism at its most rapacious" could only foment resistance and discontent.[10] Thus, it was necessary to control the population to ensure that resistance did not erupt into political activism. The machinery for repression took care of that.

In foreign policy, Banda opted for open diplomatic relations with the countries that were at the time under sanctions imposed by the Organization of African Unity (OAU). These were South Africa, Rhodesia (now Zimbabwe), and Portugal, which was involved in a tense struggle with nationalist forces in Mozambique. The crafting of Malawi's foreign policy was as much a function of global alliances, geopolitical factors, and economic incentives as it was of the personal character of Banda. In terms of global alliances, Malawi had aligned itself with the Western bloc, its pretensions to nonalignment notwithstanding. It maintained an extremely anti-Communist stance, as reflected in the banning of anything communist, especially communist literature, liberally defined as works extolling communist ideology or any publication originating from the Eastern bloc irrespective of the subject matter.

Furthermore, publications by scholars in the West that were critical of the policies of Washington or of the countries in its sphere of influence, especially those of Western Europe, were not permitted in Malawi.[11] With regard to the Middle East, Malawi's policy was very closely allied to the policies of Britain and the United States. Banda's African policy was equally pro-Western. During the Angolan civil war in 1978 Malawi did not only have to issue a public denial of allegations of its involvement with Jonas Savimbi's National Union for the Total Independence of Angola (UNITA)—along with apartheid South Africa—but during the evenly split vote of the OAU on recognition of the Popular Movement for the Liberation of Angola (MPLA) government in Luanda, Malawi voted with the "anti-

Communists" who argued for a government of national unity. Similarly, when Britain and Argentina went to war over the Falkland Islands, Malawi came out in vigorous attack of Argentina as the aggressor in the conflict.

With respect to regional geopolitics, relations between Malawi and Tanzania to the north and Zambia to the west were, to put it mildly, strained. The political asylum these countries offered to Malawian dissidents was construed as an affront by Banda. The situation was not helped by the abortive effort of a rather badly organized group of insurgents led by Yatuta Chisiza in 1967 to infiltrate the country and unseat Banda militarily. Yatuta Chisiza was killed in the ensuing engagement with the Malawian army which, to its consternation and embarrassment, sustained severe casualties in this scuffle with literally a handful of insurgents. In any case, the fact that the dissidents were allowed to organize in Tanzania and Zambia strained relations between Malawi and these two countries. Furthermore, Malawi was a landlocked country; access to the sea for its goods required passage through either Mozambique or South Africa, because shipment through Dar es Salaam was made very difficult by the lack of rail links between Malawi and Tanzania. Thus, good relations with the Portuguese in Mozambique and the apartheid regime in South Africa was a necessity. To a large extent Malawi's warm relations with the white-controlled neighboring countries derived from geopolitical considerations. However, this does not provide the full story; there is something else.

Malawi, like most other African countries, is ethnically diverse. Among the ethnic groups found within the political boundaries of Malawi are the Lomwe, Yao, Tumbuka, Tonga, Chewa (including Nyanja), Sena, Nkhonde, Lambya, Nyakyusa, and Ngoni. While the population figures of recent times do not provide a clear picture of the population distribution, it is probable that the Chewa-Nyanja group forms a numerical majority, with the Lomwe, Yao and Tumbuka groups following in second, third, and fourth positions, respectively.[12] The Tumbukas, Tongas, Lambyas, Nkhondes, Nyakyusas, and some of the Ngonis, live in the northern part of the country. The Chewas predominate in the Central region of Malawi, with some of the Yaos and Ngonis represented there as well. The southern part of the country also consists primarily of Chewas, Yaos, Lomwes and Senas.

Kamuzu Banda, a Chewa, had his power base in the central region of Malawi, where the Chewas predominate. During the colonial period most economic activities had occurred in the southern region, with the tea estates providing part of the boon. The main commercial center was Blantyre, in the south, and the administrative capital was the small town of Zomba, located some forty miles northeast of Blantyre. The central and, especially, the northern regions were relatively underdeveloped. With a Chewa president at the helm starting in 1964, it was natural for the Chewa elite to expect some shifts in economic activities and in the scope of their control of the political direction of the country. In some ways they were not to be totally disappointed. International sanctions against Rhodesia (Zimbabwe) following its Unilateral Declaration of Independence in 1965 opened a more favorable climate for Malawian tobacco, which was produced mainly in the Chewa-dominated central region. The Chewas could capitalize on the sanctions against then-Rhodesia and reap the benefits of tobacco farming.

Chewa hegemony was confirmed in 1968 at the annual convention of the MCP, when Chichewa, the language of the Chewa, was declared the national language, with English serving as the official language. Henceforth Chichewa was to be studied in the schools and used in the media, which effectively made Chewa culture the dominant strand of the Malawi cultural fabric.[13] Banda also proceeded to move the administrative capital from Zomba to the centrally located city of Lilongwe. The logic for this was simple. Economic development in the country had been concentrated in the southern region, which hosted both the administrative capital and the commercial center. The country would develop more uniformly, so the official logic went, if the administrative headquarters were in centrally located Lilongwe. Naturally, it was supposed to be purely accidental that Lilongwe was the heart of Chewaland. Donors (e.g., Great Britain, the United States, and the World Bank) expressed reluctance to support this project.

In the ensuing impasse, South Africa, noting major political and strategic advantages, offered to provide Banda with the initial capital for the project. Malawi's foreign policy immediately underwent a major shift to accommodate relations with the apartheid regime. Under the policy of contact and dialogue, Banda defended relations with South Africa on the grounds that the way to change human relations there was not through economic boycott but through discussion. It was a policy that isolated Malawi from the rest of the African countries and, for most Africans, Banda had degenerated into "the greatest rogue that went unhung."[14] Malawi's ostracism merely heightened the regime's sense of siege, which bordered on paranoia, and it made security the central concern of the government. Unabashed repression thus became a survival weapon, with human rights abuses and political detentions exploited to serve that end. Banda came to wield absolute power and Parliament was reduced to rubber stamping his whims and directives. Externally-based opposition groups were infiltrated and their leaders either assassinated, as in the case of Attati Mpakati, the leader of the Mozambique-based Socialist League of Malawi (LESOMA), or abducted from foreign soil, as in the case of Orton Chirwa, the leader of the Malawi Freedom Movement (MAFREMO) who was brought from Zambia with his wife, Vera, and their son, Fumbani.

Because they can shape multitudes of minds, the media, the churches, and the educational establishments came under the most intense scrutiny and were under constant surveillance. Malawi, like other African countries, may have "inherited a competitive, untethered press at independence," but much more than most other countries, it "managed to destroy it so effectively"[15] the expression Malawian free press acquired the air of an oxymoron. Journalism in Malawi was, quite simply, a risky business. Journalists were detained on the flimsiest of grounds. In 1973 and 1974, Parliament passed laws mandating severe penalties to "lying journalists." This was in the wake of a foreign report about Malawi-Mozambique border incidents involving Malawi and Portuguese forces, which was assumed to have been secretly transmitted by Malawian journalists. The media came under the tight control of the government with severe censorship imposed on the importation and dissemination of news.

Along with freedom of the press, academic freedom virtually disappeared. In many respects academic freedom had been quelled as soon as the University of Malawi came into existence. Opening its doors to Malawian undergraduates in 1965, the university came into existence during a period of unrest in academic institutions, especially in the United States, where colleges and universities became the centers for anti-Vietnam War activism. The opportunity to crack down on academic freedom presented itself almost immediately, with what appeared to be a blunder on the part of the students. The Chichiri campus of the University of Malawi had a debating society. In order to forge relations with the political elements, in 1967 the debating society extended an invitation to the government to debate the idea of a one-party state, with the politicians defending it and the students opposing it. Interpreting this as a sign of student opposition to the one-party state, Banda went on the attack, castigating university students as arrogant and presumptuous in thinking that they knew everything when they were "mere suckling babies."[16] Seven students were immediately expelled; all were eventually reinstated, with the exception of one Suzgo Munthali, who fled to Zambia. The university community, like the press, was under constant surveillance, with a significant number of academics eventually landing in detention for unspecified offenses.[17]

With the exception of the Jehovah's Witnesses sect, whose members had been physically harassed and driven out of the country, the other churches seemed to toe the party and government line or stay out of politics. However, as the alienation of the masses increased, the frustration at the impunity with which prominent politicians could be murdered without so much as a breath of protest from anyone, not even the institutions that preached the ten commandments, one of which clearly states that "Thou shall not kill," the relevance of the church to people's lives demanded explanation. Lessons from other countries, such as Zimbabwe and South Africa, had shown that when the oppressed could not find legitimate channels of expression for their hopes and aspirations, the church could become an important outlet.

In Zimbabwe nationalist leaders such as Ndabaningi Sithole, Joshua Nkomo, and, later, Abel Muzorewa, had come from the clergy. In South Africa Archbishop Desmond Tutu and Reverend Alan Boesak used the pulpit to articulate what the people could not express otherwise. In Malawi, the facade of independence could not eliminate or mask the oppression the people suffered, and for many the church had ceased to have relevance to their lives because it had been totally compromised, or so it seemed. It is a supreme irony that the downfall of the Banda regime and the revival of democratic ideals in Malawi was precipitated in part by the actions of the Catholic Church (more on that later).

CRACKS IN THE SYSTEM

Because authoritarianism in Malawi was highly personalized, the advanced age of Banda posed a dilemma for the regime; the question of succession was especially problematic, since Banda had no political heir apparent related to him by blood. It was common knowledge, or at least common suspicion, that Mama Kadzamira's uncle was being groomed for the post. In May 1983, a special session of Parliament was convened to ratify the appointment of John Tembo as acting president while President Banda went off to Britain on a one-year "sabbatical." Two senior ministers, Aaron Gadama (minister of the Central Region and a relative of President Banda), and Dick Matenje (secretary general and administrative secretary of the MCP), led the opposition to this unconstitutional move. They, together with Twaibu Sangala, then minister of health, and David Chiwanga, a member of Parliament, were summarily executed.

The callousness of the killings and the speed with which they were carried out were such that even the government could not come up with a coherent explanation of how the politicians had met their demise. A staged traffic accident used to account for their death was belied by the denial of funeral rights. This was noted cryptically in verse by the renowned poet Jack Mapanje who, for his "irritating" poetry, was detained for three-and-a-half years (1987–90) in Mikuyu Detention Camp near Zomba. In his poem *No Creon, There's No Virtue in Howling*, Mapanje writes:

No, Creon, you overstate your image to your People.
No, there's no virtue in howling so.
How can you hope to repair Haemon, your
Own blood, our only hope for the throne,
By reproaching his body mangled by your
Decree and put to rest without the requiem
Of our master drums?[18]

The incident not only highlighted the brazenness with which the Banda-Kadzamira-Tembo triumvirate could eliminate opposition, but also served to galvanize the conscience of the Malawi population. It gave a new rallying point for the externally based and largely fragmented opposition groups. Meeting in Lusaka, Zambia, a new opposition organization, Save Malawi Council (SAMACO), was formed, but with minimal observable impact on the regime's conduct or attitude. Effective opposition to Banda needed to be fomented within the country.

The Church and the Underground Media

There is a Chichewa proverb which warns that *Njoka yopusa idalumira ku mchira* (a foolish snake bit with its tail). The dominant religion in Malawi is Christianity, with major representations of denominations such as the Presbyterian Church, the Catholic Church, the Anglican Church, the Seventh Day Adventist, and, to a lesser extent, the Baptists, as well as some version of Zionism. The church in Malawi, which was viewed as totally compromised, engaged in activities such as running schools, and medical clinics, and saving souls. It remained detached from overt political activity, and the pulpit was never used for the articulation of the aspirations of the oppressed. Perhaps because the church appeared to have been reduced to an ally of the government, it is all the more spectacular that it became the source of mobilization of popular opposition to the government.

The brutality of the Banda regime, as reflected in politically motivated disappearances of people even outside of Malawi, economic malaise, inequity in the distribution of resources and access to medical and educational facilities, and the severe curtailment of the freedoms of speech, press, and academic inquiry, could no longer be viewed as irrelevant to the enterprise of saving souls. Malawian politics was in basic conflict with various aspects of scriptural teaching, a fact that contributed to the undermining of the credibility of the church as it projected an image of indifference to the plight of the people. Missionary activity had played a significant role in the country's development, providing schools and hospitals. The church's deep involvement in the developmental aspects of the country was curiously incommensurate with its lack of input in political matters. The attempt to rectify the inconsistency provided the immediate basis for the unraveling of the Banda regime.

In January 1992, the Episcopal Conference of Malawi met in Lilongwe. The meeting was attended not only by ministers of the episcopal faith but also by all the Catholic bishops of Malawi, five Malawians and one European. There, they "listened to a verbal report by three bishops who had met Mr. Mlambala, Minister of Education and Culture, to discuss improving partnership in education between the Church and State."[19] The report revealed that although the church made monetary contributions to education, it was not involved in determining the quality of that education; this task remained the sole concern of the government. The church was dissatisfied with the fact that in church-state ventures the operative principle was that it should pay up and shut up. At that meeting the bishops decided to act by writing a letter exposing unjust government policy in several areas of Malawian life.[20] The church finally came to realize that the silence it had maintained over those matters was simply scandalous.

The letter that was eventually drafted and signed by all the bishops turned out to be an eleven-page pastoral document entitled *Living Our Faith*, which opened with a quote from Pope Paul VI's encyclical, *The Evangelisation of Peoples:* "The Church is certainly not willing to restrict her action to the religious field and disassociate herself from man's temporal problems." The pastoral letter went on to detail the ills of Malawian society, such as increasing inequality between rich and poor, the spread of corruption, flaws in the educational system, blatant injustices, denial of basic freedoms, cutbacks in health care, and so forth. In what must go down in modern African history as one of the most effective clandestine actions, 16,000 copies of the letter were printed (10,000 in Chichewa, 5,000 in Chitumbuka, and 1,000 in English) and distributed to all the parishes to be read during the Ash Wednesday celebration on March 4, 1992.

The impact of the pastoral letter lay less in its statement of things that were already public knowledge, but more in the public articulation of those facts from the pulpit on a nationwide basis. Freedom of speech is one of the rights that the government had tried to curtail, but civil society, as represented by the church, had at last shown its resiliency. The public criticism of the government that ensued constituted the real significance of the pastoral letter, from which Banda never recovered. At first the government tried to salvage itself by striking back at the bishops with charges of sedition and disloyalty, and even by determining ways of killing them. However, the more the government tried to set the people against the bishops, the more the people flocked to the Catholic churches.

In truth, the government had underestimated the role of the church and had taken it for granted for too long. Now, like the proverbial foolish snake, it had bitten with its tail. Conversely, the church had defined a new role for itself, and, with heightened expectations from the masses, it had set itself on a course that lacked explicit directions. In brief, how could the momentum created be sustained and what direction would Malawian politics take? The church, however it might occasionaly become embroiled in man's secular problems, was definitely not going to shift focus from religious to political matters. In some ways the church now found that, having laid the groundwork for political action, it needed to transfer the leadership to politicians. It was in this state of affairs that erstwhile underground clandestine groups surfaced.

The problems of the Banda regime were compounded by the information revolution, for the longevity of the dictatorship in Malawi depended as much on the rigid control of the flow of information as it did on the coercion and repression of its citizenry. News broadcasts reflected nothing but the most positive aspects of President Banda; they exhorted people to work hard and to strengthen their pledge of loyalty to President Banda personally, the MCP, and the government. Postal services were unreliable as mail was routinely opened and read, and telecommunications were under constant surveillance, especially communication with individuals outside Malawi. Any news that might give the Malawi population "ideas" was carefully censored. Thus, the Malawi press never reported on coups and attempted or actual assassinations of politically prominent figures, and so on. For example, the attempted assassinations of President Ronald Reagan and Pope John Paul II were not carried on Malawi radio. The assassination of President Anwar Sadat of Egypt was reported several days after the fact, when there was reference to his successor, prefaced by the remark that Mubarak had taken over from the former president who had "died suddenly."[21]

To undermine the regime, ways of circumventing the control of information flow had to be found. The advent of fax machines, photocopiers, and computers turned out to be fortuitous. It became feasible to communicate without submitting the contents to the agents of repression for confiscation. Suddenly, details about Banda's misdeeds, facts about John Tembo's stranglehold on Malawi's economy and their collective designs on the future of Malawi, commentary on the need for political organization and popular uprising against Banda, and much else could be faxed or transmitted by computer to Malawi, then privately photocopied. The copies were then placed in strategic locations where they could get maximum exposure before the police or the MYP could retrieve them. The subsequent harassment of establishments with, and individuals having access to, fax machines could not stem the onslaught as the people began to comment on facts previously censored.

THE DAWN OF MULTIPARTY POLITICS

The first opposition leader to emerge and step into the political fracas in Malawi was Chakufwa Chihana, secretary general of the Southern Africa Trade Union Coordination Council (SATUCC). The very survival of the bishops gave courage to government opponents both inside and outside the country. It was natural that the externally based opposition should seize the moment to reorganize and push for democratic change in Malawi. In March 1992, a prodemocracy meeting of exiled Malawians was held in Lusaka, Zambia, where Chakufwa Chihana gave a keynote speech entitled "Prospects for Democracy in Malawi." In it he criticized the autocratic rule of Banda as "twentieth-century feudalism." During that meeting the Interim Committee for a Democratic Alliance (ICDA) was formed, and Chihana was elected chairman.

The ICDA's immediate objectives were to fight for the restoration of human rights in Malawi, the release of all political prisoners, and the granting of amnesty to all exiles. To be more effective than previous opposition movements, the committee asked Chihana to return to Malawi to organize a national conference of political forces within the country. Making a highly publicized trip back to Malawi, complete with a prepared speech to be read on arrival, Chihana flew into Malawi and straight into police custody on April 6, 1992. This was expected and his incarceration had been calculated into the publicity for the cause for democracy. That action immediately converted Chihana into a rallying point for democratic forces in Malawi. On May 1, 1992, a political organization called the Alliance for Democracy (AFORD), based in the northern region town of Rumphi, declared itself an opposition group with Chihana as chairman.

The MCP government's response to emergent changes was characteristic of its repressive methods; it sought to harass and arrest AFORD supporters, a strategy that was both unrealistic and unsound, given the shifting political climate both in the country and around the world. The strategy also played into already strained ethnic relations, as Chakufwa Chihana is a Tumbuka from the northern region. With a respectable international profile as a human rights activist—he was the recipient of the 1993 Robert F. Kennedy award—Chihana emerged not only as a credible alternative to the morally and politically bankrupt Banda regime, but, as a Tumbuka, his political stature gave hope for the possible political rehabilitation of the maligned northern region. Chihana's ethnicity and the birthplace of AFORD were not irrelevant to the composition of AFORD membership, which drew largely from the northern region. In fact, AFORD has had to contend with the image of being an ethnically based political organization, a fact that became evident in the voting pattern during the elections. The MCP government's detention of Chihana not only strengthened the resolve of the forces for democratic change, but also underscored the role of ethnicity in Malawian politics.

The emergence of AFORD gave impetus to the surfacing of another previously clandestine opposition group based in the major commercial city of Blantyre in the southern region. This was the United Democratic Front (UDF), most of whose members were successful businessmen and former MCP leaders who had fallen out with Banda. The UDF eventually elected Bakili Muluzi, a Yao and a Muslim from the south, as its chairman. Other parties were formed but their membership could not rival that of UDF and AFORD. Initially, the parties could not legally be designated political parties as the Malawi constitution had enshrined the MCP as the sole legal political party, and the democratic movement was at pains to demonstrate respect for the law and the constitution. They were thus referred to as pressure groups. However, terminological preferences could not obscure the reality that there was a major internal groundswell of anti-Banda and anti-MCP sentiment that the government could hardly ignore. The prevailing state of flux invited the exercise of other rights formerly denied or proscribed. Workers began to strike for better working conditions and higher wages, students protested on the university campuses, and, in what was a major demonstration of the crumbling of the government's grip on the flow of information and thought processes, an independent press emerged, with newspapers mushrooming at an unprecedented rate.

President Banda and the MCP were clearly on the retreat. Arrests of the leadership or supporters of the opposition groups could no longer go without comment, and the corruption of the regime became a favorite topic in the news media. International pressure had escalated to the suspension of aid to Malawi by the EEC and Great Britain, except for drought-related or refugee-related relief, until the regime could convince the international community of its readiness to respect human rights and to promote the requisite conditions for a return to democracy. This was exacerbated by a rather sustained focus by the international media, especially the BBC, and human rights organizations such as Amnesty International and Africa Watch on events in Malawi, a focus that deprived the regime of the anonymity it had previously exploited to suppress dissent and oppress its citizenry. However, the MCP was not going to give up power easily. Banda decided to put the issue of multiparty politics to a referendum on October 18, 1992, when he declared that "a referendum would be held to decide whether the people wanted to retain the one-party state or embrace a multiparty democracy."[22]

Banda's capitulation rested on the belief that multiparty politics would introduce disunity and discord among the people of Malawi, a prospect they would reject in favor of the "stable government and steady economic growth" they had enjoyed over the previous twenty eight years. Banda's calculation was in some ways shrewd and not entirely misguided. Still in control of official institutions, such as the police, the MYP, and the radio station (the MBC), Banda stood to gain politically, or so he thought, by associating multiparty politics with chaos and divisiveness. Furthermore, he could derive solace and credibility from the emergent regional and ethnic overtones of party affiliation: Banda and the MCP had their power base practically confined to the Chewa-dominated central region, with AFORD solid in the northern region, and UDF dominant in the southern region, the most populous of the three regions.

It may not have been by design, and certainly efforts to defuse the apparent ethnic or regional delineation of the parties were made by each major party, but the fact remained that multiparty politics in Malawi would be inextricably intermingled with issues of ethnicity and regionalism, at least in the short term. This could be sufficiently discouraging for a population that had enjoyed relative peace and stability, ethnic antipathy and autocratic rule notwithstanding. Banda gambled that this approach might persuade a level-headed populace to remain in the frying pan of unipartyism instead of jumping into the fire of multiparty politics. Banda decided to hold a referendum that would "give my people the chance to show their support and commitment to me and the MCP party."[23] Banda's strategy of making the referendum reflect on his standing among the people turned out to be costly for him: in June 1993 multipartyism was chosen by a ratio of almost two to one over the one-party state.

Banda's immediate response to the results of the referendum was to claim that the vote only showed that the people wanted multiparty politics, not that they rejected him as their president. As such, calls for him to step down from the presidency were misguided and beside the point. Further, while the idea of general elections was one that he or the government might give some thought to, it was not an automatic consequence of the referendum results. This may have sounded like splitting hairs or reading the fine print, but it was technically correct. Of course, Banda could choose to disregard the results of the referendum and remain in power, despite domestic and international pressure. There was also one trump card that he and the MCP held, and the opposition groups lacked: the heavily armed Malawi Youth Pioneers. This paramilitary organization had, over the years, become the armed wing of the MCP, with armaments that were the envy of the Malawi Army. It was also a heavily politicized organization that believed in exactly one doctrine or ideology: Kamuzuism.

The idea of political parties having armed wings became an issue. In a country with an army to defend it from external foes, and a police force to maintain law and order, a separate paramilitary organization detached from those functions and serving only to further the political goals of a particular political organization was plainly undesirable. Thus, among the changes sought by the opposition after the referendum was the disbanding of the MYP. Regarding this demand, Banda made no promises. In fact, the MYP went so far as to stage a brazen demonstration in Blantyre in August 1993, conveying the message rather bluntly that it would neither disband nor give up its weapons or armaments.

In the end, however, the collapse of the regime was quick and spectacular. For a start, and perhaps fittingly, Banda literally collapsed in October of 1993 from the effects of a brain tumor and had to be rushed off to South Africa. The international media and the Malawian private press were quick to publicize the story, much to the chagrin of the ruling MCP, which apparently was not keen to have the incident made public. In the interim the chairmanship of the MCP went to Gwanda Chakuamba, a former minister of youth and sports as well as Commander of the MYP. Readers familiar with Malawi politics might ask why John Tembo, the heir apparent, did not assume power following his benefactor's physical demise.

John Tembo's unpopularity was legendary; his readiness to quell competition or dissent with implacable ruthlessness was demonstrated by the killings of the ministers who had opposed his possible appointment as either prime minister or acting president. Transferring the leadership of the MCP and the government to him in the interim would have served to strengthen the belief that the presidency was being passed on, like a chieftaincy, to a family member with total disregard for the wishes of the people. Ultimately, even the most brutal dictatorships are not entirely insensitive to public opinion, especially when their political fortune is on the decline. A presidential council, as provided for by the constitution, comprising Gwanda Chakuamba as chair, John Tembo as minister of state, and Robson Chirwa, the secretary general of the MCP, was set up to run the country during Banda's hospitalization in South Africa. However, Gwanda Chakuamba quickly assumed the kind of profile that made him a de facto acting president. The confusion created by the absence of coherent leadership merely gave rise to a distinct sense of a power vacuum in Malawi. This uncertainty was to be short-lived, however. Malawi's democratic transition was put back on track at the beginning of December 1993 when the regular Malawi army effected the collapse of the MYP, the backbone of the Banda regime, through Operation Bwezani.

OPERATION BWEZANI

Without an air force or a navy, the military establishment in Malawi has traditionally consisted of the army. Maintaining the image of a professional army, it has stayed out of politics and, by and large, away from any real conflicts. During Banda's long reign, the army's public image was undermined by the government's preference for the MYP. The parallel military structure that the MYP had become made for basic strains in the relations between the two organizations. While the Malawian army was basically nonpolitical and tried to remain that way, the MYP was a political organization, the armed wing of the MCP. Thus the two organizations had nothing in common ideologically or functionally. They both just happened to be heavily armed, each with their own administrative structure and ancillary units for intelligence gathering. Of course, given the potential for armies to take over governments through coups d'états, the MYP increasingly became the force that not only spied on the army but had the muscle to quell any insurrection were the military ever to think about moving out of the barracks and into the State House. The structural arrangements seemed to project the impotence of the army; a tour de force was necessary to rectify the situation.

On December 3, 1993, while Banda was recuperating from brain surgery, the army attacked the MYP. In what was termed Operation Bwezani the army disbanded the MYP, confiscated its weapons, and sent its members scuttling into private life or into Mozambique where they allegedly sought refuge in *Resistencia Nacional Moçambicana* (RENAMO) camps. The armed conflict between the Malawi Army and the MYP was not as accidental as the accounts have suggested. The army had displayed sympathy for the transition to democracy; it was not a tool of the political parties. The differences in ideological outlook were exacerbated by the military might that the MYP had acquired. The MYP could contain any unrest within the country, irrespective of its source. Maintaining the facade of harmony between the two organizations required extra efforts, which occasionally broke down. This festering of uneasy relations was bound to explode and explode it did.

Operation Bwezani, thanks in large part to the lightning speed with which it was launched, was a military success, and it won the army major dividends in public relations. More importantly, with the playing field made level in that no party had a private army, the momentum for change was restored and real politicking could take place in earnest.

ELECTIONS: POLITICS, RESULTS, AND INTERPRETATION

The parties that sprouted to champion the cause of democracy in Malawi were not really separated by ideological differences, to the extent that these were even determinate. They had one common objective, which was to see the demise of the Banda regime. The opposition groups shared a basic antipathy toward the Banda government, but this is far from saying that they had a political ideology or an economic program. Defining political and economic platforms proved trickier for the parties, more so given the New World Order which has practically eliminated variations in the nature of political and economic debates. The absence of substantive differences in political and economic programs to provide the basis of choice among the parties meant that the appeal had to be based on other factors. The referendum had obscured the practical problems which were to beset the parties, because its objective was to decide whether Malawi should remain a one-party state under Banda or become a democratizing, multiparty state. The choice was simple and the opposition parties virtually shared the aura of being champions of democratic values and agents of change. The general elections, on the other hand, were to decide which party or persons would form the next government.

For the people it was a leap into the unknown, however much they may have longed for or anticipated the moment. For the parties, the question was, should they cooperate in order to successfully unseat or dislodge Banda, or should they campaign separately? While an alliance between AFORD and UDF, the major opposition parties, may have been desirable, there was reason to believe that it would not happen, and it did not. AFORD made it clear that the party would campaign alone, with its leader Chakufwa Chihana fielded as the presidential candidate; the MCP hung on to Kamuzu Banda for president; thus UDF had to campaign separately too, fielding Bakili Muluzi as the presidential candidate. This array of political parties immediately brought into sharp focus the factors that separated the parties and their respective agendas, to the extent that these could be articulated in clear language. The salient factor here was identification with the regions of Malawi and, along with that, aspects of ethnicity as these coincided with regional boundaries. By virtue of leadership the parties were identified with the northern, the central, and the southern regions, respectively. Polarization by regional and ethnic affiliations was made worse by popular images of the parties.

The perception of the opposition parties was that the top brass of UDF consisted of ex-MCP heavyweights who had fallen out with Banda, whereas AFORD consisted of former dissidents who had had nothing to do with the Banda government, except their incarceration or forced exile by it. This difference was exploited in a touch of negative campaigning; the campaign machinery for AFORD was quick to point out that UDF could not provide genuine change because it was nothing but "born-again MCP." Furthermore, given the dominance of prominent business people in UDF and the support the business community gave that party, with Bakili Muluzi a successful businessman himself, the party could be projected as not being worker oriented. This contrasted sharply with the image of AFORD leadership, for Chihana had been a trade unionist, and was therefore worker oriented. AFORD found these campaigns useful since they cut across boundaries of ethnicity and regionalism and ushered in perceptions of genuine differences between the parties, with AFORD probably imbued with a more socialist outlook and UDF decidedly conservative. This would give UDF the aura of a party with ideological inclinations toward further enrichment of the rich, with all the consequences that the Banda regime had made manifest. In any case, the field was thus aligned and ready for the elections.

The results of the May 17, 1994, elections not only handed Bakili Muluzi the presidency, but also gave the UDF the most seats in parliament, though not enough to give it a clear majority. The UDF secured eighty-five seats, the MCP got fifty-six seats and AFORD carried the rear with thirty-six seats. Most notable in the results was the correlation between the voting patterns and ethnic or regional boundaries.[24] In brief, the northern region overwhelmingly threw itself behind Chihana, while Bakili Muluzi captured the southern region and those parts of the central region adjacent to the south. Banda secured the rest of the central region. The demographics of the country, with the southern region as the most populous, gave Muluzi the most votes and the presidency. But the voting patterns also showed that ethnicity, which had been in the undercurrents, could no longer be ignored as a potentially divisive factor in Malawi. The more immediate problem for the newly elected UDF government was its being a minority government. Some kind of coalition, especially with AFORD, was inevitable if the UDF government was to carry out its programs. UDF and AFORD eventually agreed to cooperate after the UDF government relinquished control of a number of ministries to AFORD. The paradox here is that while Malawi appears closer to national unity, the alliance may develop into yet another big party, effectively sliding the country into a de facto one-party state again.

CONCLUSION: PROSPECTS

It is necessary to recapitulate the reasons behind Banda's fall, for the circumstances surrounding the demise of authorianism always have a bearing on the prospects of democratic transition or democratization. Credit must be given to civil society. The Church was the first to fill the vacuum that was left by the obliteration of organized political opposition to Banda. Before political parties were formed, it provided the fora for grievances against the former ruling regime and compelled it to respond. In addition, cracks developed within the security apparatus, shown most vividly by Operation Bwezani, which allowed Malawi's standing army to settle old scores with its arch paramilitary rival. The elimination of the MYP tilted the relations of forces toward the opposition, because the ruling party was deprived of its army. Banda's personal collapse meant that he was no longer in a position to manage the situation close by. Finally, international pressure, especially the cutting of aid by Britain and other donors, deprived the regime of financial liquidity; in other words, dependence may have played a role. In the end, even though Banda was personally against reform, the forces against him (i.e., domestic civil society, the international community, and his own military) were overwhelming. They were more than sufficient to overcome whatever resistance a feeble old man was willing to put up.

The prospects for democratization and democracy in Malawi hinge on a number of factors. First, as Malawi shows, it may not be necessary for a country to be rich in order to start democratizing, but wealth and everything that comes with it (e.g., a large middle class, urbanization, high literacy rates) may still be a necessary condition for consolidating the gains of democratization and moving toward democracy. Unless the new order brings out economic progress, the political gains made in 1993–94 could soon be lost. Second, Malawi's civil society institutions, much as those of Eastern Europe, were very successful in challenging Banda's authoritarian regime. Will the Catholic Church maintain an active role in post-Banda Malawi, or return to matters of greater and more immediate concerns to it, leaving politics to the politicians? An active civil society in Malawi may be the best insurance against abuse by public authority, especially if political parties move ever closer to one another in ideology and practice. In this vein, a free press, which took little time to emerge, is essential. Third, there is the Malawian military, whose decision to support prodemocracy forces may have been more strategic than principled. President Muluzi's ability to keep the Malawian military in check, by keeping its members inside the barracks and out of politics, may well determine Malawi's political fate; however, the initial signs augur well for democratization.

NOTES

1. Partly because of that perception and partly because of Banda's warm relations with the apartheid regime in South Africa, one South African remarked to the author in London during the 1970s, that in some circles in South Africa, Malawi had acquired the uncomplimentary label of "Bandastan."

2. Guy Mhone, "The Political Economy of Malawi: An Overview," Guy Mhone, ed., *Malawi at the Crossroads: The Post-Colonial Political Economy* (Harare, Zimbabwe: SAPES Books, 1992).

3. Philip Short, *Banda* (London: Routledge & Kegan Paul, 1974).

4. Ibid.

5. Africa Watch Report, *Where Silence Rules: The Suppression of Dissent in Malawi* (New York: Human Rights Watch, 1990).

6. Robert H. Jackson and Carl G. Rosberg, *Personal Rule in Black Africa* (Berkeley: University of California Press, 1982).

7. When the "rebel" Silombela "terrorized" the Mangochi area during the mid-1960s, and kept eluding the police, Banda turned to women. It was during a visit to a female friend that Silombela was apprehended.

8. Guy Mhone, op. cit.

9. Banda made no secret of the low opinion he held for Black African intellectuals. In public addresses he stated very bluntly that there would be no *mitu bii* (Black heads) teaching at the Kamuzu Academy, because he wanted to see very high standards there. The implication that Africans would lower the standards is self-evident, and the derogatory *mitu bii* label made the Kamuzu Academy highly unattractive to qualified African scholars.

10. This remark was made to the author by Tony Green, a British academic who taught Sociology of Education at Chancellor College in the University of Malawi during the 1970s.

11. The political writings of linguist Noam Chomsky, which were critical of the United States, especially its foreign policy, found themselves on the lists of banned publications in Malawi. This also applied to any publications that might be critical of, say, British policy toward Northern Ireland, regardless of the nationality of the author(s).

12. Pascal Kishindo, "The Impact of a National Language on Minority Languages: The Case of Malawi," *Journal of Contemporary African Studies* 12, no. 2 (1994).

13. Chijere Chirwa, "Regionalism, Ethnicity and the National Question in Malawi," *Sapem* (December 1994–January 1995), pp. 59–62.

14. Carolyn McMaster, *Malawi: Foreign Policy and Development* (London, UK: Julian Friedman, 1974), p. 33.

15. David Lamb, *The Africans* (New York: Vintage Books, 1983).

16. These words were in broadcasts of Banda's speeches during the debating society controversy.

17. Africa Watch Report, *Academic Freedom and Human Rights Abuses in Africa* (New York: Human Rights Watch, 1991).

18. Jack Mapanje, *The Chattering Wagtails of Mikuyu Prison* (London: Heinemann, 1985), p. 12.

19. Trevor Cullen, *Malawi: A Turning Point* (Edinburgh, UK: The Pentland Press, 1994).

20. Ibid.

21. The Malawi Broadcasting Corporation's report that Sadat had "died suddenly" was technically correct since he was assassinated in a hail of bullets and hand grenades. What was infelicitous about the report was the subtle implication that president had apparently died of natural causes.

22. Broadcast on the *Malawi Broadcasting Corporation* (MBC) on 19 October 1992.

23. Ibid.

24. For an analysis of the role of ethnicity in Malawian politics, see Leroy Vail and Lan White, "Tribalism in the Political History of Malawi," Leroy Vail, ed., *The Creation of Tribalism in Southern Africa* (London: James Curry Ltd., 1989), pp. 151–192. See also Chijere Chirwa, "Regionalism, Ethnicity and the National Question in Malawi" *Sapem* (December 1994–January 1995).

3
Cameroon:
A Flawed Transition to Democracy

Tatah Mentan

INTRODUCTION

Across the chessboard of political thought in Africa and much of the developing world, the concept of democracy remains a subject of ideological and philosophical controversy. There are three main currents in the debate on democracy: (1) the conservatives who posit that democracy is out of context with African reality, (2) the progressives who see Africa's peoples within the broad spectrum of human civilization and as deserving of democratic governance as obtains anywhere else, and (3) the moderates who advocate an adapted democracy tailored for the African condition. Opponents of democracy, as well as proponents of an adapted democracy, generally challenge its universality on grounds of social and cultural differences. Lewis, however, finds the claim that Africa is not ripe for democratic government an insult to its peoples' social development. Writing about postcolonial monolithic political systems on the continent, he noted that "all enemies of Africans are delighted to have evidence that Africans are not yet ready for the higher forms of social intercourse."[1]

The less rigid stance of the moderates, as already noted, accepts democracy, but opts for an Africanized brand shaped by the continent's peculiarities. Quite often, though, during the postcolonial period the argument for an Afrocentric democracy provided an excuse for enforcing ruthless dictatorships under the guise of "our own democracy." Adapted or not, there is one principle that validates or invalidates a country's claim to being democratic—the principle that government is created by, derives its power from, and exists to serve the people. Any political system that does not recognize that the popular will is the only legitimate basis for wielding state power cannot be called, even minimally, democratic. In other words, there are universal democratic principles and rights to which every human being—African, European, whomever—is entitled by virtue of their humanity and citizenship.

Those who argue for a relativist conception of democracy really stand on shaky ground. Cultural specificities notwithstanding, increased socioeconomic interaction between modern peoples and nations, thanks to advances in communication and transportation technologies, has been a precursor to the universalization and conventionalization of certain democratic values; globalization or interdependence has established meeting points for even the most divergent views on political democracy. This point was well enunciated by Almond and Coleman who contended that

It is still possible to discern in the movement of world history the emergence of certain conventions and even social norms which have increasingly been diffused throughout the world and which people generally feel should be recognized by any self-respecting government. . . . Mass participation, for example, has been taken to be an absolute right in the spirit of world views. Other ideas such as the demand for universalistic laws, respect for merit rather than birth, and generalized concepts of justice and citizenship, seem now to hold a place above any particular culture and thus reasonably belong to some universal standards of modern political life.[2]

Broadly speaking, the essence of political democracy is that the governed decide who governs, mainly through elections. Thus in a democracy the citizenry is vested with the fundamental rights of choosing, inter alia criticizing, and ultimately dismissing its leaders.[3] To speak about choice is to envisage alternatives, to accept, in other words, pluralism in political discussion and action. Also, in a democracy broad civil liberty guarantees are provided the populace, including press and association liberties. It is from this perspective that this chapter sizes up the transition to democracy in Cameroon since 1990, when the clamor for multiparty politics started. Democratization is examined from an institutional perspective. Institutions here refer to the legal, socioeconomic, cultural, and international framework in which political change is taking place. Of critical focus is the conjunction or disjunction between state and nation, and between what an environment conducive to pluralist politics requires and what the Cameroon Constitution actually provides. Also examined within the institutional framework is the political communication function, that is, the role of the national press in political debate, Cameroon's changing economic fortune, the increased politicization and militarization of ethnicity, the weaknesses of political society, as represented by opposition parties, and Franco-Cameroon relations in the late twentieth century.

BACKGROUND TO TRANSITION

If Cameroon embraced democratization in 1990, it was because of a number of factors. First of all, power changed hands on November 6, 1982, when President Ahidjo stepped down and was succeeded by Paul Biya. Sensing that the national mood was for freedom, Biya embarked on sermonizing for democracy. However, the brand of democracy was going to be a peculiar one: democracy was to take place within the ambit of the one-party state. This was to be a learning, drawn-out process. Between January and March of 1986, a plurality of candidates fought to be elected to the basic organs of the single party: the Cameroon People's Democratic Movement. On October 25, 1987, more competed in local council elections. On April 24, 1988, a plurality of candidates vied to be elected to the country's Parliament. Although it failed to deliver the people from the claws of authoritarian rule, the entire experience did prepare Cameroonians for the "real thing," which became a categorical imperative in 1990, in spite of the regime's best attempt to delay its arrival for as long as possible. In other words, the limited democratic opening experienced under President Biya created expectations that the regime was certainly not prepared to fullfil, but could hardly ignore.

Second, in the 1980s the Cameroonian economy was in very poor shape, although the production of oil hid its weaknesses until the second half of the decade. During the 1988–89 fiscal year, Gross Domestic Product dropped to 2.867 billion CFA francs from its 1985–86 figure of 4.071 billion CFA francs. The state budget was reduced from 800 billion to 550 billion CFA Francs.[4] Faced with this gloomy economic picture, the government could no longer justify its stay in power, much less its monopoly of power. Many other African governments that faced this same predicament witnessed an erosion of their legitimacy. They could not deliver the goods so they lost credibility. The bitter experience of economic malperformance made Cameroon a candidate for democracy, for it robbed the hitherto authoritarian political system of its legitimacy.

The economic disaster does not tell the whole story, however. The 1990s have been years of sorrow for dictators as the former Soviet empire and its satellites went crashing down, taking with them the last vestiges of authoritarianism. Ceaucescu was tracked down and ignominiously killed. This event was very significant emotionally, for Ceaucescu had developed strong ties with many African strongmen. His forcible and brutal departure was a harbinger of what could become of Africa's rulers. Closer to home, Doe had a fate not unlike that of his Romanian counterpart; Hussein Habre (Chad) and Mengistu Haile Mariam (Ethiopia) fled overnight, their palaces unable to provide the necessary security. Authoritarians of all ideological stripes and color found themselves—in some cases, literally—on the run. The democratic train was in full gear.

External support for democratization also played a role, although, as will be shown later, a timid one. French President Mitterrand told Francophone African leaders in their summit of June 1990 in La Baule, France, to make democracy their friend. He promised to condition aid on progress in democratic reforms, as did the European Union (EU) and, less explicitly, the United States, Japan, and Germany. As the EU put it: "Good government, that is, respect for human rights, efforts at democratization and the struggle against corruption and mismanagement is going to be a condition for receiving economic aid."[5] It was economic stagnation, the phenomenal syndrome of democratic craving from much of Eastern Europe and Africa by the turn of the 1990s, and donor pressure, especially that of France (however half-heartedly), that finally whipped up open defiance against a quarter-century of one-party rule in Cameroon. The illusive enigma of pursuing national cohesion and development under a unique banner had, in the course of Biya's timid flirtation with democratization, lost its narcotic power on the populace. In its stead was a new consciousness, a shift from political apathy to governmental antipathy, against which the wand of propagandist gimmicks worked no magic for the regime. The hour had come to stand up against enforced conformity, a development graphically enunciated by Rovinski:

Nothing can be achieved by a flock of sheep all bleating the same patriotic slogans. There comes a time when throats grow tired and minds suffer the nausea which is symptomatic of intellectual emptiness. The values of a society must be continually subjected to criticism, so that its individual members may feel that they are taking an effective part in the organic renewal of its various components.[6]

For all its claim to a liberalization of the country's political landscape, it was obvious that the Biya regime had been rather concerned with a limited type of popular participation while actually preventing the populace from affecting public policy, administration, and the selection of those who govern. By 1990 Cameroonians had apparently metamorphosed into the world of modern, sober politics; they had "learned to discount and distrust the pie-in-the-sky language of shallow politicians and to see through the superficial idealism of easy prophets."[7] The first episode that shook one-party rule was the so-called Yondo Black affair. In January 1990 Black chaired a meeting in Douala with fellow lawyers on the plight of democracy in Cameroon. The following month he and seven associates were arrested and charged with holding clandestine meetings and circulating seditious tracts. The sheer wave of interest whipped up nationwide by the Yondo Black trial pointed to a popular mobilization toward a showdown with the single-party system.

Following the trial and conviction of Yondo Black, the ruling party, true to style, quickly went on the offensive, organizing street demonstrations in condemnation of the advocates for pluralism and arguing that it was much too early for multiparty politics. A real test for the staying power of the CPDM conservatives turned out to be a bloody clash in Bamenda between security forces and demonstrators at the launching of the Social Democratic Front (SDF) on May 26, 1990. In a daring move to bell the cat of one-party rule, John Fru Ndi defied administrative injunctions to launch his party, citing constitutional and legal provisions corroborative of his action. (In effect, Article 3 of the 1972 Constitution allowed, at least implicitly, for the creation of political parties.) The bloody clash, which left six dead, was a strong indicator that the Biya regime was not going to give in to pluralism without a fight. As Yembe rightly observes, "[T]he regime was only reacting to the sheer challenge to the hegemony of the one-party system and the possible dislocation of its political power base, and not any legal provisions forbidding the existence of more than one party."[8]

A month after the bloody confrontation in Bamenda, Biya told delegates to the CPDM's first ordinary congress on June 28, 1990, to brace up for eventual competition. And for the first time, some big wigs of the CPDM openly took exception to an orientation coming from the chairman. They questioned the timeliness and the contextual propriety of multiparty democracy for a people who, hard-liners like Central Committee member Emah Basil, considered unschooled and unskilled in managing the liberties of democracy. But against the backdrop of an international crusade against authoritarian governments, the roof of the CPDM hegemony had to cave in. Evidently, Biya was going multiparty not out of the volition of party hard-liners or his ethnic ilk, but under pressure. On November 6, 1990, Parliament met in what was dubbed the liberty session to pass a series of laws to "liberalize" national life, notably in the sphere of civic rights and freedoms. The law on freedom of association recognized the existence of political parties, stating that they were free to "carry out activities within the framework of law." In February of the following year, a few political parties, including the *Union des Populations du Cameroun* (UPC), were legalized. (The number of opposition parties today stands at 122.)

The clamor for a multiparty system had, however, taken on a new twist: the call for a complete overhaul of the system, beginning with the constitutional review of the institutions and functions. The demand among the swelling ranks of the opposition was for a sovereign national conference, against which security forces across the country would fight running battles on the streets of major cities with crowds of demonstrators. In the early days of the civic uprising, prisons and administrative centers were attacked in Kumba, Bamenda, Tiko, Buea, Limbe, Kumbo, Banyo, Douala, Ngaoundere, and Maroua. Opposition parties, grouped under the National Coordination of Opposition Parties and Associations (NCOPA), spearheaded the campaign for civil disobedience to force the government into convening a "sovereign" national conference. But their pitched battles in the streets and the implementation of the "ghost town" strategy, crippling as they were to normal life, were no match for the resoluteness with which the regime resisted calls for genuine political reforms.

A martial law-style mobilization of the military set up national command units, with Brigadier General Jean-René Youmba commanding the littoral and southwest provinces, General Oumarou Djam for the west and northwest provinces, and General Nganso Sundjo commanding the Adamawa, north and far north operational units. A ruthless maestro in undercover police operations and repression, former Commissioner of Police Jean Fochive was recalled from retirement to head the General Secretariat of State for Internal Security. In his address to Parliament on June 27, 1991, Biya, in no uncertain terms, dismissed the idea of a sovereign national conference: *"Je l'ai dit et je le maintiens: la conférence nationale est sans objet pour le Cameroun."* ("I've said it, and I insist: a national conference is pointless for Cameroon.) It is likely that had the French backed the call for a national conference, Biya would long have organized one. But as former French Interior Minister Charles Pasqua, at the head of a visiting French delegation, told reporters in Yaoundé at the time, persons pressing for a national conference were seeking to wield power before elections—a position quite concomitant with that of the Biya regime.

Biya's obduracy vis-à-vis the opposition was clearly facilitated by his regime's cozy relationship with certain metropolitan mentors, who were rather hostile to the opposition. Castigating the opposition after the 1992 legislative election, a French senator and former special advisor on African affairs said: "Your parties don't function well. They don't amount to much because there's no pragmatic base. They are parties that rely solely on the whims of leaders."[9] Evidently, the French did not feel at home with the charismatic pull of certain opposition figures—such as Fru Ndi, who were opposed to their interest in Cameroon. For Biya, however, this was political capital. Infuriated, the opposition declared the president's dismissal an insult and called for revolt and violence. The ghost town strategy and fiscal disobedience were reinforced to the point of a stranglehold that forced the government into proposing an alternative forum: the tripartite conference of opposition leaders, so-called independent personalities, and the administration.

Called in November 1991 to elaborate on an electoral code and the modalities for access of political parties to the public media, the meeting, under pressure from the opposition, also included constitutional reform. It ended without any concrete resolutions, and a technical committee was appointed to study the question of constitutional revision. The government went ahead to organize legislative elections in March 1992, which the Social Democratic Front—at the time the regime's most formidable opponent—and a number of other parties boycotted on grounds of ill-elaborated electoral laws. The March 1 elections brought about a "multiparty" Parliament, composed of a so-called presidential majority made up largely of the ruling party, CPDM, against the National Union for Democracy and Progess (UNDP). The boycott deprived the National Assembly of a viable and vibrant SDF opposition.

Meanwhile, embittered by the failed tripartite talks, the coordination opposition reverted to its campaign for a national conference under a new and larger body, the Alliance for Change in Cameroon through a Sovereign National Conference (ARC-CNS). In a shift from the previous boycott stance, these parties, including the SDF, announced their preparedness to take part in any subsequent polls, as they anticipated local council elections. In the face of government intransigence, the new option for the opposition, championed by the SDF, was to get power progressively, starting at the council or local level. Ever shrewd, Biya put off council elections and instead called early presidential elections for October 11, 1992, which turned out to be the most controversial event in the history of pluralist politics in Cameroon. The reputable monitoring organization, the National Democratic Institute of America, reported that the elections were far from free and fair. Even after acknowledging marked irregularities in the conduct of the October 11 polls, the Cameroon Supreme Court declared the incumbent Paul Biya winner. The presidential elections of October 1997 were equally flawed, a fact that President Biya seems to admit when, speaking on Cameroon Radio and Television (CRTV), he said: "Our democracy is not perfect. We hope, however, to ameliorate it." As in 1992, President Biya and his ruling CPDM party enjoyed significant advantages over the opposition during the 1997 vote. The electronic media were (are) in government hands; the elections were managed, not by an independent commission, but by the Ministry of Territorial Administration whose titular head was (is) a Biya appointee.

The domestic and international suspicion and distrust generated by the 1992 and 1997 elections, coupled with a tightening of the government's coercive and repressive powers since then, raise questions about the regime's sincerity and commitment to the pursuit of a liberal democracy. The very substance of a claim to democratic practice has been strongly contested by some critics who believe that little has evolved from the character of one-party rule. The democratization process in Cameroon has stalled for want of consensus on the conduct of national life in a new setting. While the opposition insists on lasting constitutional guarantees, the government is content with piecemeal discretionary legislation to adapt old rules to a new situation. Sympathizers of the regime have pointed to the existence of opposition parties as a mark of democracy. Of importance here is not just the nominal existence of opposition parties, but their adversarial potency against the ruling party. As former Togolese president Olympio once put it,

The test of a democratic regime in Africa might not necessarily be the presence of a second party or several parties, so much as whether or not the regime tolerates individualists. This is the crucial point, for societies are not built or improved by conformists.[10]

Paradoxically, Olympio's hypothesis was in defense of the idea of one-party democracy. However, the same logic applies in a pluralistic setting: one-hundred-plus opposition parties in a political system where the ruling party remains intolerant of, and refuses to accommodate, alternative viewpoints constitute a sterile flock of no consequence to the order of things. Late in 1990, President Biya said in an interview with a local French radio station, Radio Monte Carlo, that he would love to be remembered as one who brought democracy and development to Cameroon. His record, though, seems to be at variance with that of a disciple of democracy. And as Professor Nnoli Okwudiba warns:

The concept of democracy has become part of the propaganda arsenal. . . . The propaganda role of democracy arises because of the positive sentiments it evokes in all the peoples of the world . . . its value is so high that practically every regime, even the most brutal, oppressive and unjust, wishes to justify its actions on democratic grounds.[11]

ANATOMY OF POLITICAL STAGNATION

That democratization in Cameroon has stalled can be explained by (1) the yet-to-be-resolved question of what it means to be a Cameroonian, (2) laws and institutions (e.g., the military) that do not make for democratic governance, (3) economic stagnation, and (4) an undemocratic power structure and culture inherited from colonialism that has made the country too dependent on France.

Who Is a Citizen?

To ask who is a citizen in Cameroon today is not an exercise in metaphysics and futility. Indeed, basic concepts such as citizenship and nationhood are problematic in many African countries, as Wole Soyinka correctly points out.[12] In Cameroon, the Anglophone-Francophone rift is real, especially for Anglophones. However, a serious examination of the current political structure, with its emphasis on a unitary state with strong presidential powers, is something that both the Biya regime and the Francophone elite in general have resisted, preferring instead to focus on elections. According to Rustow, for democracy to take off the national unity issue must be adequately addressed. It is only after this preparatory stage that the rules of the electoral game can be properly made. By conducting elections—and flawed ones at that—before reaching a national consensus as to what the structure of the Cameroon state should be, the Biya regime has consistently put the cart before the horse. In Rustow's view, "The vast majority of people in a democracy to-be must have no doubt or mental reservations as to which political community they belong."[13] For Almond and Verba, "if there is no consensus within society, there can be little potentiality for the peaceful resolution of conflict that is associated with the democratic process. If, for instance, the incumbent elite considered the opposition elite too threatening, it is unlikely that the incumbents would allow a peaceful competition for elite position."[14]

Albert Mukong even goes as far as classifying Cameroonian citizenship into three groups: the first, he says, are those whose ethnic group is in power; the second is made up of Francophones in general; and last, there are the Anglophones whom, Mukong calls, third-class citizens, the wretched of the earth or of the country.[15] The elections that have been held in Cameroon to date have essentially sidestepped the issue. If democracy necessarily entails that people are able to choose how their lives are to be governed and by whom, the following questions become decisive. Who are the people? Do they accept the terms of their membership in the political community? The decision to transform Cameroon from a federal to a unitary state was taken by presidential decree; thus, from a legal standpoint, Anglophone Cameroonians, unlike at the time of reunification when they thought that they had opted for federalism, were brought to the current, that is unitary, system without their consent. The Cameroon state, as it is presently structured, does not reflect the wishes of nearly twenty percent of those living within its borders. In the 1990s, what has been called democratization in Cameroon is a futile exercise aimed at using the stamp of democracy to legitimize a discredited system and woo foreign donors.

Constitutional Stalemate

The Cameroon constitution gives the president of the republic latitude for unrestrained overlordship. Constitutional separation of powers is as absent today as it was under the late Ahidjo. Implicitly, legislation remains the exclusive preserve of the executive in that all bills still come to Parliament at the initiative of the executive. The claim that the law allows for private members' bills lacks practical substance in so far as such bills must be routed through the presidency before being turned over to the National Assembly for study. Because the latter is not independent of the executive branch but remains susceptible to manipulative whims, it can be inferred that the executive is the main, if not the sole, legislator. Judges are appointed by the President, and may be removed and transferred at his will. As a result, judges are afraid to adjudicate in ways that might run afoul of the wishes of the executive for fear of jeopardizing their career. Laws are implemented by an administration that is more or less an auxiliary of the ruling party (i.e., the divisional and senior divisional officers, the governors, the prefects, and so on). When, for instance, the 1990 law on freedom of association provided that political parties freely carry out activities within the framework of the law, which law gave provincial, divisional, and subdivisional administrative agents discretionary powers to maintain law and order, these officials simply clamped down with impunity on opposition party activities under the guise of preempting a breach of the peace.

The excessive powers of the head of state, coupled with the loose-endedness of constitutional clauses, make government by decree a prerogative which President Biya has exploited fully to circumvent other constitutional hitches to his leadership. For example, in two successive extensions of the mandate of the present local councils, Biya has gone through the motion of legislation to have his CPDM-UPC-MDR block outvote the UNDP, the main opposition party in Parliament, to pass laws he favored. Worse still, the absence of constitutional guarantees of fundamental rights and freedoms leaves the Biya regime ample room to flirt with the notion of freedom of the press.[16] Undoubtedly, one of the hallmarks of a liberal democracy is a free press, and constant gagging of the press only serves to make a mockery of democracy. Blangden warns that "in every nation where democracy has collapsed repressive laws have been the forerunner."[17] Under what the Cameroon authorities have coined administrative censorship, the press remains under the heavy hand of the Ministry of Territorial Administration, which seized 144 newspaper editions between 1991 and 1993; the hardest hit were *La Nouvelle Expression, Le Messager,* and *Challenge Hebdo.* The electronic news media (radio and television) are yet to be liberalized, several years after Parliament passed a law to that effect, leaving the modalities for this application to an order elaborated by the minister of communications. But the order, which has been drawn up, remains blocked at the prime minister's office by hard-line conservatives, who find antigovernment hostility from the print media to be enough trouble already.

Economic Stagnation

Economic relations are, ipso facto, political relations, which explains why economic stagnation inevitably leads to political stagnation. Cameroon is no exception to this rule. The country is richly endowed with natural resources and a diversified production base. This impressive development potential combined with appropriate policies and a favorable external environment produced on average real growth of 7 percent a year from independence in 1960 through 1985. Agriculture was the mainstay of growth and foreign exchange earnings until 1978, when oil production started and quickly became the cornerstone of economic growth. This oil bonanza was not wisely invested. It instead led to higher expenditures on the civil service, subsidies to inefficient public and parastatal enterprises, accumulated debts, and capital-intensive investments with low returns. After 1986, three major shocks exposed the weaknesses in economic structure and policies. First, the external terms of trade declined by 60 percent through 1993, as the prices of coffee, cocoa, and oil fell sharply. Second, oil output began a long-term decline with the result that oil export, at $531 million in 1994, was about one third the amount reached in 1985. Third, the real exchange rate appreciated by about 54 percent from 1986–93, thus greatly reducing the country's competitiveness. By 1993, the economy and its external accounts had deteriorated significantly. Poor government services aggravated the economic situation. In 1983, about 40 percent of the population was below the poverty line. Twelve years later, about 60 percent were below the poverty line. This rife and growing poverty derived from continuous public finance deficits, as revenues fell and government expenditures continued to rise.

The burden on public finances was exaggerated by a large and inefficient public enterprise sector. Growing public sector deficits were internalized in the financial sector to the detriment of banks and the private sector. Economic decline was accompanied by increased poverty as poor farmers suffered the brunt of the fall in producer prices and the government cut spending on health and education. The Cameroon middle class, which used to be one of the most developed in sub-Saharan Africa, subsequently shrank. The outbreak of the economic crisis after 1986 was accompanied by calls for political liberalization, leading to civil disobedience. Both economic crisis and calls for political liberalization propelled the government to embark on structural adjustment in 1988–89. This structural adjustment culminated in a 60 percent cut in nominal civil service salaries in 1993 that was unique in the CFA franc zone. This strategy failed because inflation remained unchecked. In January 1994, Cameroon along with other CFA zone members, devaluated the CFA franc by 50 percent in foreign exchange terms and adopted a program of sweeping reform of trade, tariff, and transit policies. Structural Adjustment measures have left the public materially impoverished and politically apathetic.

Ethnicity Politicized and Militarized

Ethnicity is another area in which Biya has used his executive power to pursue a politics of exclusion designed to establish a Beti oligarchy, similar to the so-called Nordist one created by Ahidjo. In fact, the ethnic question, beginning right from the preindependence government of Andre-Marie Mbida down to President Biya, has been an important factor in the distribution of government portfolios. The tradition has been to weave the administrative cloth from the yarn of regional and ethnic considerations, at the expense of technical competence. In a multiparty setting, though, the oddity of this practice becomes disturbingly glaring, as it cuts directly into democratic principles of equality and fair play. For instance, on the eve of the 1992 presidential election Biya decreed the creation of new administrative units, with his south province (with less than 400,000 inhabitants) having more divisions and subdivisions than the northwest province with a population of 1.3 million (three times that of the south province). When he later appointed members of the vote counting commission, the body to validate and invalidate returns from the polls, eleven of thirteen members were people from his power base, the center and south provinces.

The political impasse has buffeted the hopes of Cameroonians. The ruling party, the CPDM, has rendered the playing field for electoral politics bumpy, using some disarming strategies: (1) exploitation of the power of incumbency to block political enemies, (2) disenfranchisement of the Cameroonian electorate, and (3) destabilization of opposition parties through fear, mutual distrust, and factionalism among them. Various means are utilized to achieve these objectives. First of all, the Biya regime does not blink in using the military and paramilitary forces to weed out unwanted opposition elements. In Cameroon, there exists a congeries of "apolitical" state security and paramilitary organizations, and an assortment of police and military figures, acting more or less as roving government vigilantes. Some security agencies, like the *Groupe Spécial d'Opération* (GSO), have their own troops and run their own detention camps. These emerging "military ethnocracies"[18] are expected to demonstrate their gratitude to the regime by doing its bidding, at least as long as the regime continues to assign military portfolios using the well-known ethnic formula. Table 3.1 shows how rewards are ethnically distributed in the ranks of the Cameroon armed forces.

Such rewards psychologically condition the military to become demonstratively loyal in obeying commands. For instance, an authorized meeting organized in the residence of the chairman of the Liberal Democratic Alliance, Njoh Litumbe, in Buea in September 1993 was disrupted by the forces of law and order, using tear gas to disperse the militants. In November 1993, security forces blocked two press conferences in Yaoundé of opposition leaders John Fru Ndi and Garga Haman. The same month Fru Ndi was denied access to the headquarters of UFDC, where a press conference had been scheduled. Fru Ndi's vehicle was later rammed and sprayed with high pressure water by a mobile police water cannon. He suffered minor lacerations and sought refuge in the Belgian ambassador's residence. On March 25, 1995, SDF militants presented their permit, no. 30/RD/J060/:SP, signed by Mbow Zanga Marcel, district officer for Yaoundé I, on March 15, authorizing them to hold a memorial service in remembrance of two SDF militants. Party chairman John Fru Ndi also had an "important message" for his followers. A combined squad of policemen and presidential guardsmen volleyed into the venue, Carrefour Warda, teargasing, flogging, kicking, and arresting militants. The indiscriminate use of troops to intimidate, beat up, and even kill SDF militants derives from the regime's fear of the crowd-pulling party.

Furthermore, the regime is very skilled at taking advantage of the patrimonial administrative environment of the Cameroon state, which is characterized by: (1) lack of accountability to civil society; (2) a lack of respect for the rule of law, that is, makers and enforcers of laws consider themselves above the law; (3) crippling regulatory burden on the private sector, which puts entrepreneurs at the mercy of political elites and rapacious bureaucrats; and (4) capricious allocation of scarce resources, that is, budgetary authorizations and appropriations generally reflect

Table 3. 1

Distribution of Generals in Cameroon Armed Forces by Province and Population

Province	Population (thousands)	Number of Generals
Adamawa	471, 200	0
Center	1,228,900	3
East	530,300	1
Far North	1,898,400	1
Littoral	770,900	1
North	672,700	1
West	1,490, 500	4
North West	1, 351,400	0
South	451,500	3
South West	942,500	1

Source: Cameroon Tribune, no. 1627, 15 March 1993, p. 3.

the relative power of the Cameroon bureaucratic elite and donor preferences, especially those of France, rather than the economic priorities of the state and the intrinsic merits of development projects. The highly centralized and all-powerful Cameroonian state makes people place a very high premium on appointed posts. To be an administrator is to have totalitarian control over one's domain. The Cameroonian civil servant, especially if he (or she) is well connected to the boss, Paul Biya, proposes and disposes all, at least as long as he (or she) does not run afoul of the ultimate benefactor. Reciprocity and unquestioned allegiance to the patron of Etoudi Palace are essential conditions for personal survival and advancement. In this way, it is easy to understand the antiopposition chicaneries of civil administrators in Cameroon. A few examples are essential to prove the case.

An SDF rally was billed for Obala, Center Province, on October 15, 1995. The administrative officers went on a door-to-door campaign to intimidate militants and persuade them to boycott the rally. They failed. But in Kribi, the SDF sought an authorization for its rally on October 28, 1995, in accordance with law N-95/55 of December 19, 1990. This was given, but the divisional officer (D.O.) announced a change of venue on the eve of the rally. But the massive attendance caused the administration to incite local militants to attack traditional dancers with the complicity of gendarmes and policemen on the spot. More dramatic scenes build up daily. The SDF scheduled two rallies on October 29, 1995, at Mbalmayo and Biyem-Assi. On Saturday October 28, 1995, the Mbalmayo SDF chief was served with prefectoral order N-028/A/J10-02/SP changing the venue of the meeting. At 11:30 P.M., the district officer himself, accompanied by the gendarmerie commander and police chief, served the SDF boss with order N-029/A/J10-02/SP banning the rally for the sake of "public order" in the town.

At Biyem-Assi, the civilian-military pillars of authoritarianism unilaterally ordered the venue to be changed. The late transfer to Biyem-Assi stadium was not easy. To make matters worse, the SDF rally started at 5:30 P.M. and was ordered to stop after thirty minutes at 6:00 P.M.! Such actions by administrators and armed forces are indicative of the lack of guarantee surrounding civil liberties, governmental arbitrariness in the application of the law, and a weak judiciary unable to review actions taken by the executive.[19] President Biya has even admitted that his regime was riddled with corruption and abuse of public office which undermined the output of the government. However, he has not condemned those who terrorize, repress, and marginalize insubordinate opposition groups to his advantage. In addition, the state-controlled electronic media are used to being the engines of the regime's need for self-serving boosterism. In spite of promises of media liberalization, the same old practices of political sloganeering and choral followership remais unscathed. Repressive laws are still on the books, notably those that tightly control both the private and public press. According to the *Encyclopedia of the Third World*:

Except for independent weeklies in Douala, Victoria and Bamenda, the Cameroon radio and press is government-owned and controlled. Criticism of the government is discouraged and the media are used as mouth-pieces of the government. Newsmen are often harassed and intimidated by the constant threat of censorship. As a result, self-censorship is widely practiced. Opposition view points are not ventilated in the media.[20]

The *Encyclopedia* reported that journalists of the official media enjoyed much less latitude than their counterparts of the private press, as they could be transferred to less desirable jobs if found contradicting government policy. It ranked Cameroon seventy-seventh among the nations of the world in press freedom, with a rating of –2.41 on a scale in which +4 is the maximum and –4 the minimum.

Other Factors

Democratic transition in Cameroon has also been stymied by factionalization of the opposition and unrelenting French backing of the regime. There is dissensus (the opposite of consensus) among opposition parties along ethnic, regional, linguistic, and religious lines, not to mention personality differences among opposition leaders. The ruling party has cleverly used these cleavages to sow disputes, rancor, and suspicion inside the opposition. The *Forces Alliées pour le Changement* (FAC) is still faction-ridden. For many opposition parties the main issue is not so much how to ease out the ruling CPDM party, but who will take over from Paul Biya as president. This unpatriotic formulation of the problem of governance in Cameroon has made the opposition as much a part of the problem as the ruling CPDM.

Moreover, there has been unequivocal French support for President Paul Biya, even though Mitterrand's exhortation at La Baule was instrumental in forcing autocratic, Francophone African heads of state to implement political change. Thus France's initial support for democratization in 1990 has been at variance with the actions of French officials, especially where Cameroon is concerned. How is the discrepancy to be explained? Cameroon is a country at the periphery of international capitalism in which the state, led by a pro-France political class, exploits and oppresses the masses of Cameroonians for the benefits of a dependent, domestic bourgeoisie and certain factions of the French bourgeoisie. As Richard Joseph has remarked, "the vicious cycle in which Cameroon has been caught by encouraging the importation of capital through facilitating its outflow in the form of profits"[21] is true of every regime in Yaoundé, colonial or postcolonial.

The "vicious cycle," to quote Gavin Williams, has "promoted the development of capitalism, foreign and domestic, by shifting resources from more competitive to less competitive producers; from craft to factory production; from agriculture to industry; from rural to urban areas; from the poor to the rich. . . . It has promoted the wealth of the nation, but only by the impoverishment of the people.[22] Vaccillations in French policy toward democratization in its *pré carré* can be attributed to the fact that the people who shape France's Africa policy do not always speak with one voice; nor do they treat all African countries in the same way. Mitterrand's statement at La Baule did not necessarily reflect the views of the many actors (e.g., government bureaucrats, French multinational executives, private arms dealers, military personnel, mercenaries) that shape Franco-African relations. It certainly was at variance with the position of the Gaullists, with whom Mitterand had to share power after 1991. As shown earlier, the irascible former interior minister Charles Pasqua made no secret of his contempt for the Cameroonian opposition's call for a "sovereign" national conference.

CONCLUSION

This anatomy of a flawed democratization in Cameroon in the 1990s shows that the two pillars upon which modern democracy rests—pluralism allowing for the displacement of those who wield state power through elections and civil liberty guarantees—have barely been erected. Instead, the barons of the Biya regime have sought to adapt the structures of an authoritarian state to a new "democratic" environment. Democratization in Cameroon thus faces some important challenges. First, the Cameroon state was not born with legitimacy; indeed, its authority was challenged on the battlefield at independence—a rare occurrence in Francophone Africa south of the Sahara. The traumatic circumstances surrounding the birth of the modern Cameroon state explain why it has been consumed with the attempt to establish its hegemony and right to rule. In terms of its monopoly over the means of coercion, the state tends to be strong in relation to Cameroonian society, but soft in regard to its ability to ensure voluntary and regular compliance to its rule and policies. Three main characteristics of the soft Cameroon state have been used to frustrate the democratization process: (1) the outright circumventing of laws and regulations by officials and their inconsistent application; (2) secret collusion between civil servants and politicians, whose task it is to supervise the implementation of policies; and (3) corruption at every level of the state.

The second challenge to democratization concerns the Cameroon economic system. The state has been the primary channel for the accumulation of wealth. Its extensive power and control over the economic life of the country make control of the state the major means of economic and social advance. The Cameroon state has thus been able to use its tenable grip on the levers of accumulation as patronage manna to buttress its security and stranglehold in an authoritarian environment. This access to state power by loyalists is guaranteed to exacerbate ethnic, religious, tribal and sectarian rivalries and tensions, as individuals and groups, reared in a parasitic system of dependence vis-à-vis the state, are likely to try to hold on to power till the end rather than allow democracy, with all of its concomitant uncertainties, to flourish.

The third challenge to the democratic transition in Cameroon flows directly from the last observation: the absence of social cohesion among Cameroon's more than 120 ethnic groups. Social cleavages can be found at two levels: the level of ethnic groups and that of the Anglophone-Francophone rift, with the latter, according to Elenga Mbuyinga, being the most explosive.[23] Other Cameroonian analysts have not failed to notice the problem. Ngniman wonders aloud whether Cameroon does not only risk being a theater for ethnic fighting with the advent of democracy but also a cultural battleground in which Francophones and Anglophones fight for dominance.[24] To Ndi Mbarga Valentine, there is no doubt that the thunderous launching of the Social Democratic Front on May 26, 1990, had something to do with what has been termed the Anglophone problem. To Susungi, if the issue of Anglophone Cameroon's existence as a distinct cultural group able to live according to its own perception of the world, or *weltanschauung*, is not adequately addressed, the eventual disintegration of Cameroon is inevitable.[25]

Cross-cutting loyalties are rare. Instead, cleavages, disassociation, and strains deriving from cultural (e.g., Anglophones versus Francophones) discrepancies are hallmarks of Cameroon's political landscape. Sharply defined barriers between culturally differentiated segments, a pronounced tendency for different groups to occupy different positions in Cameroon's economy, division of labor and social structure, and the fact that political power and authority in the postcolonial era have been seen to belong, rightly or wrongly, to one ethnic group to the exclusion of others, do not bode well for the future of Cameroon democracy. The logical outcomes of the stalled democratization process are

1. a death-grip on the reigns of power by a regime unaccustomed to power-sharing;
2. the survival of a political system conceived for absolute rule, which makes it impossible for democracy, at least in Lincolnian terms, to blossom;
3. economic dependence on external capital begetting political subservience, thereby impeding any domestication of the democratic enigma.

To surmount these challenges and build a genuine democracy, the regime has to begin seeing power through a new prism. This implies new rules embedded in a le-

gal framework conducive to democratic practice. For its part, the opposition must present a united challenge to the ruling party. It must stop defining the struggle as one of merely unseating the incumbent. (Based on past behavior, it is doubtful, however, that the ruling clique and its opposition have the capacity to overcome their respective weaknesses.) Finally, Cameroon's umbilical affiliation with France must be severed. This leaning on the former metropolis by a faction of the Cameroon elite perpetuates dependence on externally initiated agendas; in so doing, it impedes Cameroon's ability to put its development needs first and its political house in order.

NOTES

1. Arthur Lewis, *Politics in West Africa* (London, UK: George Allen and Unwin Ltd., 1985), p. 35.

2. Gabriel A. Almond and James S. Coleman, eds., *The Politics of the Developing Areas* (Princeton, NJ: Princeton University Press, 1960), p. 6.

3. With the suppression of pluralism in most African states shortly after independence, these rights were virtually surrendered to the single party, which did not tolerate dissent. See W. Arthur Lewis, op. cit., pp. 61–63.

4. Ndi Mbarga provides details of the somber economic state of Cameroon in *Ruptures et Continuité au Cameroon* (Paris: l'Harmattan, 1993).

5. See *Democratization in Cameroon*, International Delegation Report, October 1991.

6. Samuel Rovinski, *Cultural Policy in Costa Rica* (Paris: UNESCO, 1991), p. 4.

7. Lucian Pye, "Communications and Political Articulation" in Lucian Pye, ed., *Communications and Political Development* (Princeton, NJ: Princeton University Press, 1963), p. 42.

8. Omer Yembe, "Ethnic Diversity and Administration," *Ethnie et Développement,* (Yaoundé, Cameroon: CRAC, 1994), p. 118.

9. *Le Messager* (Yaoundé, Cameroon), 12 Juin 1992.

10. President Olympio is cited by K. A. Busia "The Ingredients of Democracy," in G. C. Mutiso and S. W. Rohio, eds., *Readings in African Political Thought* London, UK: Heineman Educational Books Ltd., 1986), p. 118.

11. Okwundiba Nnoli, *Introduction to Politics* (Essex, UK: Longman Group Ltd., 1986), p. 454.

12. Wole Soyinka, *The Open Sore of a Continent* (Oxford, UK: Oxford University Press, 1996).

13. Dankwart Rustow, "Transition to Democracy," *Comparative Politics* 2, no. 3 (1970), p. 116.

14. Gabriel Almond and S. Verba, *The Civic Culture* (Princeton, NJ: Princeton University Press, 1963), p. 491.

15. Albert Mukong, *Prisoner Without a Crime* (Limbe, Cameroon: Alfresco, 1985).

16. Tatah Mentan, "Press and National Liberation: Historical and Contemporary Cameroon Perspectives," unpublished, 1995. Send inquiries to Tatah Mentan, P. O. Box 1328, Yaoundé, Cameroon, Central Africa.

17. Ralph Blangden, "The Bill of Rights Today," A. N. Christensen and E. M. Kirkpatrick, eds., *The People, Politics and the Politician* (New York: Henry Holt, 1941).

18. The term is borrowed from Ali Mazuri. See Ali Mazuri, *Soldiers and Kinsmen in Uganda: The Making of Military Ethnocracy* (Beverly Hills, CA: Sage, 1975). See also Daniel Bouchard, "Améliorer la Politique Sociale dans nos Armées," *L'Union* (Libreville, Gabon), 28–29 Juillet 1992.

19. Justice Minister D. Moutome admits the powerlessness of the judiciary in *Cameroon Tribune*, 11 October 1995, p. 2. This point is also discussed very forcefully by Jean-Germain Gros in "The Hard Lessons of Cameroon," *Journal of Democracy* 6, no. 3 (July 1995).

20. George Thomas Kurian, *Encyclopedia of the Third World*, 3rd ed., vol. 1 (New York: Facts on File, 1987), p. 354.

21. Richard Joseph, ed., *Gaullist Africa: Cameroon Under Ahmadu Ahidjo* (Emegu, Nigeria: Fourth Dimension Publishers, 1978), p. 144.

22. Gavin Williams, ed., *Nigeria: Economy and Society* (London, UK: Rex Collings, 1976), p. 56.

23. Elenga Mbuyinga, *Tribalisme et Problème National en Afrique Noire: Le Cas du Kamerun* (Paris: l'Harmattan, 1989).

24. Z. Ngniman, *Cameroun: La Démocratie Emballée* (Yaoundé, Cameroon: Clé, 1993).

25. N. N. Susungi, *The Crisis of Unity and Democracy in Cameroon* (Abidjan, Ivory Coast, 1991).

4
Nigeria: Militarization and Perpetual Transition

Julius O. Ihonvbere

INTRODUCTION

It is impossible to understand the contradictions of Nigeria's seemingly unending democratic transition without considering the country's historical experience. Nigeria's contemporary crises are informed directly and indirectly by the structural distortions and disarticulations of the colonial and postcolonial state. These distortions shape the role and nature of the military, the character of the political elites, the bureaucracy, the patterns of accumulation, and Nigeria's marginal location in the international division of labor and power.[1] This chapter examines two crucial aspects of the Nigerian *problématique*: the military, whose role in politics in the postcolonial period has been paramount, and the political parties. Nigeria's unending transition can be attributed in part to the fact that both of these institutions, rather than serving society, have floated above it and engaged in a long-running battle for control of the fisc to achieve rent-seeking objectives. The behavior of the Nigerian military and the political parties is scrutinized in the contexts of the now-aborted Babangida transition, the continuing crisis in Ogoniland, and the apparent redemocratization efforts of General Sani Abacha.

REMEMBERING THE YEARS OF "INNOCENCE"

At political independence in October 1960, regional, religious, class, and ethnic differences in Nigeria were already politicized. The divide-and-rule tactics of the colonial state, the ruthless exploitation of nonbourgeois forces (especially peasant farmers), the deliberate manipulation of primordial sentiments, and the intimidation of civil society were legacies which the colonial experience bequeathed to the postcolonial elite. It pursued the same colonial politics and policies with only superficial changes. The First Republic (1963–66) was run like a leaderless, disorganized soccer team: the prime minister and ceremonial president did not get along; the army was not sure as to who had final authority to give it orders; traditional rulers had an overarching influence over politicians; the political parties remained based in the regions; and the center (i.e., the federal government) was less attractive and less credible than the regional governments, some of which maintained embassies abroad and even took some foreign policy positions that ran counter to those of the federal government. Given the fragmentation and suffocation of civil society, the general political immaturity of the new leaders, their opportunism, and the inability of the postcolonial state to contain or mediate the constraints of underdevelopment, domination, and dependence, it was clear by 1965 that the nation was headed for disaster.[2]

Nigeria experienced its first military coup in January of 1966, followed by another in July of the same year. In 1967, civil war broke out as the Eastern region tried to secede from the weak federation. It raged for thirty months and as many as one million people probably were killed.[3] If it is conceded that the period 1960–67 was one of political apprenticeship for the Nigerian political elite, there is very little evidence that they learned much that was capable of informing or conditioning their political behavior in the post-civil war period. In fact, it can be argued that members of the political elite were not really new to politics in the First Republic because many had been involved in regional and national politics for almost half a decade before political independence in 1960. They did very little to bring Nigerians together or to promote overall development. The politicians of the First Republic did not sew the seeds of democracy, accountability, and political responsibility. Rather, they promoted their personal interest, sectarianism, mismanagement, intolerance, and violence. In a society characterized by illiteracy, poverty, ignorance, and opportunistic leadership, it was easy for the military to hijack opposition to the political elite by students, workers, and other popular groups and unceremoniously dismiss the politicians.[4] This was a major setback for Nigeria's political development as it broke the political "innocence" of the nation, introduced the military as the new hegemonic faction of the dominant class, and started a pattern of undemocratic and unaccountable government.[5] This, then, has been the political story of Nigeria since the first coup of 1966, the brief period of the Second Republic (1979–83) notwithstanding.

LOCATING THE MILITARY IN NIGERIAN POLITICS

The military occupies a central place in Nigerian politics. This is largely due to the weaknesses of civil society, the tenuous hegemony of the state and its institutions, and the opportunistic and highly factionalized character of Nigeria's political elite. The main implication of its central role, however, has been the containment and distortion of democratic tendencies.[6] Military regimes are generally hierarchical, undemocratic, and repressive in character. In addition, soldiers seem to have a knack for technical solutions, which may not be appropriate where political problems are involved. True, soldiers can make decisions faster than civilians who have to consider their constituencies and houses of Parliament. However, the undemocratic character of the army, not to mention its penchant for technical quick fixes, often leads it to make the wrong political choices. Because the military has been in power for so long in Nigeria, it has been able to lay claim to some developments in the country's history. However, the post-oil boom era exposes the total emptiness of military rule and its inability to manage resources and crises, much less construct the foundations of sustainable development and democracy.[7]

Recurring military intervention has retarded development and progress in Nigeria because, in addition to being very costly in financial and human terms, it has prevented the politicians from learning from their mistakes, strengthening their constituencies, and forging the kinds of political alliances which can contain crisis and instability. Military rule also closes existing democratic spaces, promotes sycophancy and mediocrity, encourages waste and corruption, and, more important, encourages political arrogance, intolerance, and generally undemocratic attitudes. It is undeniable that the military successfully prosecuted the civil war and has carried out policies which have become landmarks in the country's political terrain, including: the creation of several states, a new national anthem and currency, a constitution fashioned after the U.S. presidential model, a new federal capital in Abuja, the demystification of the regions and the strengthening of the federal government, infrastructure development, the establishment of several educational institutions, the creation of political institutions and agencies to facilitate administration, and more. Unfortunately, these innovations have been insufficient to strengthen civil society, check corruption and irresponsibility, and ensure the effective and efficient utilization of scarce resources. On the contrary, some of them seem to have been designed to insure military hegemony over society and to promote corruption. It has become a truism in Nigeria that the best time to loot the treasury is under military rule as this almost guarantees that excesses will not be probed.

However one looks at the Nigerian experience, the military has been a disaster to the process of political development. Its frequent intervention has subverted the possibilities for development in several areas. It has failed to nurture the emergence of a rational and responsible political class. It has failed to give the country a workable political structure worth the name, as reflected in the creation of ever more states. It has reduced the worth of the judiciary and the academy through constant harassment and the politics of domestication and incorporation.[8] The military in Nigeria has virtually convinced all young and able-bodied people that hard work is a waste of time. It is faster and easier to become a millionaire through extra-legal and illegal means. The military has also convinced the younger generation of Nigerians that forming or joining political parties is an expensive, uncertain, and long route to power. Joining the army, however, is faster and more secure, which the lifestyle of military officers makes plainly evident. The Nigerian military has elevated ethnic, regional, and religious differences to new heights; there have been more religious riots under the military regimes of Babangida and Abacha than at any other point in the nation's history. Under such conditions, political development can hardly take place as the processes and institutions of politics become privatized and subject to manipulation. It is in this context of military encapsulation of political praxis that the failure of party politics in Nigeria can best be explained.

PARTY POLITICS IN POSTCOLONIAL NIGERIA

Prior to and since political independence in Nigeria, the patterns of party formation have remained rather constant. There has never been a genuine attempt to use political parties to draw sharp ideological or philosophical differences within and between classes. The parties have devoted practically no attention to mass mobilization and education, the selection of the best candidates for political offices, or the articulation of matters of interest to the Nigerian masses. Nigerian political parties have been conservative, elitist, urban based, and downright pedestrian in spelling out their goals and strategies for capturing power. This is one reason why they have failed to attract public support, resist the military, and maintain a lasting presence. Political parties in Nigeria have relied heavily on the manipulation of region, religion, ethnicity, ignorance, and fears of the rural and urban poor.[9] They are often formed by particular individuals or a group of individuals, usually with very little in common other than an interest in capturing power to facilitate the theft of public resources. Their concern is hardly with the need to consolidate democracy, contain the military, strengthen civil society, empower the people and their communities, build consensus within and between classes and constituencies, establish channels for negotiating interests, and legitimating power through open, competitive and honest elections.[10]

In most of the political parties before and since Nigeria's political independence, the members have had no say, women have been largely invisible, and the interests articulated in the party platforms have been close to those of the urban-based, corrupt, and highly factionalized elites. It has been these narrow interests that have been expressed in public policies in the often brief periods of civilian rule. The political parties, without exception, have been dominated by their founders and their close friends. Even a populist party like the Peoples' Revolutionary Party (PRP) in the defunct Second Republic, which made claims to grassroots legitimacy, was dominated and controlled by a handful of individuals who were not necessarily the most qualified or popular. Almost without exception, the political parties have relied heavily on the use of money.[11] In fact, money has been the main qualification for anyone aspiring to run for office in postcolonial Nigeria. It is needed to create visibility inside one's party, to attract outside "supporters," and to be taken seriously by rival party leaders, the military, and the government (when the last two are not one and the same).

Money is necessary to hire and train political thugs, to buy votes at national conventions, to bribe the electoral officers, the police, and other security personnel, and to organize a "campaign" around the country. Without money, politicians like Bashir Tofa and Chief M. K. O. Abiola would not have been able to hijack the march to the Third Republic and present themselves as presidential candidates, even though they had joined their respective parties only a few months prior to the 1993 elections. As Femi Falana has noted,

Nigeria has been unfortunate with political parties. True, a few have been set up based on ideological positions. However, everyone knows that only one or two people in such parties believed in such ideologies. . . . They have never succeeded in providing a serious sense of direction. Most importantly, they have acted as a sort of magnet: they have attracted the military through their disorganization and irresponsibility. The military has wasted no time in disbanding them.[12]

Nigerian political parties have never succeeded in critically inserting themselves into civil society. They have remained, like the military, suspended above the people, failing to address their needs and hopes. Because their linkages to society are often tenuous, it has been easy for the military to dismantle and proscribe the parties. When the military intervenes, the politicians and parties get no support from the people, as confirmed in the following comment: "Though I do not like military rule, it was good that they chased those useless politicians and their useless parties away. All they did was eat, drink, and gamble in Abuja. I cannot recall one major law they passed to help us. They spent time talking about their salaries and allowances or looking for contracts. Politicians and political parties have been a curse to our dear country."[13] Because the politicians and their parties have not made a coordinated effort at nation building, constituency organization and education, mobilization of the people, and the construction and strengthening of a democratic political culture, they have served as obstacles to democratization. Thus, aside from the direct containment of democracy by the military, the other critical factor militating against the construction of a viable democratic order in Nigeria is party formation and party politics. An examination of the debacle of Nigeria's most recent transition underscores the twin bankruptcy of party politics and military rule there.

"TRANSITION" BABANGIDA-STYLE

In January 1986, General Babangida, then in power for three years, announced that the military would return to the barracks in October 1990 and hand power over to elected civilians. In March 1986, a political bureau was set up to organize a national debate on Nigeria's political future. In March 1987, the government released its recommendations on the political bureau's report and announced that it had shifted the transition date to 1992. In September 1987, the Constitutional Review Committee (CRC) was established to review the 1979 constitution. Local government elections on a nonparty basis were held in the same year; there were 15,000 candidates vying for 301 seats. In 1988, a Constituent Assembly of 450 members was inaugurated to review the recommendations of the CRC. It presented its report to General Babangida in April 1989. In May 1989, the government lifted the ban on politics and promulgated the 1989 constitution. Nigerians were urged to form political parties under established guidelines, which attempted to eliminate the kinds of parochial interests which had plagued past political parties. About thirty-five political parties and organizations vied for registration with the National Electoral Commission (NEC). Thirteen political associations met the requirements to be considered for registration. The NEC eventually recommended six of the political associations to the Armed Forces Ruling Council (AFRC).

In October 1989, General Babangida announced that all political associations, including the six recommended by the NEC, had been dissolved because they were dominated by corrupt politicians, practically "owned" by individuals and, as such, were definite reincarnations of the parties of the First Republic. He went on to inform Nigerians that the government had, instead, created two "grassroots" political parties: one "a little to the right"—The National Republican Convention (NRC), and another "a little to the left"—The Social Democratic Party (SDP). As if to underscore the parties' lack of independence, the military government, through the NEC, drafted their manifestoes and constitutions, built their secretariats, appointed their administrative secretaries, selected their logos, and provided them with funding. In spite of several revisions to the electoral rules, changes in personnel, the banning and unbanning of politicians, and tight government control of the political process, elected politicians had taken charge at local, state, and federal levels by the end of 1992.

The presidential vote was held on June 12, 1993. The SDP had a wealthy Muslim millionaire from the West, Chief M. K. O. Abiola, as its presidential candidate. The NRC had a wealthy Muslim millionaire from Kano in the North, Bashir Tofa, as its flag bearer. Though the elections were judged to be the most free and fair in Nigeria's political history by most national and international observers, General Babangida annulled the results. In his broadcast to the nation, General Babangida argued that "lasting democracy is not a temporary show of excitement and manipulation by an over-articulate section of the elite. . . . Lasting democracy is a permanent diet to nurture the soul of the whole nation and the political process. Lasting democracy must be equated with political stability. Informed by our sad experience of history, we require nothing short of a foundation for lasting democracy."[14] He noted that the transition program, if allowed to continue, would lead the country into a "Third Republic with epileptic convulsions in its democratic health." Ironically, the General listed the "prerequisites which constitute an irreducible minimum for democracy" to include: free and fair elections, uncoerced expression of voters' preferences in elections, respect for the electorate as an unfettered arbiter of elections, decorum and fairness on the part of electoral umpires, and absolute respect for the rule of law.[15]

Based on the reports by the NEC, the International Observer Team (IOT), the government-sponsored Center for Democratic Studies (CDS), and other prodemocracy groups and observer teams, the June 12 elections satisfied all of the above requirements. Yet General Babangida, who was widely known to have a hidden agenda, claimed in his broadcast that

The recently annulled presidential election was . . . afflicted by these problems. Even before the presidential election and, indeed, at the party conventions, we had full knowledge of the bad signals pertaining to the enormous breaches of the rules and regulations of democratic elections. . . . We overlooked the reported breaches. Unfortunately, these breaches continued into the presidential election of June 12, 1993, on an even greater proportion.[16]

This allegation shocked many Nigerians who witnessed the event. As a prodemocracy activist put it, "We knew that the man was treacherous. But we also assumed that he had some self-respect and would not openly lie to the nation and the world. It is a reflection on his poor leadership qualities if he was in this country, was aware of the so-called breaches, but decided to let the nation waste so much money and time before annulling the election."[17]

Local opposition forces and the international community did not find Babangida's action funny; they moved swiftly to condemn it and reject the general's new proposals. Within the country, especially in Lagos, the annulment precipitated massive demonstrations and acts of violence. The United States, the European Union (EU), and Canada imposed limited sanctions on Nigeria and called on General Babangida to release the election results and inaugurate the winner. Babangida refused. Exploiting the corruption, weaknesses, and divisions of the political class, General Babangida hurriedly installed an illegal Interim National Government (ING) headed by Chief Ernest Shonekan, who had been head of the powerless transitional government.[18] It is interesting to note here the role of the two political parties. The NRC supported the annulment of the election because it was actually behind in the released results. An annulment would allow Tofa or another candidate to run again. The National Republican Convention thus largely agreed with Babangida.

The Social Democratic Party was split in two. Those who had failed in their bid against Abiola for the presidential ticket and felt that they had a renewed chance of being hand picked by the party supported Babangida's action. They worked with the military to install the ING and helped to nominate SDP members into the cabinet. This group was led by Shehu Yar'Adua, a former military head of state who was outdistanced by M. K. O. Abiola after winning only two primaries.[19] The other faction of the SDP opposed the annulment and the ING and stood by Abiola. This group included those who were later to invite the military to seize power in the hope that it would hand power over to Abiola. To be sure, there were groups like the members of the largest and most powerful prodemocracy movement, the Campaign for Democracy (CD), who supported the Abiola camp on principles, but most had ulterior motives.[20] In any event, the political parties showed that they were divided, had very limited linkages with popular constituencies beyond their ethnic bases (not insignificantly, Yoruba politicians were by far the most vociferous in their protest), and had no agenda for preventing or resisting military intervention.

In the absence of political parties capable of challenging the military, the human rights and prodemocracy movements took center stage. The protests against Babangida widened democratic spaces in Nigeria and challenged the military. They showed that civil society, though long dormant and repressed, had an inherent capacity, with the right leadership and set of issues, to awaken and assert itself even against a very cunning and ruthless dictator. The opposition to Babangida also enabled new constituencies (e.g., the Ogonis) to emerge, articulate a set of democratic and environmental demands, initiate new strategies of resistance, and gain international publicity for their plight.

Although General Babangida was eventually forced out by a combination of local and external pressures, he left power in a hurry and the country in confusion. The ING could not mobilize support from within or outside the country. Governors belonging to the SDP refused to recognize or cooperate with it. The interim government's legality was challenged by the SDP in the courts and on November 10, 1993, the High Court ruled that the ING was illegal because General Babangida had signed the ING decree one day after he had ceased to be president of the republic. This immediately created a power vacuum that the disorganized and divided politicians, especially those of the SDP, could not fill. Once again, the political parties and politicians opened the way for the military to seize the initiative, hijack popular struggles and present itself as the savior of the nation. Shortly after the High Court's decision, in a not unexpected palace coup, the secretary for defense in the ING, General Sani Abacha, restored full military rule and disbanded all political institutions set up during the transition program. Nigeria was back to square one.

THE ABACHA JUNTA

The Abacha junta wasted no time in establishing its authority. It was certain that in order to maintain law and order and effectively consolidate its rule, it had to contain growing popular consciousness and destroy the prodemocracy groups. The formation of a liberal political coalition, the National Democratic Coalition (NADECO), in May 1994 was seen as a very dangerous threat to the interests of the military. In the ranks of NADECO were highly respected politicians of the early years of independence like Anthony Enahoro and Michael Ajasin, retired military leaders like Dan Suleiman and Ebitu Ukiwe, and intellectuals and new generation politicians like Kofoworola Akerele, Bola Tinubu, Ralph Obiorah, and Bolaii Akinyemi. With its declared goals, which included getting the military out of office and reinstating the June 12 mandate of the SDP and Chief Abiola, NADECO was on a collision course with the junta.

Unfortunately, NADECO's effort fizzled out when disbanded governors and legislators failed to respond to its call to reconvene the national assembly. Instead, many political leaders, including Abiola's running mate and the former president of the Senate, joined the Abacha cabinet as ministers! In any case, the response of the military to NADECO's initiative was swift: it arrested the uncooperative politicians and detained them without charge at Kirikiri prisons. It also had trade union leaders arrested and dissolved the executive council of the Nigeria Labor Congress (NLC) for refusing to cooperate with the new junta. Journalists who were seen to be sympathetic to the cause of NADECO were arrested and detained as well; those working for newspapers such as Tell, New Tempo, and Concord were special targets for arrest and intimidation. When students of Edo State University organized a public protest over ethnic cleansing in Ogoniland (see below) and indiscriminate arrests, some were simply massacred by the police.[21]

In early September 1994, the military government promulgated eight new decrees aimed at expanding its arbitrary powers. The decrees were backdated to cover events which had taken place earlier. Decrees 12 and 14, for instance, eliminated the jurisdiction of the law courts and the use of habeas corpus. To demonstrate its intolerance of any dissenting opinion, General Abacha sacked Olu Onagoruwa, the attorney general and minister for justice, when he distanced himself from the decrees and threatened to resign unless they were amended. With these draconian decrees, many innocent Nigerians and activists were detained by the notorious State Security Service (SSS). When Ogoni leaders mobilized their people for a peaceful protest against Shell Oil for decades of environmental degradation, the Abacha junta moved swiftly to restore investor confidence, especially in the oil industry, and to teach a lesson to other minority groups as to how far it was prepared to go to keep law and order (more on the Ogonis later).[22]

By the end of 1996, Abacha had more or less contained civil society, or at least driven it underground or abroad. The list of Nigerians in exile in the United States and Europe reads like a Who is Who in Nigeria: Chief Anthony Enahoro; Nobel Laureate Wole Soyinka; Dapo Olorunomi, a prominent internationally acclaimed journalist; retired General Alani Akirinade; and Chief Ralph Obiorah, among others. To counter the effectiveness of prominent individuals and groups in mobilizing international support against it, the junta has spent millions of dollars on lobbying Western governments, newspaper advertising and subsidizing the activities of Western politicians and organizations. In retaliation against Western nations like the United Kingdom and the United States for imposing limited sanctions and travel restrictions on supporters of the junta, the Abacha government has imposed its own travel restrictions on citizens of such countries in Nigeria. It is also building a new circle of friends which now includes China, South and North Korea, Turkey, and France—the latter aiming to supplant the United Kingdom and United States in oil exploitation. Internally, the brutal assassination of prominent political figures like Chief Alfred Rewane, a prominent NADECO leader, and Alhaja Kudirat Abiola, one of the wives of Moshood Abiola, sent shivers down the spines of prodemocracy activists. Many felt that if such prominent persons could be killed with impunity, then less well-known figures would pose no problem to the strategy of silence by elimination.

In some ways, the Abacha junta is merely a continuation of the Babangida dispensation, only more brutal. Aside from the fact that Abacha was a full participant in the construction of the Babangida regime, his style of governance and relationship to civil society have only extended the frontiers of a very hostile, violent, and conflict-ridden engagement. The Sani Abacha coup of November 1993 has posed fundamental challenges to the survival of Nigeria as a nation and may have set the cause of democracy back by decades. On the one hand, it has brought out the worst in Nigerian politics: repression, intimidation, violence, corruption, betrayals, manipulation of primordial loyalties, and the suffocation of democratic aspirations. On the other hand, the character of politics since 1993 has exposed the underbelly of Nigeria's political rot and provided added strength and legitimacy to the still factionalized and weak fledgling prodemocracy camp. Thus, as hard as it is to find, there is a positive side to the Abacha coup: the crystallization of political forces and positions, the internationalization of the Nigerian agenda for democracy, the emergence of broad-based movements inside and outside Nigeria in opposition to the junta and the further delegitimization of the military. In addition, one of the major consequences of the zigzag march to political pluralism and the eventual annulment of the June 1993 election has been the intensification of struggles for identity, visibility, and political space by ethnic minorities and other communities. The ongoing Ogoni crisis is a case in point.

THE OGONI CRISIS: STATE VERSUS NATION AND CIVIL SOCIETY

The basis of the conflict between the Ogonis and the Nigerian state can be found in the flawed, unequal, and exploitative nature of center-periphery relations in the country; the domination and exploitation of oil-producing communities by the state and foreign capital; the neglect and marginalization of those communities; and in the insecurity, instability, and general weaknesses of the neo-colonial state.[23] The Ogonis have always complained of marginalization, neglect, exploitation, and disrespect. The Nigerian federal and state governments and the oil corporations have taken much from the Ogoni community and put very little or nothing back. The various formulas for revenue allocation and state and local government creation in Nigeria have simply disregarded the complaints and claims of the Ogonis, although several commissions of inquiry set up since the late 1950s have always given credence to Ogoni claims and complaints. The 1979 constitution of Nigeria simply vested all oil resources in the federal government.

The Land Use Decree written into the 1979 Constitution transferred ownership of all land to the government. Thus the Ogonis not only lost their land, they lost control of all oil discovered within their territory. The joint venture agreement between the Nigerian government and Shell Oil, following the nationalization of British Petroleum (BP) in 1979, simply strengthened the power and control of Shell over economic activities in the oil producing territory of Ogoni. Given the history of neglect and deepening socio-economic dislocations and decay, the Ogonis decided to intensify their struggles. Ogoni leaders realized that only international attention brought to their claims would force the Nigerian government to take them seriously. The strategy was to challenge the government and then use its expected brutal response as a basis for international appeal. Ogoni grievances were outlined by Saro-Wiwa thus:

In 1990, the Ogoni took stock of their situation in Nigeria and found that for all the wealth of their land, and in spite of the fact that an estimated 100 billion US dollars had been taken from their land in thirty-two years of oil mining, they had no schools, no hospitals and no roads. They found that there was an intense pressure on their land and that they lived in a poisoned environment in which wildlife, etc. could not survive. They found that the few Ogoni men and women who had some education had no access whatsoever to jobs and that when they had jobs at all, they did not obtain promotion, no matter their competence. They found that from time to time, their leaders had laid faith in cooperation with the rest of Nigeria but that this faith had been grossly misplaced as each ethnic group has its own agenda quite unrelated to the notion of cooperation in a multi-ethnic nation.[24]

In October 1990, the chiefs and people of Ogoni prepared and submitted an Ogoni Bill of Rights to the federal government. The document demanded political autonomy for the Ogonis as a distinct and separate unit. This autonomy was to include: political control of Ogoni affairs by Ogoni people, the right to the control and use of their economic resources, adequate and direct representation as a right in all Nigerian institutions, use and development of Ogoni languages, the full development of Ogoni culture, the right to religious freedom, and the right to protect the Ogoni environment and ecology from further degradation. As negotiations progressed, the demands came to include the creation of an Ogoni state with thirteen local government areas. The Nigerian government ignored the Bill of Rights. On August 26, 1991, the Chiefs and people of Ogoni sent the Addendum to the Ogoni Bill of Rights to the Nigerian government and international community. It was at this point that the Ogonis noted that "without the intervention of the international community, the Government of the Federal Republic of Nigeria and the ethnic majority will continue [their] obnoxious policies until the Ogoni people are obliterated from the face of the earth."[25]

What followed was massive internal mobilization, the creation of relevant organizations such as the Movement for the Survival of Ogoni People (MOSOP), the National Youth Council of Ogoni People (NYCOP), the Conference of Ogoni Traditional Rulers (COTR), the Council for Ogoni Rights (COR), and others. These were very militant and active organizations. There were mass demonstrations, press statements and conferences; public opinion in support of the Ogonis was mobilized in the Nigerian media; more importantly, the Ogoni community itself was educated on the nature of the demands. MOSOP constantly restated the commitment of the Ogonis to peaceful strategies of struggle for their demands. In addition, MOSOP disseminated its agenda through other Non Governmental Organizations (NGOs) and prodemocracy groups across the country. MOSOP also worked closely with grassroots movements and professional organizations outside Nigeria. Specifically, MOSOP took the case of the Ogonis to the Underrepresented Nations and Peoples Organization (UNPO), the United Nations, and international environmental and human rights organizations to enlist their support in pressuring the Nigerian military and the Shell Petroleum Development Company to compensate the Ogonis for decades of exploitation and abuse of their environment.[26]

The Nigerian military and Shell had other ideas. The military responded with intimidation, the arrest of Ogoni leaders, and support for conservative politicians and traditional rulers in Ogoniland to create divisions and counter-propaganda. It drafted police and army units to protect oil executives and workers in the area and to demonstrate its strong alliance with Shell Oil. Shell Oil, for its part, refused to dialogue seriously with the community, claiming that it was the responsibility of the host government to compensate the Ogonis. In April 1993, violence broke out when a U.S. contracting company, Wilbros, bulldozed crops in Biara to make way for the laying of new pipelines in total defiance of the demands of the community. The police, called in to protect company employees, fired and killed an Ogoni man and wounded twenty others. This development strengthened the belief of the Ogonis that the government and oil companies were ganged up against them.

By July 1993, non-Ogoni neighbors who had traditionally depended on Ogoni trade routes and markets and who had maintained peaceful relations attacked the Ogonis with automatic weapons, grenades, and other sophisticated arms. This attack by the Andonis led to the death of more than 1,000 people and displaced 20,000. Neither the state nor federal governments responded to the appeals of MOSOP and the Ogonis. In December 1993, the Ogonis were attacked by the Okrikas.[27] This incident, which lasted for several days, left 95 Ogonis dead and thousands wounded and displaced. As before, the authorities refused to act, even though military and police installations were close by. In April 1994, the Ogonis were attacked by their northern neighbors, the Ndokis. This time the attackers were aided by Nigerian soldiers who raided seven Ogoni villages destroying lives and property. One village, Ledor, was completely burned to the ground and all the inhabitants rendered homeless. These acts of violence, clearly orchestrated by powerful forces beyond the warring communities, sent clear signals to the Ogonis, the prodemocracy groups, the international NGOs, and other minority communities that the military regime would not flinch at crushing any challenge, peaceful or otherwise, to its power.

In May 1994, four prominent and conservative Ogoni leaders were murdered while attending a meeting at Giokoo, Gokhana Kingdom. The murdered chiefs, Edward Kobani, Samuel Orage, Albert Badey, and Theophilus Orage, had been members of MOSOP but had disagreed with the more militant positions of younger members. Their resignation from MOSOP saw the election of Ken Saro-Wiwa as MOSOP president and the intensification of grassroots mobilization and the internationalization of MOSOP's demands. It also led to a division within the Ogoni community between the so-called conservatives, who were seen as government stooges and opportunists, and the younger, more militant members. This division was exploited by the military government which tried to present MOSOP as unreasonable, irresponsible, and not representative of the genuine interests of the Ogonis. With the murder of the four chiefs, the military government, this time, responded immediately. It blamed the murders on MOSOP and NYCOP, arrested Ken Saro-Wiwa, the spokesperson for the Ogonis and president of MOSOP, and sent a brutal military expedition to occupy Ogoniland. The military commandant in charge of the expedition, Major (later Colonel) Paul Okuntimo, saw it as an opportunity to "waste" the Ogonis. He treated the operation like the Nigerian involvement in the civil war in Liberia.[28]

Although the strategy of MOSOP was largely peaceful—that is, letter writing, demonstrations, press releases, and international campaigns—the Nigerian military under Abacha saw the growing influence of MOSOP President Ken Saro-Wiwa and the publicity surrounding the Ogoni predicament as a threat to its agenda for consolidating military rule and containing existing pockets of opposition. The military needed urgently to contain the tide of opposition and protest by showing an example. It also needed to keep the proceeds from oil flowing to reward its supporters. The Ogoni situation provided an ample opportunity, for the Ogonis, by virtue of their small number and historical marginalization in the Nigerian political system, could be picked apart more easily than other groups opposing the military. Following a clearly flawed trial by a military tribunal without the right of appeal, and in defiance of global appeals for clemency, nine MOSOP leaders, including Ken Saro-Wiwa, were put to death by hanging on November 10, 1995.[29]

The executions marked a turning point in Nigeria's struggle for democracy. The junta was condemned by the entire world, by African leaders, the United Nations, international NGOs, and by Nigerian communities abroad. The country was suspended from the British Commonwealth following a motion by president Nelson Mandela of South Africa, a country, which ironically, had benefited from Nigeria's antiapartheid stance. The European Union and other Western nations reviewed diplomatic relations. The Canadian government imposed sanctions and in November 1995, the Standing Committee on International Trade and Foreign Affairs of the Canadian House of Commons voted unanimously to impose a trade embargo, stop buying Nigerian oil, freeze all foreign aid, and work hard with the United States and the Commonwealth to impose stiffer sanctions on Nigeria. City councils in North America—such as Toronto, Oakland, and New York—imposed sanctions on Nigeria. Rallies were organized around the world by Nigerians, human rights organizations, and NGOs like Greenpeace, Friends of the Earth, Amnesty International, and TransAfrica in front of Nigerian missions to protest the killings and continued detention of political activists. The executions had not only exposed the brutality and arrogance of the junta to the world, but also may have forced the government, in the face of mounting protests, to construct an agenda for redemocratization.

CONCLUSION: YET ANOTHER TRANSITION TO DEMOCRACY?

The advent of General Abacha in Nigerian politics (whose regime is really an extension of that of Babangida, 1985–93) represents the triumph of irrationality, corruption, mediocrity, and the negation of all norms of dialogue and consensus. This made it possible for atavistic, sectional, and opportunistic interests to emerge in all sectors of society at the expense of popular and democratic interests. It also has made it possible for disgraced ethnic, religious, and regional warlords to be rehabilitated and for their rather sinister objectives to be articulated anew. More importantly, it has severely bifurcated the country along ethnic and regional lines: the North against the South, the North and East against the West, Christians against Muslims, and the military against civilians. These divisions have far reaching implications for state-society relations and for democratic revival. In fact, the politics of the Abacha junta—in particular, the way in which the regime has treated the Abiola and June 12 election issue, the minority question, and military disengagement from politics—has hardened positions and forced many usually liberal and nationalist politicians to return to their regional enclaves to articulate separatist positions. The so-called new transition initiative is more of the same old game; very little, if anything, has changed.

The five registered parties—United Nigeria Congress Party (UNCP), Committee for National Consensus (CNC), National Center Party of Nigeria (NCPN), Grassroots Democratic Movement (GDM), and Democratic Party of Nigeria (DPN)—have not demonstrated any new ideas and programs; worse still, they have no plan for resisting and keeping the military out of politics. They are led by the very same characters who precipitated the demise of the Second Republic and the nonactualization of the Third Republic. Some of the parties have been falling all over each other, pleading with Abacha to "civilianize" himself and become their presidential candidate. For virtually all of the prominent political figures in the five parties, politics is still a business, an opportunity to penetrate the state and engage in rapid accumulation. Once again, Nigeria appears to be embarking on another false march to democracy, and the military may simply be warming up to either continue the Abacha dispensation or supplant him with another variant of the same military arrangement.

It is true that only the expansion and consolidation of civil society can guarantee the success of democratic transition. Yet, the Nigerian experience presents many ambiguities. The emergence of scores of narrowly focused, opportunistic, irredentist, ethnically and regionally based interest groups like the Afenifere and Egbe Omo Yoruba in the West, the Oha'Eze in the East, the Northern Elements Coalition in the North, the National Unity Club, the Peoples' Consultative Forum, the New Dimension, Club '95, Club 258, the Justice Forum and the Progressives' Summit, to mention only a few, have implications for civil society, the national project and democratization. Only if they are democratic (and they are mostly not) can these organizations serve as platforms for articulating the interests of the people as part of a larger national movement. At the moment, many are led or sponsored by persons with very questionable political credentials and dubious sources of wealth. Many in the opposition are there only because they have been marginalized from current power dispensations. At the same time, there is hope. The executions of the Ogoni leaders and the continued detention of prodemocracy leaders, which have attracted international calls for sanctions, have further isolated Nigeria's military regime.[30]

In its desperation, the Nigerian military has responded like a caged animal, lashing out at opponents, insisting on its sovereignty, and blaming foreign governments, NGOs, and Nigerians abroad for its predicament. This response, which clearly is not remorseful, has only hardened domestic opposition and attracted international attention. In the United States, the Clinton administration remains publicly committed to the restoration of democracy in Nigeria and has openly stated that stiffer responses would follow more human rights abuses by the junta. The Commonwealth, the European Union, as well as the Tony Blair government in the United Kingdom, have expressed opposition to military dictatorships and have provided support for Nigerian opposition movements. Canada virtually has no diplomatic relations with Nigeria. Even Jamaica has refused to continue some bilateral agreements with Nigeria. At the same time, commercial interests in some of these countries and the apparent success of the Nigeria-led forces of the Economic Community of West African States (ECOWAS) in Liberia may have prevented the imposition of harsher economic sanctions, thus raising questions about the seriousness with which the West takes democracy efforts in Africa's most populous country.

As long as the Nigerian military remains untamed, floating, as it were, above society, and as long as the Nigerian political parties are little more than tools for ambitious individuals who seldom embrace the aspirations of the masses, democratization in Nigeria is likely to remain a mirage. Given the military's continued hegemony, Abacha's apparent interest in keeping the reigns of power (either as a civilian or a general), and opportunism and division within Nigeria's political elite, Nigeria will continue to be an unfortunate example of democratic failure in an increasingly changing global order.

EDITOR'S POSTCRIPT

The chapter on Nigeria was submitted in 1997, one year before the death of General Sani Abacha. What impact will this unexpected turn of events have on Nigerian politics? The passing of Abacha has undoubtedly changed the balance of forces in Nigerian politics in favor of the democratic opposition. Since transition outcomes essentially hinge on the relative power and influence of competing groups at crucial time periods, the death of Sani Abacha may turn out to be the coup de grâce that breaks the Nigerian military's stranglehold over civilian society. General Abdulsalam Abubakar's decision to release some prominent political prisoners, including former head of state Olasegun Obasanjo, may be a reflection of the Nigerian military's weaknesses and the ascendency of prodemocracy forces. Thus, some of Abubakar's initial gestures give reason for hope. At the same time, his promise to continue with Abacha's so-called transition program is worrisome, as is the uncertainty surrounding whether Abubakar can hold in check the more hawkish and anti-democratic elements within the Nigerian armed forces. It is also an open question whether the political parties and ethnic groups of Nigeria, especially the Igbos and Yorubas, will see Abacha's death as an opportunity to set aside their differences and form a coalition that would dislodge the generals who have ruled Nigeria on behalf of a dying semifeudal order for much of the country's postcolonial history. In this connection, the arguments made by professor Ihonvbere are as valid today as they were in 1997.

NOTES

1. See Julius O. Ihonvbere and Toyin Falola, "The Illusion of Economic Development," and "Colonialism and Exploitation," in Toyin Falola, ed., *Britain and Nigeria: Exploitation or Development?* (London: Zed Books, 1987).

2. See Billy Dudley, *Instability and Political Order: Politics and Crisis in Nigeria* (Ibadan, Nigeria: Ibadan University Press, 1973).

3. See Adewale Ademoyega, *Why We Struck: The Story of the First Nigerian Coup* (Ibadan, Nigeria: Evans Brothers Publishers, 1981). See also N. U. Akpan, *The Struggle for Secession 1966–1970: A Personal Account of the Nigerian Civil War* (London: Frank Cass, 1971).

4. See Richard Joseph, "Affluence and Underdevelopment: The Nigerian Experience," *Journal of Modern African Studies* 16, no. 2 (1978), pp. 64–85. See also B. J. Dudley, *Instability and Political Order: Politics and Crisis in Nigeria* (Ibadan, Nigeria: Ibadan University Press, 1973).

5. See Terisa Turner, "Nigeria," in John Dunn, ed., *West African States: Failure and Promise* (Cambridge, UK: Cambridge University Press, 1978). See also J. P. Mackintosh, *Nigerian Government and Politics* (London, UK: Longman, 1985).

6. See S. K. Panther-Brick, ed., *Nigerian Politics and Military Rule* (London, UK: Athlone, 1970). By the same author, *Soldiers and Oil: The Political Transformation of Nigeria* (London, UK: Frank Cass, 1978).

7. Dare Babarinsa, "The New Inheritors," *Tell* (Lagos), 6 December 1993.

8. Julius O. Ihonvbere, "The Military and Political Engineering Under Structural Adjustment: The Nigerian Experience Since 1985," *Journal of Political and Military Sociology* 20 (1991), pp. 14–28.

9. See Julius O. Ihonvbere and Toyin Falola, *The Rise and Fall of Nigeria's Second Republic: 1979–84* (London, UK: Zed Press, 1985).

10. See Sam C. Nolutshungu, "Fragments of a Democracy: Reflections on Class and Politics in Nigeria," *Third World Quarterly* 12, no. 1 (1990), pp. 40–57.

11. Of course, this is not peculiar to Nigeria. In the United States the use of so-called street money to get out the votes is common practice. The ability of Ross Perot and The United We Stand campaign to gain visibility and create a following in a short period of time is directly related to Mr. Perot's personal wealth. The difference, however, is that, in the United States, there are still checks and balances, as well as predictable rules guiding the political game.

12. Author interview with Femi Falana, Obafemi Awolowo House, Ikeja, Lagos, December 1993.

13. Author interview with a prodemocracy activist, Campaign for Democracy Headquarters, Anthony, Lagos, December 1993.

14. Ibrahim Babangida, "Laying the Foundation of a Viable Democracy and the Path of Honour," June 26, 1993. Reproduced in full in *Newswatch*, 5 July 1993.

15. Ibid.

16. Ibid.

17. Author interview with a prodemocracy activist, Campaign for Democracy Headquarters, Anthony, Lagos, December 1993.

18. The 1989 constitution did not make provisions for an interim government. More importantly, at the time the ING was sworn into power, there was no decree supporting its creation and legitimacy. Ibrahim Babangida actually signed the decree after he ceased to be president of Nigeria. It was largely on this ground that the courts were to declare the Shonekan government and the ING unconstitutional and illegal.

19. See Ola Rotimi Ajayi and Julius O. Ihonvbere, "Democratic Impasse: Remilitarization in Nigeria," *Third World Quarterly* 15, no. 4 (1994), pp. 102–118.

20. The CD had initially opposed Abiola as SDP presidential candidate. The CD reasoned that Abiola was corrupt, too close to the military, and had a rather unreliable relationship with popular communities. However, following the election and its subsequent annulment, the CD changed its position, arguing that the will of the people had to be respected. In all of its press releases, the CD urged Nigerians to stand by democracy. It argued that its support for Abiola had nothing to do with religious or ethnic consideration. It was simply a matter of principle.

21. See "Massacres in Nigeria," *Committee for Academic Freedom in Africa Newsletter* no. 8, (spring 1995), pp. 4–6. According to this document, over twenty-five persons were shot to death, thirty-eight were arrested, and thirty-four, including some well known human rights and prodemocracy activists in the Edo state, were declared wanted.

22. See E. I. Udogu, "The Allurement of Ethnonationalism in Nigerian Politics: The Contemporary Debate," *Journal of Asian and African Studies* 29, no. 34 (1994). See also, by the same author, "National Integration Attempts in Nigerian Politics," *Canadian Review of Studies in Nationalism* 27 (1990), pp. 60–84.

23. See "Nigeria: The Unacceptable Marginalization of the East," *Daily Champion,* 7 October 1993; "Abacha, What Have the Igalas Done?" *The Guardian,* 18 December 1993; Adeiza Shamsudeen, "The Realities of Ethnicity and Marginalization in Kogi State," *New Nigerian,* 8 January 1993.

24. See Ken Saro-Wiwa, *Genocide in Nigeria* (London, UK, and Port Harcourt, Nigeria: Saros International, 1994), p. 92. As part of its campaign to discredit Saro-Wiwa and eventually justify the executions of the Ogoni activists, the Nigerian government deliberately misinterpreted the Movement for the Survival of the Ogoni People's (MOSOP) call for local autonomy as a desire to secede from the federal republic of Nigeria.

25. Ibid., 99.

26. See Emmanuel Efeni, "When Ogoni Got UN Hearing," *The Guardian,* 14 September 1995. For a scholarly treatment of the Ogonis' plight, see Ben Naanen, "Oil Producing Minorities and the Restructuring of Nigerian Federalism: The Case of the Ogoni People," *Journal of Commonwealth and Comparative Politics* 33, no. 1 (1995).

27. Underrepresented Nations and Peoples Organization (UNPO), *Ogoni* (The Hague: UNPO, 1995), 26.

28. Restricted memo by Major Paul Okuntimo, RSIS/MLAD/LOO/94004, to Rivers State military administrators, 12 July 1994.

29. See "Ogoni Verdicts-Abacha's Final Revenge," *Tell,* 13 November 1995.

30. See Chris Ogmonna, "Sanctions: Shape Up or Ship Out," *Tell,* 18 December 1995.

5
Democracy, State-Building, and "Nations" in Ethiopia: 1974–95

Kassahun Berhanu

INTRODUCTION

This chapter aims to shed light on the course, causes, and possible outcomes of the struggle for democratic governance in Ethiopia from 1974 to 1995. The thrust of the argument can be summarized as follows: Ethiopian politics has essentially been about how best to incorporate the different "nations" that make up the Ethiopian state—first the empire state, and after 1974, the Marxist state—without trampling on popular aspirations for local and regional autonomy from centralized authority. In spite of initial expectations and promises of building Ethiopia on democratic principles and structures, both Emperor Selassie and Mengistu eventually dropped all pretenses of adhering to those ideals and resorted to force to preserve the country's unity and, more importantly for them, secure their own power. They both failed, with tragic consequences for their respective regimes and Ethiopia as a whole.

The current Ethiopian Peoples' Revolutionary Democratic Front–led government's official commitment to democracy through so-called ethnic federalism is a continuation of the long-running quest for the type of governance that would make the forementioned goals achievable. It is by no means clear that the outcome of current efforts will be different from those of the past. The singling out of the 1974–95 period as a point of entry is meant to provide historical boundaries to the chapter, but it also underscores one important point. The quest for democratic governance in Ethiopia did not begin with the fall of the Berlin Wall and the euphoria that followed in its wake throughout Africa; it has been at the heart of modern Ethiopian political life and will continue to be until the underlying issues which gave that quest its raison d'être are satisfactorily resolved.

BACKGROUND

Strategically located in the region commonly known as the Horn of Africa and with a population of over 50 million people inhabiting a territory of about 1.1 million square kilometers, Ethiopia is a land of diversity, a mosaic of ethnic and language groups, cultures, contrasting ecological zones, and physical configurations. The marked ethnic heterogeneity of the polity is an outcome of protracted migration and continuous settlements resulting from conquests, displacements, and resettlements. The varied demographic distribution pertaining to the different ecological zones has been influenced by topography, climate, and historical occurrences, which in turn explains the entrenchment of predominant livelihood systems and peculiar modes of existence relating to the different peoples and localities. According to Kuhlman, amid bewildering variations some important patterns can, nonetheless, be discerned.[1]

In spite of the fact that historical relationships between the peoples of Ethiopia have gone through complex and intricate processes of disharmony and conflict over the years, ample instances of amity and peaceful coexistence also have been featured. The collision-collusion syndrome could be explained by the lust for control and hegemony on the one hand and common denominators revolving around mutual interests and complementary affinities on the other. Available historical records bring to light the fact that the initiation of the state took shape in the northern part centuries before the birth of Christ with the formation of the Axumite kingdom. During subsequent periods, the kingdom of Axum transformed itself into a kind of quasi-empire by annexing and incorporating territories and localities around and beyond the Red Sea coastal regions and frontiers to the south away from the center.[2]

Christianity was introduced to and adopted in Axum around the beginning of the fourth century and in the years to come it was instrumental in molding the Abyssinian element with the Geez language. Markakis argues that this blending pervaded all aspects of traditional Ethiopian culture and became a potent social force with manifold ramifications.[3] In terms of ethnicity, what was regarded as the Abyssinian central element was constituted by the Tigrayans (including those inhabiting the highlands of present-day Eritrea) and the Amharas, at a later stage.[4] These two groups, sharing closely related languages originating from the same source and a common religion in the form of Coptic Christianity, were among those that played a significant role in shaping modern Ethiopia. The situation in the south during the period under discussion was quite different. The south was, as it is at present, a broad conglomeration of diverse peoples, cultures, beliefs, value systems, and social organizations. Communities of hunter-gatherers, pastoralists, and sedentary farmers with egalitarian and fairly differentiated structures prevailed there. The lack of common, cultural denominators, as they existed in the north, probably accounted for the delay in the emergence of a more or less homogenous formation in the south.

Around the end of the last millennium, the center of the Abyssinian state began to effect a gradual but steady shift toward the south of the ancient heartland. This was caused by factors such as demographic pressures calling for new and more hospitable lands, insurgencies by subject peoples threatening the security of the centralized state, and the progressive intrusion of Islam, which was hostile to the status quo; hence Axum declined as the center of influence in Ethiopia. In the process of such a retreat, the northerners (i.e., Abyssinians) interacted with new peoples and cultures. The new polity included diverse national and religious groups with differing economies, ideologies, and kinship systems. According to Markakis, while Abyssinia proper was a more or less homogenous state, with a solid national base (i.e., the Solomonic myth legitimizing the authority of the state and Orthodox Christianity sanctioning its preeminence), Ethiopia was a multiethnic empire.[5]

Subsequent periods were marked by instability, prompted by regional and dynastic rivalries, internal centrifugalism, and external invasions. Significant among these were the difficulties of maintaining a "Solomonic" heir at the helm of state power against the wishes and aspirations of other pretenders (thirteenth century); the rise and expansion of the Ottoman empire, which triggered the assertive stance of Ethiopian coreligionists aspiring to supreme power (sixteenth century); and the weakening of central authority caused by the proliferation of warlordism and fragmented regionalism, as expressed in what is known as the Era of Princes (the eighteenth and the first half of the nineteenth centuries). With the successful rise of Theodros II, chaos and anarchy ended. Centralized authority was consolidated, and Ethiopia became an empire state at the turn of the nineteenth century. However, in attempting to contain the challenges that had previously led to its decadence, the state came to be increasingly immersed in its self-preservation.

Apart from striving to retain whatever lands were at its disposal, the state was simultaneously engaged in the exercise of territorial expansion by way of annexation and incorporation of new principalities. With an admixture of diplomacy and military prowess, Menelik II ruled over a formidable empire. Menelik was responsible for ushering in the phenomenon of "modernity" on the one hand and effecting the subjugation of peoples of the annexed territories on the other. According to Bulcha, the coercive annexation of the peoples of the conquered territories to facilitate the creation of the empire state became the incarnation of all kinds of alienation and marginalization, thereby forming the basis upon which future antagonisms that have proved detrimental to the polity have flourished.[6] Markakis agrees with this thesis when he argues that the expansion stored great potential for conflict in the nature of the relationships between those who controlled the state and those who became its subjects.[7]

With some qualifying corrections, Addis Hiwot appears to concur with Bulcha and Markakis:

After the creation of the multi-national empire state by the shoan feudal principality, especially after the conquest and effective occupation and incorporation of the south, south-western and south-eastern areas, a classical system of feudal serfdom was established. An extensive process of land confiscation and the enslavement of the indigenous peasants took place. The religious, cultural and linguistic differences between the feudal conquistadors and the indigenous peoples gave the process of enslavement a still more brutal dimension.[8]

Nevertheless, it should be noted that not all the people in the north benefited from such an enterprise, save the ruling classes and the soldiers that participated in it for their ends. Nor were all southerners losers, owing to the fact that the local gentry had been attracted by the incentives and rewards for cooperating. But the masses of the people, in both the north and south, were probably either non benefi- ciaries or net losers of the Ethiopian empire state. The coming onto the scene of elite or ruling-class politics shaped the modus operandi of the political system. In all fairness, however, the negative implications of such an undertaking for the nationality-ethnicity makeup of the peoples of the incorporated territories should not be overrated, for the system had simultaneously tried to prevent ethnicity from becoming a base for political supremacy by introducing interethnic arrangements of convenience, at least at the level of ruling circles.[9]

In general terms, both before and after the forming of the empire, elite politics and rivalry persisted in shaping the interactions among protagonists vying for ac- cess and control of state power, while at the same time rallying support from class or ethnicity-based constituencies by presenting issues presumed to be matters of common concern. As Harbeson notes, such a state of affairs has rendered Ethio- pian history to be characterized by endemic competition and military struggle among diverse political entities and ethnic groups included within its bounda- ries.[10] Nevertheless, it should be noted that not every occurrence that led to dishar- mony and conflict was fueled by elite politics alone. One finds ample instances of class-based confrontation, the causes of which are rooted in disaffection of the masses, whose legitimate claims and demands elites had failed to address. Peasant revolts and insurgencies, and, at later stages, workers' strikes and student riots di- rected their fury against those symbolizing and representing the system, regardless of their ethnic affinity.

The further tasks of empire-building and the consolidation of the accomplish- ments of Menelik II fell on Haile Selassie I, in the first decades of the twentieth century. From the early days of his regency until he was ousted by the revolution- ary upsurge of 1974, Haile Selassie sought to infuse changes into the veins of the political system in line with new developments both at home and abroad. These in- cluded strengthening the power of centralized authority vis-à-vis local ones. This policy coincided with Selassie's preference for personalized rule; as a result, the factors that were deemed critical to the entrenchment of that style of governing were given the utmost attention from the very beginning. Despite some socio- economic and political changes experienced during Haile Selassie's long reign, state-society relations were hardly as smooth as claimed by his nostalgic and revi- sionist admirers.

Ethiopia's relative integration into the wider framework of the global political economy and the concomitant progressive retreat of some aspects of traditional values led to greater awareness in the masses of Ethiopians of developments in other parts of the world on the one hand and a better understanding of the situation at home on the other, which in turn prompted demands for fair and equitable distribution of societal resources. The very nature of the political economy (feudal and centralized as it was) precluded any change of significance within the status quo. Ethiopia's erstwhile imperial rulers' reluctance (if not to say incapacity) to respond to popular aspirations for change served as a hotbed of contradictions, which then prepared the ground for subsequent confrontations. When Selassie did respond in the 1960s and early 1970s the reforms introduced were late and were viewed as measures intended to increase the efficiency of centralized rule, as opposed to genuine reforms intended to drastically alter state-society power relations within the empire state.

The ascendance of Haile Selassie thus entailed the centralization of both power and prestige.[11] However, unlike Western Europe where the advent of the modern nation-state was accompanied by the centralization of power by Weberian-type public bureaucracies, centralized administration inside the empire state of Ethiopia did not approach Weber's ideal bureaucracy because of its highly personalized nature.[12] Failing to transcend the confines of limited goals and purposes for which they were designed, the cosmetic changes, as proved later, were rendered powerless to offset the effects of the thrust made to overthrow the edifice upon which the status quo had rested. The crises-ridden fabric of state-society relations, therefore, had to go through fragmented processes, infested by unfriendly encounters between ruling groups (intraelite struggles) on the one hand and between segments of society and the state on the other. The situation was so complex and intricate that there was no united opposition based on identical programs of action in challenging the establishment.

As Selassie's reign reached its terminal stage, a plethora of demands, at times antagonistic and appearing mutually exclusive, were advanced and advocated. These ranged from calling for reforms and adjustments within the framework of existing structures to dismantling the entire establishment and supplanting it with a radically different arrangement. The situation is expressed by Holcomb, who argues that the causes for the discontent of the different groups antagonized by the regime were in no way similar.[13] In other words, the underlying reasons for disaffection varied, assuming class, national, regional, and even personal overtones at times. One exception, however, was the coming onto the scene of the Ethiopian Student Movement, which was radically oriented toward the need for effecting a fundamental alteration of the entire system through revolutionary means.

Both at home and abroad, and despite certain limitations in approaches, tactics, and strategies, the Ethiopian Student Movement did manage to transcend the shortsightedness and fragmented parochialism of other disaffected groups. By advancing such slogans as Land to the Tiller, National and Religious Equality, Representative Government and Democratic Rights, and so on, the movement effectively echoed the grievances of all victims of autocratic outrages. In doing so, it became an embodiment of the wishes and aspirations of the forces of change in society without subscribing to the individualistic desires of any one ethnic group, power center, or subsystem.[14] On the contrary, rather than paying allegiance to narrowly defined sectarian dispositions, it developed a sound Marxist orientation thus posing as one of the most militant groups in the Third World.[15] Its offsprings, the All Ethiopia Socialist Movement (MEISON) and the Ethiopian People's Revolutionary Movement (EPRP), were responsible for determining the radical orientation of the 1974 revolution, although they failed to steer it to a glorious end.

It is against this background that the events of the 1974 revolutionary upsurge need to be assessed. On the eve of the unfolding of the revolutionary process, all the major forces that participated in it were convinced that in the face of the persistent reluctance of the political system to be responsive and amenable to changes, the quest for democratic transformation would remain an illusion beyond doubt. The regime was widely viewed as plodding, evasive, basically conservative, and mainly interested in perpetuating itself, rather than in bringing about change.[16] The need to do away with it became increasingly attractive and indispensable. A mix of both endogenous and exogenous factors coming together at the right time provided the *casus belli* of the revolution.

First, the progressive deterioration of the quality of life for many Ethiopians was aggravated by a major drought-induced famine (1973–74) that killed hundreds of thousands. This increased the unpopularity of the regime, especially following reports that it had refrained from publicizing the crisis and done nothing to help the afflicted. Second, in the urban areas there were growing student activism, labor unrest, and dissidence among members of the intelligentsia and professional groups. Third, the apparent opening up of an arena of struggle and competition within the ranks of the ruling elite was witnessed. Fourth, army support was wavering. Fifth, there was widespread disaffection among the urban population due to the effects of the 1973 oil shock. Sixth, nationalist, regionalist, and religious dissidents, who resented the handling of issues by the regime in the past, came to represent a readily available support base in favor of any move against the existing arrangement.

The disarray in the ranks of the forces of repression became clear when some segments went to the extent of making their own claims and demands to be settled by the regime in a manner that was incompatible with previous practice. This led to the gathering of momentum of mass protests in the form of student riots, workers' strikes, and soldiers' mutiny, which began to take leaps and bounds in succession. Those who engaged in semiopen and clandestine activities added fuel to the fire. They branded the regime as the villain responsible for all the mishaps that had befallen the country and called for the termination of Selassie's reign. It is worth noting, however, that there was no organized political party, no vanguard, that could guide such a wave of discontent to a positive outcome.

Apart from concurrence on the general goal of dismantling imperial rule, the forces of change did not, by and large, give much thought to what needed to be done in the aftermath of the fall of Selassie. As Marcus rightly affirms, there were no political parties that could generate competing agendas for action.[17] This want of a political machinery can be explained by the reluctance of the autocracy to allow for autonomous political space and action, thus inhibiting the prospects for creating an alternative to itself when such crisis situations came to the fore. Such shortsightedness was to prove detrimental to the proponents of absolute control in the immediate aftermath of their overthrow. Nor did this spare society at a later stage. According to Hess, in maintaining Ethiopia as a no-party state, the emperor had walked a tightrope between traditionalism and modernism, stability and change.[18] As proved later, this precarious balance could not be maintained indefinitely.

Posing as the armed wing of the popular protest movement, the new regime that supplanted imperial rule in 1974 was constituted by a group of noncommissioned and junior officers. It was presented as an elected representative of the various units and contingents of the defense and security establishments and designated as the Provisional Military Administrative Council (PMAC), alias, the *Derg*. This body was vested with responsibilities for carrying out the functions of the state, on an interim basis, "until such time that a popularly elected constitutional government takes over." A series of major ideological and general policy shifts were made, presumed to be instrumental in effecting fundamental changes and symbolizing drives toward overall betterment.

Despite timid and haphazard resistance by some proponents of the status quo ante, particularly in the ranks of the rural gentry, the much expected reform measures began to take full swing around the first months of 1975. Indoctrination by individual members of the revolutionary intelligentsia, pressure from overzealous and militant labor and student unions, pragmatic dispositions of some influential PMAC members, and so on, probably contributed toward endorsing the socialist orientation both as an ideology and a framework for praxis. Thus, it could be argued that revolutionary visions inspired by adherence to Marxist-Leninist ideology clearly and heavily influenced the reform policies and the organizational structures of the Ethiopian transformation.[19] They also impinged on the country's foreign policy after 1974.[20]

Because the severing of the umbilical chord connecting state and society over a period of several centuries was not a task to be easily disposed, considerable measures of politicization and mobilization, complemented by a host of legislation and proclamations in tune with the new drives, were necessary and appropriate. At the same time, dismantling the edifice upon which the old order had rested in terms of functions, institutions, personnel, values, and modus operandi became one of the major preoccupations of the early period. The most outstanding accomplishments, which were then considered to be congruent with the goals of the revolution, were the nationalization of land, the creation of new units and nuclei of local government known as Peasant and Urban Dwellers' Associations (March–July 1975), and "public" ownership of the commanding heights of the economy. Simultaneously, neutralizing resistance by the forces of counterrevolution aimed at containing advances in this direction was well underway by early 1975.

STATE-SOCIETY RELATIONS AND POLITICAL ECONOMY (1974–91)

Frustration and disillusionment caused by the failure of the imperial regime to improve the lot of society gave way to new hopes and expectations triggered by the dismantling of the old order. The Land Reform Act of 1975, which terminated exploitative landlordism, and other similar measures initially created a formidable constituency of support in favor of the revolution. Notwithstanding this, however, resistance and antipathy to either the Derg or the revolutionary process, and in some cases both, were present from the very beginning. Apart from the Marxist-oriented EPRP and the conservative Ethiopian Democratic Union (EDU), the ranks of the camp of the discontent also included the long entrenched Eritrean separatist movements like the Eritrean Liberation Front (ELF) and the Ethiopian Peoples' Liberation Front (EPLF) and nascent nationalist groups like the Tigray Peoples' Liberation Front (TPLF).

Based on a comparatively wider constituency of support, the thrust of the revolutionary process was too strong to be contained by the action of its adversaries. The zeal displayed by the forces favoring the unmitigated continuation of the process of change was responsible for wresting the initiative from those forces that were ready to benefit by exploiting prevalent confusion in Ethiopian high politics in a manner attempted by Somali irredentism. The period was also characterized by the unleashing of long-repressed sectarian sentiments and loyalty to the Ethiopian revolution.[21] Whether the firm allegiance that the revolution managed to command in the early days was to persist depended, as proved later, on the accomplishments or drawbacks of its opponents. Marcus has noted that the regime succeeded in defeating the Somali invasion and effectively contained threats from the Eritrean insurgents and other opposition forces, including those within the ruling body, by 1978.[22]

The opposition movements squandered their energies by administering deadly blows against each other, which subsequently made them easy prey for the then emerging dictatorship of Mengistu Haile Mariam. Those who remained were cowed into absolute obedience, abdicating their pretentious autonomy for fear of being treated like their departed counterparts. An undeclared Bonapartism that resolved to make maximum use of the executive branch of government, including its means of repression, soon surfaced. It was at this point in time that the Mengistu clique reneged on its promise to go back to the barracks and began to prepare for an indefinite stay in power. The opportunity was provided by the weaknesses and indeed progressive disintegration of the political opposition and the subduing of civil society, using a combination of threats, security control, and, above all, terror, epitomized by the most extreme forms of physical violence.

Concrete manifestations of such abuses included arbitrary arrests, torture, and summary executions directed against all suspected of sympathizing with, or belonging to, groups opposed to the regime. The so-called red terror was declared as a revolutionary response to the urban violence, or white terror, of the EPRP that had commenced around the second half of 1976, and was in full swing in 1977, eventually obtaining legal sanction by October of the same year. These tragic phenomena (the white and red terrors) were characterized by killing orgies targeting individual opponents and at times involving personal vendettas.

Religious institutions, trade unions, and professional associations—in short, civil society itself—were not immune from these abuses. The private sector, particularly the wealthy members of the business community who were labeled economic saboteurs also were not spared. Massive purges were intensified against the leadership and rank-and-file members of these components of civil society who were suspected of harboring discontent in one form or another. Many were subjected to long-term imprisonment or killed, while others were dismissed, carrying with them the specter of some unidentified misfortune that might visit them in the future. The regime's organized opponents were promptly replaced by those who were handpicked and ready to serve in order to ensure their survival in the face of unpredictable odds and uncertainties.

Bloody purges also visited military personnel in different divisions and barracks. Accusations by political commissars and security officers, serving as the henchmen of the Mengistu clique, sufficed to carry out executions of numerous highly trained officers and professional soldiers, who were often deprived of the benefit of hearings by court martial. The entire country, with the exception of the strongholds of the Tigrayan and Eritrean guerrillas in the remote corners of their respective regions, was entangled by chaos, anarchy, and terror. The insurgents, entrenched in the northern parts of Ethiopia, underwent a period of consolidation, the opportunity for which was provided by the regime's preoccupation with cleansing its opponents that were within easy reach. Furthermore, the TPLF and the EPLF were strengthened considerably by the growing support of their local populations, who were antagonized by the changed behavior of the regime, and by the increased number of disgruntled elements joining their ranks over time. Elites from other ethnic groups that supported and served the revolutionary cause at one time concluded that the lofty ideals of the 1974 mass upheaval had been betrayed. They opted to use the various nationalist movements as a basis for struggle against the emerging despotism.

The people were required to surrender, in a gradual and piecemeal manner, the gains of the early years of the revolution. Participation was replaced by demobilization and depoliticization; local unit elected representatives gave way to handpicked favorites; consultation and consensus-building were supplanted by orders from above. The relative autonomy of all components of civil society was eventually wiped out without a trace. Harbeson sums up the situation that led to the nullification of the expected outcomes of land reform as follows:

The implementation of the land reform has yielded generally extremely modest, discouraging results for reasons attributable to an implementation strategy featuring inadequate farmgate prices, diversion of administrative resources from agricultural to regime maintenance purposes, extreme concentration of scarce public resources on state farms at the expense of a majority of rural producers, inadequate support for agricultural research, energetic but only partially effective efforts to restrict the access of rural producers to private traders, and excessive centralization and bureaucratization of administrative machinery.[23]

The historical prominence of peasant agriculture, which was the most outstanding source of surplus, was pushed to the background, giving way to such ideology-driven projects as state farms and collectivist ventures in the form of Producers' and Service Cooperatives organized under the auspices of Peasant Associations (PAs). The latter also served as administrative machineries appended to the state bureaucracy, particularly after losing their democratic and representative features of the early years. Accordingly, about thirteen million members were organized under 19,500 PAs in thirteen administrative regions by 1984. Five million members among these were reported to have been embraced in 3,651 Service Cooperatives and 1,000 Producers' Cooperatives during the same period.[24]

The neglect of the subsistence farming subsector is illustrated by Cohen, who alleges that only 8 percent of the government budget for agriculture was allocated to peasant farms and less than 20 percent of the agricultural credit was provided to the sub-sector by the Agricultural and the Industrial Development Bank (AIDB) of the Ethiopian government.[25] The number of peasant producers who had access to improved inputs like fertilizers was only 25 percent of the total farming population. On the other hand, state-sponsored projects received preferential treatments, mostly at the expense of household producers. Thus, the peasant subsistence subsector was stymied by the workings of the political economy. The introduction of ill-considered grandiose schemes such as villagization, collectivization, and resettlement were aimed mainly at bolstering the image of the regime by portraying it as an agent of socialist-oriented development.

The intention here is neither to argue in favor of the fragmented holdings characteristic of peasant agriculture nor to rule out the advantages of cooperatives, collective ventures, villagization, and resettlement schemes. While it is possible to endorse the usefulness of such enterprises in principle, what took place in Ethiopia, with regard to the implementation of these schemes and their consequences, cannot be justified. Consultations with and persuasion of the stakeholders about the wisdom of opting for a given course of action was virtually absent, and recourse to coercion in executing plans worked out by party zealots, who cared little about assessing objective conditions, became routine. Structures of command anchored in central planning dogma led to the proliferation of disaffection caused by drastic falls in producer prices and growing planting restrictions. Not surprisingly, these disincentives had a negative impact on peasant initiatives and productivity, and were costly in both financial and human terms.[26] Apart from being required to pay heavy taxes for land use, peasants often were forced to make periodic contributions for the maintenance of local administrative apparatus, support the families of those recruited as members of the militia, meet quota requirements by surrendering a fixed amount of their produce to the agricultural marketing parastatal at drastically reduced prices, and pay fines for their absence from the regular meetings and campaign works.

The dismal performance of the industrial sector prevented it from offsetting strains and setbacks weighing on the economy at large. The industrial base was too small, accounting for only 20 percent of the GDP in 1978 before falling to 17 percent by 1982. At about this time, the state owned 80 percent of the existing industrial enterprises and was involved in 65 percent of the export trade and 77 percent of the import trade.[27] The distribution of goods and services was run mainly by parastatals headed by corrupt and inefficient managers whose major preoccupation was self-enrichment through graft and fraud. Lack of foreign exchange, industrial inputs, spare parts, poor infrastructure, and mismanagement augmented the already precarious situation of all sectors. Exports originating from the agricultural sector, the bastion of surplus despite odds militating against it, were beset by a wide range of problems, which included recurrent drought, backward technology, and government policies relating to prices and marketing.[28] Deprived of ancillary support and optimal conditions facilitating its sustainable development, and rendered fragile by various state exactions and restrictions, peasant production failed to serve as a buffer against mounting food shortages, which led to full-scale famine by 1984–85.

The 1984–85 famine was more devastating and deadly compared to that of 1973–74. According to the Relief and Rehabilitation Commission of the Ethiopian Government, the number of those affected grew from 1.85 million in 1981 to 10 million in 1985, out of which 8 million were reported to be in need of relief aid.[29] This hazard entailed a marked decline in the potential for economic growth and, at the same time, forced society to shoulder added burdens. The intensification of civil war in the traditionally risk-prone areas of the north undoubtedly exacerbated the situation, owing to military actions by the armed protagonists and intensified repression by the state against the civilian population. By outnumbering the rebels and devoting a huge amount of resources to its war efforts, the regime had hoped to emerge victorious quickly. The slogan Everything to the War Front led to the conscription of productive manpower into the army while other assets (material and financial) were commandeered to serve the same destructive ends. Rather than seeking a negotiated political solution to the claims of nationality groups that were calling for self-determination or of opponents who were demanding popular democracy, the regime responded with force and bureaucratic centralism, which further eroded its support and legitimacy.[30]

At the apex of the famine and civil war, the regime inaugurated the so-called Workers' Party, which was deemed useful in the creation of another fallacy: the Peoples' Democratic Republic. But the real aim was to legitimize the perpetuation of the Mengistu clique in power. The high hopes and lofty ideals espoused during the early days of the revolution were thus completely shattered; in fact, the socioeconomic policies and political methods of the Mengistu regime only succeeded in effectively antagonizing each and every religious and national group, peasants and workers, civil servants and factions within the army, the intelligentsia and the business community. By the same token, the regime also failed on the diplomatic and military fronts to match its adversaries, who continued to gain ground, literally. The institutions and structures that Mengistu had developed to control society, and the catchwords and slogans coined to appeal to Ethiopian nationalism failed in the end to prevent the inevitable collapse.

Military setbacks with far-reaching implications for the regime began to be experienced in the late 1980s. The bloody purge of the military top brass following a foiled coup in 1988 rocked the military establishment to its foundation. Low morale, defeatist attitudes, and poor leadership forced the regime's fighting force to crumble in the face of rebel advances, often assisted by the local population in the vicinities of the theaters of military operations. The harrowing accounts relating to the fall of well-fortified garrisons and whole regiments into the hands of the rebels one after the other are indicative of the decadence and stagnation of the presumptuous dictatorship. The first months of 1990 saw dramatic encirclements of cities by rebel armies, whose march to the major towns and the capital was made with relative ease. Mengistu fled the country a few days before the fall of Asmara to the Eritrean Peoples' Liberation Front, which was followed by the victorious entry of the TPLF-led Ethiopian Peoples' Revolutionary Democratic Front (EPRDF) into Addis Ababa on May 27, 1991.

ANOTHER ATTEMPT AT DEMOCRATIC TRANSITION?

After dismantling the political and war machineries of the defunct regime, the incumbent EPRDF formed a transitional government in collusion with other groups, most of which claimed to represent nationality and ethnic groups from different parts of the country. The basis on which the Transitional Government of Ethiopia (TGE) was formed was enshrined in a charter designed to serve as an interim constitution. The charter, composed of five parts and twenty articles, pledged respect for human rights as outlined by the United Nations Declaration of December 1948; freedoms of conscience, expression, and association; the right of nationalities and peoples to self-determination, including secession; the establishment of national, regional, and local councils for the purpose of self-rule; and so on. Whereas the ousting of the dictatorship received overwhelming applause from the population at large—much as happened after the overthrow of Emperor Selassie in 1974—skepticism and anxiety relating to the democratic credentials of the EPRDF were vocally expressed as well. The reason appears to be, among other things, the Marxist orientation espoused by the groups prior to their accession to power. In fact, it was alleged that the radicalism of the victors excelled that of their defeated antagonist. Furthermore, there was widespread belief that the EPRDF had employed considerable heavy-handedness in instilling iron discipline in its ranks, and those who believed this hesitated little in branding it as an organization with considerable potential for unleashing repression. However, the EPRDF more or less abandoned its avowed radicalism by the time it controlled the whole country. Merera attributes this change, at the level of rhetoric at least, to rapidly changing political events on the international scene, which the EPRDF was not prepared for and was incapable to challenge.[31]

Some of the measures and policy directions of the new government also raised the ire of the populace. They included decisions such as the prohibition of some multiethnic political organizations (e.g., MEISON and EPRP) from participating in the new political process, the endorsement of secession, and the wholesale disbanding of the defense and security forces of the fallen regime. The condoning of the dismemberment of Ethiopia by a regime that claimed to have taken power in order to promote the interest of the country raised questions as to whether the TGE had a hidden agenda revolving around the destruction of the entire country. Furthermore, the TGE's acceptance of the Structural Adjustment Program (SAP), whose harsh effects were exhibited in the laying off of thousands of allegedly redundant workers and civil servants, and the withdrawal of government subsidy for basic consumer goods, quickly made the new government unpopular, especially in the urban areas.

Another point of contention was the distribution of power within the new dispensation. The Council of Representatives and the Council of Ministers, two of the bodies in charge of shaping political life in post-Mengistu Ethiopia, were dominated by the EPRDF. For example, the EPRDF appropriated nearly 40 per cent of the seats in the legislature, whose chairman was the EPRDF chief and the head of state. The prime minister was second in command in the EPRDF, and important cabinet portfolios (e.g., defense, foreign affairs, interior and information) went to the EPRDF as well. Most diplomatic posts and key positions in the local councils were likewise distributed, and the new defense forces were exclusively formed from among the ranks of former guerrilla units of the EPRDF. From a legal standpoint, all these steps were undertaken in accord with the provisions of the charter, which was cunningly designed to insure EPRDF hegemony in the new order.

Surprisingly, the first challenges to the charter came from some of its original signatories, like the Oromo Liberation Front (OLF), which in due course withdrew from the coalition on grounds of breach of concord by the major partner, the EPRDF. Thus controlling the reins of power to a considerable degree, the EPRDF-led transitional government set out to effect measures presumed to be instrumental for instituting a "democratically elected" government. A series of national, regional, and local councils were established, in accord with a 1992 proclamation providing for their coming into being. The EPRDF succeeded in controlling the regional and local councils amid wide protests, including by some groups in the ruling coalition. They accused the incumbent of failing to adhere to the standard democratic requirement of free and fair elections. The Constitution Drafting Commission was formed in 1993, and the appointed leadership resorted to coopting members from the ranks of the non-EPRDF groups into joining it. This was viewed as an attempt to lend a semblance of pluralism to the commission's composition and final decisions.

The Constitution Drafting Commission of the TGE carried out its assignment and in 1994 presented a draft constitution for deliberation and adoption by the Council of Representatives. Given the overwhelming presence of the EPRDF in the Council, and given that articles dealing with almost all important issues of national concern were mirror images of the EPRDF's position on those same issues, the draft was adopted with little change. Pursuant to the provision of the Charter, instituting an elected Constituent Assembly vested with the power of ratifying the adopted draft became necessary. A National Election Board (NEB) entrusted with the tasks of organizing elections was set up by the TGE in 1994. The neutrality of the board, however, became suspect because many of its members were appointed by the new government. The board was often accused of being biased in favor of the EPRDF in its handling of affairs that involve the latter as one of the litigants.

Constituent Assembly elections were held in June 1994. Officially, the EPRDF won in 460 (89.3 percent) of the 515 electoral constituencies. The opposition groups, including those that were excluded from the constitution-making process from the very start, largely boycotted the Constituent Assembly elections, despite half-hearted invitations from the transitional government for them to participate. The reasons given for the opposition's behavior vary. They range from a priori conclusions that free and fair elections could not be realized without a truly inclusive transitional government of national reconciliation to pressures of various kinds, including repression perpetrated by the new regime. Nevertheless, given the fact that the EPRDF had cultivated a solid base of support in the regions where it had been mobilizing and organizing during the years of its relentless struggle against the Mengistu regime, it is difficult to fathom that it could have lost the elections even if those groups that boycotted had entered the race. On the other hand, the EPRDF's apparent victory would probably have been less sweeping if the rules governing the elections were free and fair and the opposition had participated.

Convened more or less as scheduled, the EPRDF-dominated Constituent Assembly ratified the new Constitution, which envisaged a Federal Democratic Republic of Ethiopia, the creation of a bicameral parliament (the Council of Peoples' Representatives and the Federal Council), power-sharing between a federal government and its federating units, and so on. The conglomerate was to be constituted on the basis of so-called ethnic federalism, which was presented at the time as a radical democratic solution to the ever present problem of the right of nationalities to self-determination. The approach was also dubbed a breakthrough that could nurture a sense of belonging vital to building a new Ethiopia based on the free will of peoples. Thus ethnicity became the epicenter of political life and nation-building. At the same time, Article 39 of the Constitution categorically pronounces "the right of nations/nationalities and peoples to self-determination including and up to secession." The passing of Article 39 was unparalleled in the history of constitution-making in Ethiopia, which had always regarded the territorial integrity and continuity of the empire state turned People's Democratic Republic as sacrosanct. Elections to the leading bodies of the federal and regional state governments were conducted on May 7, 1995, which the EPRDF handily won. The Federal Democratic Republic of Ethiopia was officially inaugurated in August 1995, with the EPRDF qualifying as the ruling political organization.

Ethnic Federalism: Solution or Time Bomb?

Ethiopia has come full circle: from a strong center which hitherto insisted on annihilating the periphery to a periphery which now has the right to completely detach itself from the center. The right to self-determination, including and up to secession, was elevated to the status of the ultimate password after 1991. The problem is not the recognition of this principle as a democratic ideal. As Bahru cautioned,

To deny the principle of national self-determination is both unprincipled and impolitic. But to elevate that principle—which is only a working principle—to the level of creed and not to relate it to the country's pressing economic needs and the international context in which it finds itself can only bring trouble.[32]

There are, indeed, practical difficulties in crafting an ethnicity-based federated entity in Ethiopia, which far from resolving the problems federation was intended to solve, may worsen them. Ethnicity as a central factor for establishing self-governing regions first took effect in 1992 under Proclamation 7 of the transitional government. National, regional, zonal, and district-level units of government were instituted with little regard for socioeconomic and political conditions. The sin of overlooking these factors, however, began to militate against the efforts to implement the project as envisaged, because it was impractical to create a corresponding number of local units in a country that had eighty ethnic groups. To overcome this problem, Ethiopia was divided into fourteen national-regional state governments, which were later reduced to nine when five of them (Regions 7, 8, 9, 10, and 11) decided to regroup under one broad framework, namely, the Southern Ethiopian Peoples' National-Regional Administration.

The criteria relating to language and ethnicity as the exclusive cornerstones of the new structure of self-government were equally problematic. There is hardly a region in Ethiopia that is ethnically pure. Regardless of the rhetoric of irredentist elites, there has been a good deal of mutation and social intermingling among Ethiopia's so-called nations. Population pressure, civil wars, famines, and the migratory life style of some livestock-raising groups have been responsible for this. As a result, it is extremely difficult to draw a clear line in the proverbial sand, based on ethnic-linguistic homogeneity. The other problem encountered in the process of implementing the ethnic federalism plan was not merely confined to the absence of regions with ethnically pure and homogenous territories. Territorial contiguity also endangered the project. More specifically, pockets of the larger ethnic groups can be found in more than one area; which one of these, therefore, represents the natural domain of those groups? The history of settlements and demographic movements of peoples in the various localities within the polity, which did not anticipate their possible displacement at a certain point in time, also came to threaten the new course of action. Even today, claims and counter-claims to a given territory, or enclaves thereof, are on the rise. The following examples are illuminating:

1. Setit Humera and Wolqait, formerly under the Amhara Region of Gonder, are put under the Tigray Region. The people inhabiting these areas being both Amharas and Tigrayans, there appears to be controversies as to where they really belong, as far as administrative jurisdiction is concerned.
2. Metema has a considerable Amhara population and is placed under the Benishangul Region. This, reportedly, has created resentments by the majority of the inhabitants.
3. Territories claimed by the Maji and Bench ethnic groups are incorporated into the Oromiya Region. This has provoked controversy between all claimants.
4. The Yem and the Oromo ethnic groups, led by their respective political organizations, are at loggerheads on the issue of the town Sokoru being placed under the jurisdiction of the Oromiya national-regional state.
5. Oromos and Somalis are quarreling over territories along the Harar-Jijiga road.

6. Urban enclaves, such as Addis Ababa, Harar, Dire Dawa, Jimma, Nazareth, and Shashemene that have more or less evenly distributed multiethnic populations have become bones of contention between ethnic organizations.

Thus, the ethnic federalism formula has tended to exacerbate the so-called national question by pitting people against people.[33]

Another problem that can be expected to arise in the future is rooted in the uneven resource endowments of regions. Some regions enjoy advantages in terms of size and quality of land, minerals, and skilled manpower. Given the fact that internal sovereignty to run one's own affairs and have command over one's own resources is the order of the day, at least de jure, the taking effect of such a policy could amount to condemning disadvantaged regions to a state of perpetual stagnation. This is likely to occur despite expectations that such mishaps will be offset by subsidy and support from other sources. Regional imbalance is bound to lead to fierce competition for resources, which in the past has often been one of the prime factors causing conflicts. There are already signs of discontent among some organized groups, whose members feel that they might be better off if they disengaged from a federal partnership in which the have-nots are suspected of benefiting at their expense. A perverse sense of centrifugalism resulting from what might be called the politics of greed could disturb the foundations upon which the new status quo is expected to be anchored.

Finally, it is important to note that federalism was chosen in post-1991 Ethiopia on the assumption that it qualifies as a concrete expression of democratic governance. This is not necessarily true. Whereas a given form of government, such as federalism, may be adopted by some states, equating it with democracy is erroneous. If this had been the case, federal Nigeria would have qualified as more democratic than unitary Britain! The example points to the banal and simplistic foundation of the equation. Forms and structures do not beget substance. Even if one is inclined to accept the desirability of federalism in Ethiopia, why need it be ethnic? Why not simply federalism, based on more conventional considerations such as territories or regions? Furthermore, the notion that democracy is capable of solving problems of all kinds, at all places and times is of questionable validity. As Haynes argues, "The establishment of democracy is by no means a panacea for all socio-economic ills."[34] There have been ample instances—not the least of which is neighboring Somalia—where disintegration and chaos were harvested following attempts to ostensibly rid the world of tyrants and make it safe for democracy.

CONCLUSION

Although much has changed in Ethiopia since 1991, the country's march toward democracy deserves close scrutiny. A balance sheet of the accomplishments and failures of the EPRDF-led government presents a mixed picture. The civil war has been ended, though at the cost of forfeiting Eritrea. Press censorship has been lifted and a host of private media (exclusively the print media, mostly in tabloid form) have flourished, despite intensified assaults against them by a hypersensitive government. The movement of goods and services and people, both within the country and abroad, is taking place with fewer restrictions than before. Official statistics depict encouraging signs of economic recovery. In 1992–93, the level of both imports and exports grew as compared to the preceding year, and an economic growth rate of 7.6 percent in real terms was experienced. Sectoral growth rate for agriculture, industry, distribution and services was registered as 5, 12, 8.9, and 9.3 percent respectively.[35]

However, the harsh effects of the economic reform program, which has made the recovery possible in part, are forcing many citizens to undergo a trying process, often with dire consequences for their livelihood and entailing significant social costs (e.g., urban prostitution, juvenile delinquency, and crime). Bilateral and multilateral aid and economic cooperation have also intensified, allegedly due to liberal economic reforms, pluralist politics, and improvement in respect for human rights. Western governments and donors, in fact, have been overenthusiastic in their dealings with the new regime, and at times have gone to great lengths to unconditionally condone its actions under the pretext that it is laying the basis for democracy. This has often been done by way of comparing incomparables: the new government and the heinous Mengistu dictatorship.

In foreign relations, aspects of both change and continuity are being witnessed. Cordial and amicable relations with Kenya and Djibouti are maintained while Sudan has been marked as an enemy and a pariah that the region has to bear. Ironically, Sudan had been placed in the same position by the military regime for hosting and assisting the present incumbents. The old friendship between the present rulers of Ethiopia and Sudan was officially suspended when the Karthoum regime was accused of orchestrating terrorism that targeted the Egyptian leader while he was visiting Ethiopia in May of 1995. There are speculations that the Ethiopian government took the issue further than was necessary because it wanted to find a pretext to come to the aid of its Eritrean comrades, who had come under pressure from Sudan prior to the terrorist incident. The bellicose stance of the Ethiopian leadership has been attributed to opportunism also. By appearing tough on Karthoum, Ethiopia may have wanted to court the favors of the West—the United States in particular—which has labeled Sudan a terrorist state.

Perhaps the most ominous threat to the establishment of democratic governance in Ethiopia is the attitude of the EPRD-led government vis-à-vis the opposition and other nonconformists. In its craving for monopolizing power, the government does not seem to be positively disposed toward national reconciliation.[36] Numerous leaders and members of opposition groups are held in detention, often without being charged. There are detainees who are held contrary to court rulings ordering their release. Despite the apparent multiethnic composition of those who wield legislative, executive, and judicial powers, most probably belong to satellite organizations associated with the EPRDF in one way or other. In sum, what began as a pluralist affair with an attractive democratic semblance, much like the 1974 revolution and the early years of Selassie, may be in the process of being transformed into the consolidation of one-party hegemony and perhaps even one-man rule. Lessons from past experiences caution that reneging on pledges and abusing popular trust with impunity are disastrous for peace, stability, and state-building in Ethiopia.

NOTES

1. Thomas Kuhlman, *Asylum or Aid? The Economic Integration of Ethiopian Refugees in the Sudan* (Leiden, Netherlands: African Studies Center, 1994).

2. Tadesse Tamrat, *Church and State In Ethiopia: 1270–1527* (Oxford, UK: Oxford University Press, 1972). See also B. Thomson, *Ethiopia: The Country That Cut Off Its Head* (London,UK: Robson Books, 1975).

3. John Markakis, *Ethiopia: Anatomy of Traditional Polity* (Oxford, UK and Addis Ababa, Ethiopia: Oxford University Press, 1974).

4. Edward, Ullendorf, *The Ethiopians: An Introduction to Country and People* (Oxford, UK: Oxford University Press, 1973).

5. John Markakis, *National and Class Conflict in the Horn of Africa* (Cambridge, UK: Cambridge University Press, 1987).

6. Mark Bulcha, *Flight and Integration: Causes of Mass Exodus From Ethiopia and Problems of Integration in the Sudan* (Uppsala, Sweden: Scandinavian Institute of African Studies, 1988).

7. John Markakis, "Ethnic Conflict and the State in the Horn of Africa," in K. Fuki and J. Markakis, eds., *Ethnicity and Conflict in the Horn of Africa* (London: James Currey, 1994).

8. Addis Hiwot, "Ethiopia: From Autocracy to Revolution," *Review of African Political Economy* 1 (1975).

9. Teshale Tibebu, *The Making of Modern Ethiopia* (Lawrenceville, NJ: Red Sea Press, 1995).

10. John Harbeson, *The Ethiopian Transformation: The Quest for the Post Imperial State* (Boulder, CO and London, UK: Westview Press, 1988).

11. Donald Levine, *Wax and Gold: Tradition and Innovation in Ethiopian Culture* (Chicago, IL and London, UK: University of Chicago Press, 1965).

12. Donald Donham, ed., *The Southern Marches of Imperial Ethiopia: Essays in History and Social Anthropology* (Cambridge, UK: Cambridge University Press, 1986).

13. Bonnie Holcomb and Sisai Ibssa, *The Invention of Ethiopia: The Making of a Dependent Colonial State in North-East Africa* (Trenton, NJ: Red Sea Press, 1990).

14. Fentahun Tiruneh, *The Ethiopian Students: The Struggle to Articulate the Ethiopian Revolution* (Chicago, IL: Nyala Type, 1990).

15. Randi Balsvic, *Haile Selassie's Students: The Intellectual and Social Background to Revolution, 1952–1977* (East Lansing, MI: Michigan State University, African Studies Center, 1985). See also Kiflu Tadesse, *The Generation* (Silver Spring, MD: Independent Publishers, 1993).

16. Edward Keller, *Revolutionary Ethiopia: From Empire to People's Republic* (Bloomington and Indianapolis, IN: Indiana University Press, 1988).

17. Harold Marcus, *A History of Ethiopia* (Berkeley, CA and London, UK:University of California Press, 1994).

18. Robert Hess, *Ethiopia: The Modernization of Autocracy* (Ithaca, NY and London, UK: Cornell University Press, 1970).

19. Harbeson, op. cit., p. 17.

20. Keller, op. cit., p. 193.

21. Gebru Tareke, *Ethiopia: Power and Protest: Peasant Revolts in the Twentieth Century* (Cambridge, UK: Cambridge University Press, 1991).

22. Marcus, op. cit., p. 201.

23. Harbeson, op. cit., p. 223.

24. Tegegne Teka, "Cooperatives and National Development: The Ethiopian Experience," in *IDR Working Paper No. 18* (Addis Ababa, Ethiopia: Institute of Development Research, 1984).

25. James Cohen, "Agrarian Reform in Ethiopia: The Situation on the Eve of the Revolution's Tenth Anniversary," in *Development Discussion Paper No. 164* (Cambridge, MA: Harvard Institute for International Development, 1984).

26. Edward Keller, "Drought, War and the Politics of Famine in Ethiopia and Eritrea," *Journal of Modern African Studies* 30, no. 4 (1992).

27. Ibid., pp. 247–248.

28. Eshetu Chole, "Ethiopia's Balance of Payments: 1975–1985," *Journal of Ethiopian Studies* 22 (November 1989).

29. Relief & Rehabilitation Commission, PMAC, "Regional Vulnerability Profile," *Report to Donors' Meeting*, Addis Ababa, Ethiopia, 1985.

30. Keller, op. cit., p. 267.

31. Merera, Gudina, "The Ethiopian Transition From Military Autocracy to Popular Democracy: Some Major Issues for Consideration in Crossing the Crossroads," *UFAHAMU* 22, nos. 1 and 2 (1994).

32. Bahru Zewde, "Haile Selassie: From Progressive to Reactionary," paper presented at the Sixth Michigan State University Conference on North-East Africa, East Lansing, MI, April 1992.

33. Research and Action Group for Peace in Ethiopia and the Horn of Africa (RAGPEHA), *ADDIS DIGEST,* nos. 6–7 (September–October 1995).

34. Jeff Haynes, "The State, Governance and Democracy in Sub-Saharan Africa," *Journal of Modern African Studies* 31, no. 3 (1993).

35. *Ethiopian Herald*, 20 May 1995.

36. Kassahun Berhanu, "Ethiopia Elects a Constituent Assembly," *Review of African Political Economy* 22, no. 63 (1995).

6
Leadership and Democratization: The Case of Tanzania

Jean-Germain Gros

INTRODUCTION

This chapter links democratization in Tanzania to the country's founding father and spiritual leader Julius Nyerere. It should not be construed as a wholesale endorsement of the so-called Great Man theory of history, but rather as an acknowledgment that political change is shaped by a variety of factors, one of which is individual leadership. Indeed, during the transition it matters a great deal whether a country is led by a Julius Nyerere or a Nelson Mandela, as opposed to a Mobutu Sese Seko or his ilk. This is because a leader who takes democracy seriously in principle is also more likely to practice it than one who does not. What leaders think, their cognitive ability to interpret the world and the events around them, is always crucial to what they do. In the case of Tanzania, the ideas of Julius Nyerere have often, but not always, become public policies. In particular, democracy has been at the heart of Nyerere's political philosophy, even though his notion of the concept has not always matched the Western (bourgeois) model. Nyerere's concern about democracy has had a major influence in tempering the worse effects of the Tanzanian one-party state, and in launching the country on the path of political reform. By focusing on Nyerere's role, this chapter highlights the promises and pitfalls of one-man-led democratization. Nyerere the philosopher and *mwalimu* (teacher) is mixed with Nyerere "the king" in a methodology that straddles political theory, biography, and policy analysis.

DEMOCRACY ACCORDING TO NYERERE

As his writings and speeches demonstrate, Julius Nyerere has had a deep interest in democracy. As a statesman, he was keen to seeing his vision of democracy implemented in Tanzania in tandem with his vision of socialism. In fact, for Nyerere the two were inseparable. This is evident in the following comment: "True socialism cannot exist without democracy also existing in the society."[1] Nyerere's understanding of democracy was probably informed by his knowledge of Western political theory (from his days at Edinburgh) and his Christian faith. His rejection of it in the African context probably had to do with his perception (some might say glorification) of traditional African society, and the shortcomings of bourgeois democracy in the West.[2] Nyerere articulated his views on democracy most succinctly in January of 1963 at the Annual Conference of the Tanganyika African National Union (TANU).

Democracy, in Africa or anywhere else, is Government by the People. Ideally, it is a form of government whereby the people, all the people, settle their affairs through free discussions. The appropriate setting for this basic, or pure, democracy is a small community. . . . After pure democracy, the next best thing is Government by the People's Representatives. . . . So free elections are the essential instruments of Representative Democracy.[3]

The problem for Nyerere lay in the implementation of democracy in Tanzania and, by extension, sub-Saharan Africa. Nyerere was deeply suspicious of political parties and spoke of them thus:

Now my argument is that a two-party system can be justified only when the parties are divided over some fundamental issue; otherwise it merely encourages the growth of factionalism. If, on the other hand, you have a two-party system where the differences between the parties are not fundamental, then you immediately reduce politics to the level of a football match.[4]

Using the football analogy, Nyerere further asserted with great insight and prescience into contemporary Western, especially U.S., politics that

a football match may, of course, attract some very able players; it may also be entertaining; but it is still only a game, and only the most ardent fans (who are not usually the most intelligent) take the game very seriously. This, in fact, is not unlike what has happened in many of the so-called democratic countries today, where some of the most intelligent members of society have become disgusted with the hypocrisy of the party games called politics, and take no interest in them.[5]

To Nyerere, the only time the multiparty system is justified is when parties reflect fundamental social cleavages, which, by definition, cannot go on for long, lest society runs the risk of tearing itself apart through civil war and revolution. In his words, "where there is no difference over policy (and I repeat that a difference over policy is a difference over fundamentals), the only choice which make sense must be choice between individuals. That is, the choice of the best individual for the job." Nyerere drew no distinction between policy differences and fundamental differences; the two were one and the same and of a temporary nature. In cases where parties fundamentally agree, Nyerere asked, "Is it not absurd, then, that every few years the country should be asked to choose which of the 'opposing' parties should do the job which both agree should be done?"[6]

Where Tanzania was concerned, Nyerere felt that there was little justification for opposition parties since TANU already represented the interests and aspirations of the masses and was trying to fulfill those aspirations. The evidence that Nyerere used to bolster this claim was the 1960 multiparty election held just before independence, when TANU captured 100 percent of the contested seats in the legislature. As long as the party was striving toward an egalitarian, that is, classless, society, there was no need for opposition parties, which tend to reflect class cleavages. Nyerere only envisaged multipartyism under extraordinary circumstances.[7] He even suggested that a democratic one-party state was superior to a democratic multiparty one.[8]

Thus in the 1960s Nyerere did not see any contradiction between democracy and the one-party state, which was orchestrated by him de jure in 1965, although de facto it existed at independence. Following his resignation as prime minister in January of 1962, Nyerere returned to power as president in December of the same year along with some key allies who were also elected to the National Executive Committee (NEC) of TANU, the policy-making arm of the party. The first resolution calling for the one-party state was submitted by Nyerere to the NEC and was then officially endorsed at TANU's annual conference in January 1963. Thereafter, the NEC "authorized" Nyerere to set up a commission to study, not the feasibility of a one-party system in Tanzania, but its modalities. The commission submitted its favorable report to the NEC in 1965, and the NEC approved the recommendations at its annual conference held the same year. Thus, the formation of the Tanzanian one-party state can be traced directly to the ideas and actions of Nyerere; not only was the NEC packed with Nyerere's allies, but members of the "investigating" commission were appointed by him.

What was unique about Tanzania was the extent to which its leaders sought to give TANU preeminence over all other institutions while subjecting it to a significant dose of internal competition. Credit, to the extent that any is due, must go to Nyerere, who really felt that internal, or intraparty, democracy was more important than interparty democracy. TANU did become the most important institution in Tanzania, supplanting Parliament and even the armed forces (more on that later). Nyerere's view of the role of the party was made clear on June 7, 1968. Speaking at the Uganda People's Congress Conference, he affirmed:

For the truth is that it is not the Party which is the instrument of the Government. It is the Government which is the instrument through which the Party tries to implement the wishes of the people and serve their interests. And the Party has therefore to determine the basic principles on which Government should act; it has to determine the policies its government will follow.[9]

TANU was not merely a subterfuge for one-man rule, although within it Nyerere clearly wielded considerable influence. TANU was truly a national institution that had to be reckoned with: cells, complete with gender and age-based wings, were established throughout the country; songs, plays, and poems praising TANU were written; school children were taught the party's virtues; political commissars were posted inside barracks to watch over military men (which created resentment within the ranks);[10] and TANU membership was compulsory for the personal advancement of ambitious Tanzanians. In Nyerere's vision, TANU was to be a policy-making body while the government was to be the implementer.[11] TANU's near supremacy having been noted, Tanzania's socialist one-party state was far from totalitarian, as one recent revisionist work has suggested.[12] TANU-led socialism was definitely more Fabian than Marxist-Leninist, thanks in large part to the political philosophy of Julius Nyerere. Evidence in support of this contention can readily be found in Nyerere's speeches as well as in practice.

In building Tanzanian socialism Nyerere argued against the creation of a vanguard party with restricted membership.[13] Unlike the Eastern European countries and the former Soviet Union, with which Tanzania admittedly had close ties, there was no attempt to substitute TANU for organized religion; in fact, Nyerere remained a devout Christian. Furthermore, he explicitly forbade the use of force in moving farmers from scattered homesteads to *ujamaa* (familyhood) villages, which is not to say that force or other forms of coercion were never used. Force did, in fact, become the preferred operational method during the forced villagization period that followed voluntary *ujamaa*, but there is no question that it was not used on a scale as massive as, say, in Russia during the period of Stalinist collectivization, and, closer to Africa, in Ethiopia during Mengistu's own effort at collectivization in the 1980s. Nyerere always felt that rural socialism in Tanzania had to be built gradually and voluntarily by peasant farmers, with TANU cadres leading by example and exhortation.

Perhaps more important for this chapter, within TANU there was a modicum of competition as measured by the fact that TANU candidates were able to compete, at times fiercely, for the national legislature and local offices. National parliamentary elections often resulted in the defeat of a rather high percentage of incumbents, dating back to 1965 when only twenty-one members of parliament up for reelection were returned to their posts out of a total of fifty.[14] By 1985, more than half of the incumbents who ran for reelection lost their seats.[15] High turnover rates among Tanzanian national legislators may have been linked to their dual status and responsibilities, as they were expected to represent both local and national interests. Thus, one way of measuring the substance of intraparty democracy under the Tanzania one-party state is to ask whether politicians had real constituencies and whether their survival depended on their perceived effectiveness at serving those who elected them to office. In other words, was there accountability in Tanzania's one-party system? At least one early study showed that the ability of members of Parliament to deliver to their constituencies was the determining factor in their success (or failure) to renew their mandate.[16] The one-party elections arrangement may well have laid the foundation for the multiparty elections of the 1990s.

However, Nyerere's vision of a democratic, one-party, socialist state was profoundly flawed. By denying a role to those who had a different view of what policy choices should be made, Nyerere's approach violated a fundamental tenet of democratic governance. Interparty competition, to the extent that it allows for the formulation of alternative public policies, is even more important to the health of a democracy than intraparty contests, which have to do with the rather limited realm of personnel circulation. Political monopoly by the Tanganyka African National Union (TANU) and its successor, *Chama Cha Mapinduzi* (CCM or Revolutionary Party), also led to the elimination of the kinds of automatic safeguards that make ruling parties in multiparty systems vigilant. Even under Nyerere the ruling party was not exactly the bastion of egalitarian democracy that he had envisaged; within CCM there were militants and there were militants. Those who had Nyerere's ears were in a more enviable position than those who had not.

Worse, the party's dominant role in every facet of public life led to the virtual breakdown of its internal span of control. In the countryside, local party bosses and government bureaucrats created their own fiefdoms and ruled as petty tyrants, utterly oblivious to party dictates and the teachings of Nyerere. A healthy multiparty system might have helped to create more accountable governance, but alas it was not allowed until 1994. What explains the relative tardiness of democratization in Tanzania; why was democratization triggered not by violent protests from below, but by pressure from above, especially from Julius Nyerere? The roots of the answers to both of these questions can be found in Tanzania's most famous social experiment, that is, *ujamaa vijijini* of which Nyerere was the ideological architect.

REVISITING *UJAMAA VIJIJINI*

No other policy decision made in postcolonial Tanzania has been studied as extensively as *ujamaa vijijini* or familyhood. It is unlikely that the policy edict that officially embarked Tanzania on the path of rural socialism, the Arusha Declaration of 1967, would have been possible without Nyerere. Over the years *ujamaa* has had its apologists as well as its distracters. In the latter category, some, like the Tanzanian scholar Issa Shivji, have argued that *ujamaa* was not designed to bring about rural socialism at all, but was rather an attempt by the Tanzanian state, as the local arm of international capital, to integrate subsistence agriculture into the cash economy and appropriate the surpluses of the Tanzanian peasantry more effectively. If this line of argument is taken to its logical conclusion, *ujamaa* was basically the benign expression of a sinister conspiracy between Tanzanian state leaders and external imperialist forces.[17] Others, like Goran Hyden, are more sanguine in their analysis of the motive behind *ujamaa*, but leave no doubt about their assessment of its outcome. Hyden asserts that rural socialism was doomed because historical stages cannot in effect be skipped.[18] The "economy of affection" and the absence of a truly rural capitalist class in Tanzania, according to Hyden, made *ujamaa* a utopia which the country could ill afford.

Anyone analyzing the economic results of *ujamaa* would be tempted to concur that it was indeed a failure. By the late 1970s Tanzania was a net importer of food; if one compares the influx of foreign aid before the policy (before the 1967 Arusha Declaration) and after, it is also clear that Nyerere's stated goal of self-reliance (*kujitegemea*) was not met. Tanzania became more dependent on foreign aid, especially from the Scandinavian countries, to balance its budgets. Nevertheless, some progress was made in the social sphere. Life expectancy was increased in Tanzania from thirty-five years at independence to fifty-five by the early 1980s; over the same period, literacy grew from 30 percent to 69 percent, making Tanzania a highly literate society by African standards.[19] Income inequality between the elite and the masses was not as pronounced in Tanzania as it was in other African countries, although this may have had more to do with the fact that the state had succeeded in making everyone poor. In sum, the one-party state was not as illegitimate in Tanzania as it was elsewhere in Africa, which explains why it did not come under much political strain, at least on the mainland, in the early 1990s.

Professor Baregu's claim that the Tanzanian state suffered from a legitimacy crisis is somewhat exaggerated, if legitimacy is measured in terms of popular support.[20] On the eve of the government's decision to liberalize the political system, a strong majority of Tanzanians (77 percent) professed support for the one-party state.[21] Tanzanians did not take to the streets—as Kenyans, Zambians, and other Africans did—because the one-party system, in spite of rising corruption, had a modicum of legitimacy, thanks to its past successes in the social sphere dating back to the Arusha Declaration. More importantly, Nyerere's continued association with the *Chama Cha Mapinduzi* (he remained party chairman seven years after leaving office) probably helped to sanitize the party's image. Finally, the corporatist authoritarian structures erected by Nyerere, specifically, the participation of the military in governing and the emasculation of labor unions, made for a remarkably united ruling elite, especially where political reform was concerned.[22]

Thus, the transition to multiparty democracy in Tanzania has had a peculiar character: it was not initiated because of mass pressure but in the near absence of it. Furthermore, it was not led by a civil society-based counter-elite, à la Zambia and Malawi, but by an influential member within the ruling elite who was not even officially in power. This development is all the more intriguing, since Nyerere, as shown earlier, had been one of the most eloquent African ideologues of the "democratic" one-party state. In essence, he helped to dismantle the political edifice he had spent a lifetime building and defending. Why the *volte-face*? It is, of course, always risky to gauge the motives of political actors; fortunately, in the case of the loquacious Nyerere, recent statements allow for reasonable conjectures.

NYERERE: FROM ONE-PARTY IDEOLOGUE TO MULTIPARTY PREACHER

Great statesmen, especially in the twilight of their existence, often become concerned about how they are likely to be remembered; they are also generally very sensitive to the possibility that their lifelong vision and efforts might be ended by their successors. The moral dimension of Nyerere's leadership helps to explain his turnabout. Even though CCM still had wide popular support in the early 1990s, this may not have been good enough for Nyerere. Nyerere always expected the party to be above reproach. In fact, its justification for monopolizing power rested, as stated earlier, on its commitment to equality through socialism. Tanzania had clearly opted for capitalism in 1986 when it signed a structural adjustment agreement with the World Bank, which, although it improved the country's macroeconomic situation, probably accentuated inequality. Part of the pact required the Mwinyi government to introduce a number of unpopular measures, including user fees to cover the cost of services hitherto provided by the state for "free."

In addition, with the relaxation of the Leadership Code of the Arusha Declaration (repealed formally in 1991 by the Zanzibar Declaration), which explicitly forbade public servants from having second incomes, party and government officials no longer felt compelled to maintain a façade of probity. In any event, the sudden appearance on the streets, shores, and shops of Dar es Salaam of Mercedes Benz vehicles, seaside villas, and other manifestations of ostentatious consumption would only have made any claim by party members of their commitment to equality a cruel joke. The ruling party had become too corrupt for Nyerere to morally justify its monopoly. Nyerere admitted as much when he remarked in February of 1995 that "Tanzania stinks with corruption."[23]

Much as the Arusha Declaration of 1967 was meant to reenergize TANU by committing it to rural socialism, Nyerere's conversion may have been propelled by the desire to rid CCM of corruption and the arrogance of constitutionally protected one-party incumbency.[24] As long as the party was not subject to competition, acts of corruption could be expected to occur and go unpunished. What motivation did CCM officials have to clean up their acts if they did not have to worry about losing power? For Nyerere, multipartyism became the disinfecting solution which would permit CCM to reconnect with the people. The party could no longer rely on institutional memory—it had abandoned its socialist principles—to justify its hold on power; it had to earn it at the ballot box. Nyerere certainly did not want CCM to lose power as a result of democratization; he "only" wanted it to change its ways, to become closer to his vision. Nyerere did not hide his partisanship when he declared: "I don't propagate long live one-party system, but I do propagate long live CCM. I want it to live forever and crush all opposition parties that may crop up in the future."[25]

Nyerere's conversion also was probably due to the increasing vocality of centrifugal forces on Zanzibar and, to a lesser extent, the mainland. Nyerere has always considered the federation with Zanzibar one of the high points of his tenure, a kind of pan-Africanism in miniature. Since globalization and dependence had forced Tanzania to give up rural socialism, there was one remaining concrete evidence of Nyerere's legacy: the union. He was probably loath to see this achievement unraveled on account of the rigidity of the one-party state. Managed democratization may have been part of a deliberate strategy to satisfy those who wanted a greater voice in running the country without, so to speak, giving away the store. Nyerere probably felt that if the ruling party waited to be pushed to embrace change, it might lose control of the process, whereupon anything could happen. Having witnessed the ignominy with which other African founding fathers had had to exit the political scene, Nyerere did not want to be remembered as the one who stood against democratization in Tanzania. At the same time, he did not want to see the experience of the former Soviet Union repeated in "his" union. He appears to provide some support for this conjecture when he stated with characteristic bluntness: "We cannot remain an island. We must manage our own change— don't wait to be pushed."[26]

Nyerere's subsequent role throughout 1995 in maintaining continuous dialogues with island opposition parties such as the Civic United Front (CUF) to insure that they supported the continuation of the union and his castigation of antiunion mainland politicians, underscore the importance of the issue to him. Of course, the fact that multipartyism could be seen by Nyerere as an instrument of, and not a threat to, political stability represents a complete reversal of earlier positions. The one-party state, it will be recalled, was adopted in Tanzania, as in the rest of Africa, ostensibly to do away with regional, religious, and ethnic cleavages; by 1990, Nyerere came to understand that multiparty democracy, properly managed, far from contributing to the implosion of those cleavages, could help mitigate their worse effects.

The wind-from-the-East argument is not being rejected in its entirety, for Nyerere's change of heart was clearly influenced by external factors as well. This is evident in what is perhaps one of his most humorous yet penetrating comments: "When you see your neighbor getting a shave, you had better wet your hair to avoid a dry shave."[27] By themselves, however, external events do not determine what happens in individual countries; it is how political leaders respond to those events that is of consequence. The late Mobutu Sese Seko, thanks to his many secret service agents and international contacts, was probably as aware as anyone of the crumbling of Leninist regimes in Eastern Europe, yet this knowledge apparently was insufficient to compel him to get on with democratization. Nyerere's response to the same international events was quite different (although it must be acknowledged that by that time he also was safely out of office).

Leaders do matter; how they receive, process, and respond to outside pressure can make a difference in both the pace and outcome of democratization. Part of Nyerere's immense talent is that he anticipates events and seeks to stay one step ahead of them, even if that puts him at odds with members of his own party. This does not make Nyerere a master opportunist in the mold of Omar Bongo of Gabon; instead, Nyerere is someone who seems to hold very strong beliefs, but he is not incapable of admitting failure and changing course even if this means going against his party. The essence of leadership is in fact the ability of the leader to see what followers cannot yet see and the willingness to take them where they do not yet want to go. The argument bears repeating: perspicacity and the ability to persuade are crucial elements of leadership. Some CCM officials, including former president Ali Hassan Mwinyi, were initially reluctant to follow Nyerere's lead (as were apparently most Tanzanians), but he convinced them. Scholars have paid relatively little attention to the role that individual leaders play in the ongoing democratic transition in Africa. Yet in societies that generally pay attention to their elders, especially untainted ones, as well as in those where the institutionalization of politics is just getting started, this dimension can only be ignored at one's peril.[28] The Tanzania case also reveals that individuals do not necessarily have to be formally in power to be influential. Indeed, Nyerere's position as a so-called outsider, as someone who was perceived (wrongly) to be above partisan politics, may have made him more, not less, consequential to Tanzania's democratization.

NYERERE AND ELECTORAL MULTIPARTY POLITICS

The most vivid evidence of political change in Tanzania were the 1995 presidential and legislative multiparty elections and Nyerere's paramount role therein from start to finish. Nyerere played a key role in the selection of the final CCM candidate, who was to become the third president of Tanzania. The selection process had the aura of both competitive and Byzantine politics. Historically in Tanzania the NEC of the ruling party was the highest governing body of the party, although nominally the National Conference, which met only twice a year, was the supreme organ. In national elections the NEC chose whom to nominate as the party's final candidates, with input from regional and district-level party secretaries. Until Nyerere resigned in 1983, he was president of Tanzania and president of TANU-CCM; thereafter, he remained chairman of the party until 1990.

The party's chairmanship was reunited with the post of head of state in 1990 when Mwinyi was given both portfolios. Accordingly, more than anyone in Tanzania, Mwinyi was superbly suited to use his position as party chairman and head of state to push for the nomination of any candidate he preferred (with due allowance for regional protocol), much as Nyerere had done before him. Yet, once again, it was Nyerere who prevailed. His protégé, former education minister (and current president), Benjamin Mkapa, in the end got the nod, in spite of the fact that Mkapa was relatively unknown among ordinary Tanzanians and was seen as a party lightweight.[29] Mwinyi's failure to get CCM to choose his preferred candidate—Cleopa Msuya, his prime minister and first vice-president—demonstrated his lower standing inside the party, compared to Nyerere's, as well as the latter's greater political skills.[30]

Tanzania's first transition election took place on October 21, 1995, in Zanzibar. At stake were fifty seats in the newly created Zanzibari legislature and the Zanzibari presidency. Voter participation was extremely high, with 95 percent of the islands' 348,934 registered voters apparently turning out to vote. According to official results, the opposition party Civic United Front (CUF) got twenty-four and CCM twenty-six of the fifty seats in Parliament, giving the latter a slim parliamentary majority. However, virtually all of the seats won by the two parties were won almost exclusively on their home turf. CUF had a clean sweep on Pemba island, winning all twenty-one seats; CCM swept Unguja, except in the Stone Town part of Zanzibar, winning twenty-six of the twenty-nine contested seats. The presidential race also was officially very close. CCM incumbent Salmin Amour was declared the winner with 50.2 percent of the votes while Hamad got 49.8 percent.

The election results were not free of controversy. Although voting was apparently peaceful, the process of vote counting, according to foreign election observers, was less than transparent. First, there was a ninety-six-hour delay in the counting of the votes, which led the CUF to believe that enough time had lapsed for votes to be padded and doctored. In a bizarre development, the CCM initially called for the votes to be annulled, but, after the final results were announced, CCM officials, not surprisingly, accepted the verdict. Did the initial call for cancellation reflect CCM's fear that it could lose in a free and fair election and, if so, what, if anything, was done during the vote-counting process to insure that this would not happen? Was the apparent delay due, as the electoral commission director, Mr. Abou Talib, put it, to heavy rain and late voting, or was the extra time needed to falsify the ballots? The CUF also charged that ballot papers were late to arrive in voting districts in which it had strong support, and this caused people not to vote at all. If true, the delay may have had a significant impact on the outcome, since only 1,500 votes separated Mr. Armour from the CUF candidate.

Elections on the mainland took place on October 29, 1995. At stake were 232 seats for the new federal Parliament and the presidency. Serious irregularities were reported by foreign and domestic election observers.[31] Accusations of vote rigging by the ruling party were especially loud in Dar es Salaam where the voting process broke down almost completely. This prompted the NEC to annul the Dar es Salaam results and reschedule elections there for November 19. Meanwhile, the opposition called on the Supreme Court to annul the entire exercise, create a government of national unity, and reschedule elections in six months. Their request denied, the presidential aspirants of the opposition then decided to boycott the Dar es Salaam rerun, although it was less united on whether to continue fielding candidates for Parliament. Perhaps because of confusion and fatigue, fewer Dar es Salaam voters went to the polls on November 19 (voter turnout was less than 20 percent of eligible voters) than they did on the October 29. In the end, CCM obtained a commanding share of the seats in the new Parliament, officially winning 180 of the 232 contested slots; CUF got 24 seats; and NCCR won, somewhat surprisingly, only 12 seats. In the presidential election, the CCM candidate, Mr. Benjamin Mkapa, won.

Table 6.1 shows the CCM candidate (and current president) winning against the nearest challenger by a margin greater than two to one (62.8 percent for Mkapa versus 27.8 percent for Mrema). This is in stark contrast to neighboring Kenya, where Moi was barely able to gain a plurality in the 1992 presidential election. The overwhelming victory for Mkapa also suggests that a more unified opposition would not have changed the outcome. The ruling party, CCM, had such an overwhelming advantage in public resources (more on that later) that a pooling of private resources by the opposition in support of one candidate probably would not have allowed the opposition to make a significant dent in the asymmetry between the ruling party and its challengers.

If one assumes that Tanzania's first post-one-party election was essentially a contest between the ruling CCM and NCCR (at least on the mainland and in the popular mind), and if one gauges the two parties' strength on the basis of whether their respective candidates received a majority of the votes in specific constituencies, it is clear, as Table 6.2 shows, that Mr. Mrema, in spite of his popularity, had a very limited electoral support base.

Table 6.2 shows Mrema obtaining a strong voting majority only in Kilimanjaro, which was considered his home turf; in the remaining twenty-four regions he re-

Table 6.1
Presidential Election Results

Candidate	Party	Votes	%
John Cheyo	UDP	258,734	4.0
Ibrahim Lipumba	CUF	418,973	6.4
Benjamin Mkapa	CCM	4,026,422	61.8
Augustine Mrema	NCCR-MAGEUZI	1,808,616	27.8

Source: NEC-Tanzania. *Presidential Election Official Results.* Dar es Salaam: NEC HQ, 1995.

ceived less than 50 percent of the votes, and in many places considerably less than this number.[32] Again, it should be emphasized that serious irregularities were recorded throughout Tanzania, which means that the official results must be taken with a grain of salt. Nevertheless, the size of the ruling party's victory in both the legislative and presidential elections calls for explanations that go beyond cheating and incompetence by election officials. Two factors responsible for CCM's strong performance were the party's resource endowments, its presence throughout the country, and, more important for this chapter, the fact that it had Julius Nyerere on its side. Given how well Mkapa did throughout Tanzania, one is somewhat suspicious of the opposition charge that the results of the 1995 presidential election do not reflect the will of Tanzanian voters.

Indeed, the legitimacy of election results in Africa can never be assessed by the reaction of the opposition. African opposition parties seldom, if ever, accept defeat at the polls. They generally adhere to a false syllogism: if they end up losing, the election, ipso facto, must have been fraudulent; on the other hand, if they win, the election must have been free and fair. While African incumbents have, in fact, engaged in acts of fraud, opposition parties have tended to overestimate their electoral strength. When led especially by people with acknowledged oratory skills (e.g., Mrema in Tanzania, Fru Ndi in Cameroon, and Abdoulaye Wade in Senegal), the rallies of opposition parties tend to attract huge and enthusiastic crowds in the urban centers. Leaders then extrapolate that support for them must be equally strong in the rural areas, where most Africans live. Often, however, this extrapolation ends up being false, primarily for one reason: opposition rallies tend to attract the converted and disenchanted but not necessarily the apathetic, who may constitute the largest voting bloc and are to be found in the countryside. The core of African opposition support, however, tends to be in the urban areas; it includes groups such as students, intellectuals, the unemployed and underemployed, and frustrated political elites. In the countryside, peasant apathy, logistical impediments, and lack of money hinder the capacity of opposition parties to make serious inroads.

Table 6.2
Presidential Election Results in Selected (Mainland) Regions (%)

Region	Mkapa	Mrema	Others
Arusha	60.5	37.0	2.5
Coast	71.6	13.3	15.1
Dar es Salaam	72.0	21.2	6.8
Dodoma	75.2	18.0	6.8
Iringa	68.0	28.7	3.3
Kagera	56.1	39.7	4.2
Kigoma	56.4	30.1	13.5
Kilimanjaro*	20.4	77.5	2.1
Lindi	86.1	7.9	6.0
Mara	56.1	39.6	4.3
Mbeya	57.8	39.0	3.2
Morogoro	64.7	29.2	6.1
Mtwara	89.5	4.8	5.7
Mwanza	56.5	23.6	19.9
Ruvuma	78.0	18.6	3.4
Shinyanga	52.2	19.8	28.0
Singida	75.2	17.4	7.4
Tanga	75.5	5.4	9.1

Source: NEC-Tanzania. *Presidential Election Official Results.* Dar es Salaam: NEC HQ, 1995.

* Region where main opposition candidate obtained a voting majority.

In Tanzania, where CCM was not merely a decoy for one-man rule but had instead established a genuine party machine, it is not difficult to imagine that local party bosses could deliver the votes in support of CCM candidates in a way that few of their rivals could do for opposition candidates. The ruling party had a number of advantages over the opposition, which it could use to secure a victory: experience in running a government and elections, money, and greater access to, if not control of, the electronic media (e.g., Radio Tanzania). CCM parliamentary candidates could use these resources to their advantage. In addition, as a result of the economic liberalization efforts undertaken by the CCM government, prices paid to peasant farmers for their crops have been on the increase since 1986. Tanzanian farmers might have felt that they had more to lose by abandoning CCM than to gain by embracing the opposition.[33] In a country where voter exit surveys have barely existed, this hypothesis is hard to prove. The point, however, is to suggest that election results that maintain incumbents in power may not be due solely to acts of fraud. The size of Mkapa's victory can be explained by the factors just mentioned plus Nyerere's support, who actively campaigned for him. Nyerere's coattail is indeed long, so much so that one of his sons was able to capture a parliamentary seat for the opposition! The Nyerere name may well transcend party politics in Tanzania.

CONCLUSION

This chapter ends where it began: focusing on the man who has dominated Tanzanian politics in a way that few, if any, African founding fathers have. Julius Nyerere's success, both in and out of office, is due to both interpersonal skills and the nature of the society from which he came. In the first instance, the strength of Nyerere's character, his integrity, articulateness, down-to-earth demeanor, and political cunning have, in the main, served him and Tanzania well. Julius Nyerere is that rare political specimen who had all the powers necessary to be a dictator, yet did not become one. In this, he resembles Charles de Gaulle of France, Leopold Senghor of Senegal and Nelson Mandela of South Africa. These giants of late twentieth-century politics owe their success not to charisma, which is by nature messianic, uncompromising, and thaumaturgical, but to the strength of their intellect and the clarity with which they express their ideas. They evince an admixture of courage, intellectual profundity, and personal charm.

Also, sub-Saharan Africa's overwhelmingly paternal social structure and its reverence for the alleged wisdom of the elderly explain Nyerere's fortune. It is a pity that few other African heads of states were gracious and wise enough to leave office under conditions that would allow them to play a constructive role in the affairs of their country. Much blood spilling and pain might have been avoided. Nyerere's influence has been especially critical in two issues that have torn asunder other African states: corruption and the management of regional and ethnic differences. He took a multiethnic, multireligious and territorially bifurcated polity and transformed it into one of the most stable countries in sub-Saharan Africa—all while trying to keep inequality in check. Nyerere's concern about these issues, as well as his appreciation of democracy for its own sake, probably led him to embrace political reform in Tanzania.

The above is in no way meant to suggest that Nyerere has always had his way. Indeed, he lost one of the most important political battles in postcolonial Tanzania: he had to abandon his vision of an egalitarian, socialist society to make way for capitalism. Nor have the fights Nyerere won always had their expected effects.

Therein lies the danger of ongoing democratization efforts. While it is clearly preferable for democratization to be supported by elites than to be resisted by them, it is important for the process to assume its own course, to become, in other words, institutionalized. Nyerere's continuous foray may have retarded this development in Tanzania, since decisions of national importance have been strongly influenced by his views. He has come very close to being the political equivalent of judge and prosecutor, making and breaking careers even years after leaving office.

As long as Tanzania was a one-party state, it may have been fine for Nyerere to play a preponderant role, since the performance of the ruling party and its policy choices could not be judged by the electorate at large through multiparty elections, and since "lesser" members of the CCM, including former president Mwinyi, were hesitant to criticize the apparent excesses of their colleagues. In the absence of the automatic external checks and balances imposed by an effective multiparty system, an ombudsperson was needed to temper the opportunistic impulses of party and government officials. However, Tanzania entered a new day with the October 1995 elections, and the rule of law must henceforth prevail over Nyerere's personal charm. In the absence of this happening in Tanzania, continued influence by a man who is officially out of power—and therefore not subject to strictures placed on government officials—may undermine democratic rule.

The question now is whether Nyerere will step back from the limelight and allow the impersonal norms of the competitive political marketplace to dominate, or whether he will continue to act as Tanzania's version of Superman. The initial signs are good. President Mkapa has moved in with a new team, the unicameral Parliament, even though dominated by CCM legislators, is asserting institutional independence.[34] Nyerere has been relatively quiet since the 1995 elections, devoting his time to the crisis in the Great Lakes countries of Burundi and Rwanda and to his farm. For the long-term future of democratization in Tanzania, this is surely a welcome development. Nevertheless, one has to wonder what will become of Tanzania as a federated, democratizing state when Nyerere's mortality deprives the country of the leader that has guided it through difficult periods in the latter part of the twentieth century.

NOTES

1. Julius K. Nyerere, "The Arusha Declaration," in *Freedom and Socialism* (Dar es Salaam, Tanzania: Oxford University Press, 1968), p. 234.

2. This point is also made in Colin Legum and Geoffrey Mmari, eds., *Mwalim: The Influence of Nyerere* (Trenton, NJ: Africa World Press, 1995).

3. Julius K. Nyerere, "Democracy and the Party System," in *Freedom and Unity: Uhuru na Umoja* (Oxford,UK: Oxford University Press, 1967), p. 195. This speech was first delivered by Nyerere at the January 1963 TANU Annual Conference. It is perhaps the most detailed exposé of Nyerere's view on democracy; at its roots, however, lies the notion that multiparty politics and nation-building are incompatible.

4. Ibid., p. 196.

5. Ibid., p. 197.

6. Ibid.

7. Those so-called extraordinary circumstances had to with the existence of fundamental social cleavages, and since those could not be expected to exist for very long before society disintegrates, neither could multiparty politics. The argument, in so far as one can be deciphered, is rather circular.

8. Julius K. Nyerere, "Democracy and the Party System," p. 200.

9. Julius K. Nyerere, *Freedom and Development: A Selection from Writings and Speeches 1968–1978* (Oxford, UK: Oxford University Press, 1973), pp. 32–33.

10. Author interview with a Tanzanian colonel on 11 July 1995. His name is being withheld upon his request. Also, research rules at the University of Missouri, which financed the trip that made the writing of the chapter possible, prohibit exposing human subjects to any possible risk.

11. This vision was not to be fulfilled. The government did emerge to supplant the party, a fact that Nyerere himself acknowledged in 1981. See *Bulletin of Tanzanian Affairs*, no. 12, March 1981, pp. 6–7.

12. See *The Transition to Democratic Governance in Tanzania: An Assessment and Guidelines for Near-Term Action*, Contract No. AFR-0542-Q-00-1109-00, ARD and MSI for USAID, 1994. Section I of this donor-sponsored study provides a devastating, but historically inaccurate, and ideologically partisan, critique of Tanzania's effort at achieving socialism.

13. Julius K. Nyerere, "Democracy and the Party System," p. 201.

14. Lionel Cliffe, "Democracy in a One-Party State: The Tanzanian Experience," in Lionel Cliffe and John S. Saul, ed., *Socialism in Tanzania* (Nairobi,Kenya: East African Publishing House, 1972).

15. Joel Samoff, "Single-Party Competitive Elections in Tanzania," in Fred Hayward, ed., *Elections in Independent Africa* (Boulder, CO: Westview, 1987), pp. 149–186.

16. Lionel Cliffe, *One-Party Democracy in Tanzania* (Dar es Salaam, Tanzania: East African Publishing House, 1967).

17. Issa Shivji, *Class Struggles in Tanzania* (Dar es Salaam, Tanzania: Tanzania Publishing House, 1976).

18. Goran Hyden, *No Shortcuts to Progress* (Berkeley: University of California Press, 1980).

19. Peter Iane, *The State of the Tanzanian Economy* (Dar es Salaam, Tanzania: University of Dar es Salaam, Economic Research Bureau, paper no. 84.1, 1984).

20. Mwesiga Baregu, "The Rise and Fall of the One-Party State in Tanzania," in Jennifer Widener, ed., *Economic Change and Political Liberalization in Sub-Saharan Africa* (Baltimore, MD: Johns Hopkins University Press, 1994), p. 165.

21. This finding came from a study by the Commission on the Democratic System in Tanzania, whose members were officially appointed on 5 March 1991, to determine whether Tanzania should maintain its one-party system or adopt multipartyism. See *Report and Recommendations of the Commission on the Democratic System Tanzania*, vol. 1 (Dar es Salaam, Tanzania: University Press, 1991), p. 8. Dean McHenry has made the astute remark that it took an "undemocratic" act to bring about multiparty democracy to Tanzania. If one fundamental tenet of democracy is majority rule, then it could be argued that Tanzania's embrace of multipartyism violated that principle when the minority position was adopted. See Dean McHenry, *Limited Choices* (Boulder, CO: Lynne Rienner Publishers, 1994), especially Chapter 4.

22. See Constantine Danopoulos, *Civilian Rule in the Developing World* (Boulder, CO: Westview Press, 1992). This book contains analyses of civilian-military relations in Cameroon and Tanzania.

23. *The Guardian*, 11 February 1995.

24. An excellent, if also overly generous, treatment of Julius Nyerere and the Arusha Declaration is provided by Cranford Pratt in *The Critical Phase in Tanzania, 1945–1968* (Cambridge, UK: Cambridge University Press, 1976).

25. *Daily News*, 18 July 1990.

26. *Daily News*, 11 July 1992.

27. *Daily News*, 22 February 1990.

28. One encouraging sign that scholars are beginning to pay attention to the important role that individual leaders play in the transition to multiparty democracy is found in the work of LeMarchand on South Africa, Burundi and Rwanda. See René LeMarchand, "Managing Transition Anarchies " *Journal of Modern African Studies* 32, no. 4 (December 1994), pp. 581–604. French social scientists are perhaps ahead of their English-speaking counterparts in recognizing the role of individuals in post-Cold War politics. See Michel Girard, *Les Individus dans la Politique Internationale* (Paris: Economica, 1994).

29. Anaclet Rwegayura, "Tanzania Election Updates" *Inter Press Service* (IPS), 15 October 1995.

30. CCM was hardly unified during this time, as strife between various aspirants to the party's presidential slate became open, frequent, and bitter by July of 1995. See Daily News Reporters, "Kikwete Accuses Gama of Bias," 14 July 1995. See also Nimi Nweta, "Cracks Emerge as CCM Presidential Nomination Nears," *The East African*, 17–23 July 1995. However, CCM's internal problems ceased to be aired in public once the party's presidential candidate was chosen. The opposition, on the other hand, remained divided to the end, in spite of occasional talks of forming a united front.

31. Author interview with Rwekaza S. Mukandala, Chairman of the Tanzania Election Monitoring Committee (TEMCO), December, 1995. This Tanzania-based organization, along with foreign election observers, reported the irregularities in its report. See TEMCO, *Report of Tanzania Election Monitoring Committee on the October 1995 Legislative and Presidential Elections* (Dar es Salaam, Tanzania: University of Dar es Salaam, 1995).

32. For complete, official reports of the parliamentary and presidential elections on both the mainland and Zanzibar, see National Electoral Commission, *Parliamentary Election Official Results*, and *Presidential Election Official Results* (Dar es Salaam, Tanzania: NEC HQ, 1995).

33. Author interview with Philip Momoh, former minister of communications, Dar es Salaam, July 1995.

34. Robert Greenberger, "New Leaders Replace Yesterday's 'Big Men,' and Tanzania Benefits," *Wall Street Journal*, 10 December 1996.

7
Elections and Democratic Transition in Ghana: 1991–96

Kwamina Panford

INTRODUCTION

The phenomenon that is commonly referred to as the transition to democracy con-stitutes a major political change in contemporary Africa. In 1996 alone, eighteen different polls were held in the subregion. Using Ghana's 1992 and 1996 presiden-tial and parliamentary elections, as well as developments in the area of civil liber-ties, this chapter assesses the apparent rebirth of democratic governance in sub-Saharan Africa's first postcolonial independent state. However, a note of cau-tion should be sounded first. The confusion over whether elections per se consti-tute democracy should be acknowledged. The fallacy of equating elections with democracy has real-life implications for Ghanaians and other Africans. If it is as-sumed that elections constitute the sole condition for democracy, then Rawlings, after two consecutive multiparty elections, can rightly assert that he is the legiti-mate ruler of a democratic Ghana. On the other hand, if democracy requires more than a finite number of elections, it needs to be investigated what the additional re-quirements are and whether they exist in modern-day Ghana. Second, assuming that elections attest to the democratic credentials of a country, there is the problem of evaluating them in specific contexts to determine whether they meet free and fair criteria. With respect to Ghana, there is controversy over whether the 1992 elections were fair. Prominent Ghanaian scholars such as Boahen, Oquaye, and Ninsin have argued that the unfair nature of the Ghanaian elections of 1992 casts doubt on claims of a successful transition to democratic rule.[1] Westerners, for their part, have been much more enthusiastic over what has been happening in Ghana. Where does the truth, if it exists, lie? Critical examination of the processes, the ma-jor personalities, and groups involved in the transition is called for. Since political developments in Ghana are still evolving, any observation made about them can be only tentative.

GHANA'S POSTCOLONIAL HISTORY: THE RAWLINGS FACTOR

A turning point in Ghana's transition occurred at exactly 4:00 P.M. on January 7, 1993, when Ghana's erstwhile military leader, former Flight Lieutenant Jerry John Rawlings, in the presence of representatives of foreign governments, including those of the United States and other Western nations, took the oath of office as president of the Fourth Republic. Before this event power in postcolonial Ghana (Table 7.1) alternated between elected civilian rulers and soldiers, as well as between one-party and multiparty systems of government.

Indeed, I recall the loud booms and other sounds as gun fights raged in Accra on June 4, 1979. While the gun battles went on, Rawlings came on Radio Ghana (the state-owned national radio station) and announced the overthrow of the military government, the Supreme Military Council II. Following this coup, a group of junior military officers took over the government and formed the Armed Forces Revolutionary Council (AFRC), led by Rawlings. The AFRC declared a revolution to rid Ghana of corruption, which resulted in the execution of eight senior military officers, including members of the defunct SMC and three former military rulers.

Elections were held in 1979 to establish a Third Republic. They were won by the People's National Party (PNP), a loose coalition of Convention people's Party (PCP) elements led by Dr. Hilla Limann. While turning the government over to Dr. Limann, Rawlings cautioned the new regime that he would be back if it failed to meet the expectations of Ghanaians. True to his warning, on December 31, 1981, Rawlings seized power again and formed the Provisional National Defense Council (PNDC). Rawlings became the only political leader in Africa to come to power by force twice; the legend was thus born. Although the word "provisional" was included in the title of the new ruling clique, members of the PNDC, especially Rawlings, made it clear that not only was the government to remain permanent but it would also complete the housecleaning task initiated by its predecessor, the AFRC. Rawlings and his colleagues were determined not to hand over the reigns of government to anyone else. Instead, the PNDC planned to create a new form of "democracy" based on so-called people power.[2] The PNDC blamed the nation's problems on politicians and party politics.

From December 31, 1981, to mid-1983, various versions of people power reigned in Ghana under the PNDC. The government backed numerous pseudorevolutionary groups. They included the June 4 Movement (named after June 4, 1979, when Rawlings first seized power), the 31st December Women's Movement (31st DWM) and the People's and Workers' Defense Committees. However, in the second half of 1983 Rawlings made a major U-turn in economic policy. His government went from radical populism, which emphasized economic redistribution, to implementation of one of the most far-reaching neoliberal economic programs on the African continent. During this time, and throughout the 1980s, the PNDC consistently refused to hand over power to an elected government, with Rawlings personally deriding multiparty politics. In 1989 things began to change politically in Ghana; a timid transition was begun. Why? This important question

Table 7.1
Chronology of Governments in Ghana (1874–1997)

1874–1957	British colonial rule; Ghana then known as Gold Coast
1957–1966	First Ghanaian government Nkrumah and Convention People's Party (PCP)
1957–1964	British parliamentary form of government
1964–1966	One-party state under the PCP
1966–1969	National Liberation Council (NLC); first military government
1969–1972	Second Republic Progress Party (PP) led by K. A. Busia; British parliamentary model of government
1972–1978	Second military coup; Ghana led by Ignatius K. Acheampong and his National Redemption Council (NRC) and Supreme Military Council (NRC/SMC)
1979	Third military coup; creation of Armed Forces Revolutionary Council (AFRC), also known as Rawlings's First Coming (3½-month rule)
1979–1981	Third Republic; Dr. Hilla Limann elected to office
Dec. 30, 1981	Fourth military coup; Rawlings's Second Coming; creation of Provisional National Defense Council (PNDC)
Nov. 1992	Presidential elections: Rawlings declared winner in first round
Dec. 1992	Presidential elections: NDC won heavily following opposition boycott
Jan. 7, 1993	Government of the National Democratic Convention (NDC) Party, led by Rawlings, forms first government of the Fourth Republic
Dec. 7, 1996	Presidential and parliamentary elections, first back-to-back elections in more than a decade
Jan. 10, 1997	Rawlings takes office for his second and expected final term as head of state of the Fourth Republic

goes to the heart of the seriousness or credibility of Ghana's political transformation.

WHY THE CONVERSION TO MULTIPARTY POLITICS?

Several factors explain why the PNDC began a program of transition to multiparty politics.[3] For ease of analysis I identify two causes which operated in tandem with each other. These causes, which are not presented in any order of significance, are external and internal in their origin or nature.[4] First, as in the case of several African countries, Ghana could not insulate itself from the prodemocracy movements that pressed for multiparty systems of government and elections. By 1990, the Ghanaian middle class, whose members had been excluded from power and stripped of their economic and social standing in favor of cash-crop producers, began to organize to oppose Rawlings and the PNDC, especially under the banner of the Movement for Freedom and Justice (MFJ). Lawyers were especially active in challenging the PNDC; their income had fallen drastically because of the loss of lucrative litigation caused by the setting up of so-called people's courts and public tribunals.[5] Thus, as a group accustomed to economic and political privilege, lawyers suffered severe losses under the PNDC. Professor Adu Boahen's famous Sphinx Speech, which severely criticized the PNDC for stifling freedom of opinion and implanting a culture of silence in the country, may have served as the clarion call for an end to PNDC rule. One important difference between the prodemocracy movement in Ghana and its counterparts elsewhere should be noted, however: the pressure for a return to constitutional rule had begun a decade earlier during the reign of the Supreme Military Council led by General I. K. Acheampong.[6]

Second, some have correctly identified donor pressure as a major factor responsible for Ghana's transition. According to Oquaye, "the principle adopted by the World Bank and the West that aid would be given in future based on the application of the good governance principle motivated Rawlings to launch the program that led to a parliamentary government under the Fourth Republic."[7] It is my understanding (based on information obtained from a PNDC source) that the PNDC agreed in principle with Western donors to hold elections in 1989 to convert itself into a civilian elected government.[8] The agreement was aborted by the PNDC when Daniel Ortega and the Sandinistas lost their bid to retain power in Nicaragua. The loss incurred by the Sandinistas may have deterred the PNDC from testing its own popularity at the polls, as a follow-up to the non-party-based District Assembly elections of 1989. But why did donors change their tune, after they had supported authoritarian regimes inside and outside of Africa throughout the Cold War?

Two major world events may have motivated Western donors, led by the United States, the World Bank, and the European Community, to become advocates of multiparty democracy in Africa. These were the disintegration of the Soviet bloc of old and the decreased attraction of socialism as a political and economic ideology. By 1989, with the virtual demise of Soviet domination of Eastern and Central

Europe, it was no longer necessary for the United States and other Western capitalist nations to stick to the Cold War policy of providing support to both civilian and military dictators simply because they were avowed anticommunists. Without the Cold War, Western nations have no strategic need for propping up non-democratic rulers. Their interests have become more economic, with the search for and control over commercial and strategic raw materials and expanded markets attaining primary importance. The interplay of these new international economic phenomena are captured by Clark:

It can hardly be an accident that the recent wave of democratization ensued immediately after the collapse of Eastern Europe's communist regimes. Even if one prefers Marxian materialism to Hegelian idealism as the source of social mobilization, one cannot usefully deny the "demonstration effect" produced by the European events in 1989. The World Bank only strengthened the prevailing *zeitgeist* of that fateful year with its call for improved "governance" in Africa. Since 1989, the international factor has favored democratic change.[9]

The International Monetary Fund (IMF), the World Bank, and other Western donors were especially interested in Ghana's democratization because of its status in Africa in the late 1980s and early 1990s. Specifically, by 1991 Rawlings had emerged not only as the longest reigning ruler in Ghana, but also had overseen the implementation of one of Africa's most enduring package of economic reforms under the two Bretton Woods institutions' supervision. These donors may have pushed hard and supported elections in Ghana to legitimize the PNDC and safeguard the Structural Adjustment Program (SAP) they had initiated in June, 1983.[10] To them, even the most nominal type of democracy would serve one of their most favored African governments. After crowning Ghana as an example of successful economic liberalization in Africa, the time had come to proclaim it the champion of political liberalization via an elected government.[11]

In response to both internal demands and encouragement from its Western benefactors, in 1991 the PNDC began to open up the political system to limited competition as shown in Table 7.2. The transition from a military to an elected civilian government and republican constitutional order was, however, micromanaged by the PNDC to optimize its chances of remaining in power. In 1991, the National Commission on Democracy, which the PNDC had created in 1982 to develop a "new" form of democracy based on Ghana's culture and society, started courting public opinion. In its work, however, the NCD excluded views which it deemed contrary to those of the PNDC. The next step was the creation of a Committee of Experts to draft a new constitution. The terms of reference of this committee included a review of the previous Ghanaian constitutions of 1957, 1960, 1969, and 1979. It was comprised of a chairperson and seven members, who commenced deliberations on June 11, 1991, and submitted their report to the PNDC on July 31, 1991. The Report of the Committee was forwarded to a Consultative Assembly. The Assembly's members included government appointees, members elected by District Assemblies, and identifiable bodies or organizations such as trade unions, army, police, and professional groups.

As shown in Table 7.2, the Assembly completed its task of proposing a new constitution on March 12, 1992. On April 28, 1992, the proposed constitution was submitted to a national referendum for adoption or rejection. With the opposition urging Ghanaians to vote for acceptance of the new constitution, the endorsement was substantial. In August 1992, the PNDC officially declared the contest open for the presidency and a 200-seat parliament. It lifted the decade-old ban on party politics prior to announcing the scheduled elections. For the first time in more than ten years, non-PNDC political operatives were permitted to engage openly in partisan politics without censure from the government or security agents. The elections of 1992, were, however, quite unique: for the first time, presidential and parliamentary polls were to be held on separate days. The presidential elections were scheduled for and held on November 3, 1992, and the parliamentary polls, after a postponement due in part to opposition boycott, were held on December 10, 1992.[12] Ghana's multiparty system had been resurrected.

Table 7.2
Chronology of Events Leading to Transition in Ghana

1982	National Commission for Democracy (NCD) is formed by the PNDC.
1991	The NCD is charged by the PNDC to collate public opinions on appropriate forms of government for Ghana.
	On July 31, Committee of Experts appointed by the PNDC submits its report on proposals for a draft constitution of Ghana.
	Consultative Assembly, made of one-third PNDC appointees, drafts a new constitution based on proposals submitted by the Committee of Experts.
	In November, the NCD is replaced with an Interim National Electoral Commission to oversee national elections.
1992	On March 12, Consultative Assembly submits draft of constitution to the PNDC.
	On April 28, new constitution is approved in a national referendum.
	In August, the ban on party politics is lifted.
	On November 3, Presidential elections are held.
	On December 10, after one postponement, parliamentary elections are held.
1993	On January 7, Rawlings and his National Democratic Party (NDC) form the first government of the Fourth Republic.

Source: Adapted from Ninsin (1993: 6).

1992 AND 1996 ELECTIONS

Rawlings and his National Democratic Convention were declared the official winners of both the presidential and parliamentary elections of 1992. As Table 7.3 shows, in the presidential polls Rawlings garnered 58 percent of the vote with a voter turnout of approximately 40 percent. With the opposition parties' boycott of the parliamentary polls, the NDC took 189 of the 200 seats in the new legislature.

As shown in Table 7.4, the results of the 1996 presidential election did not vary significantly from those of the 1992 presidential election, especially where Rawlings' performance was concerned. Rawlings officially obtained 57 percent of the votes in 1996 as compared to 58 percent in 1992. However, in terms of the legislative polls, there were notable changes. Whereas in 1992 the controversy surrounding the presidential election led the opposition to boycott the legislative elections that followed, thereby giving the NDC a virtual parliamentary monopoly, in 1996 the opposition fielded candidates for Parliament. As a result, the number of NDC lawmakers was reduced to 133 while the opposition gained 66 seats. Also, in 1996 the turnout for the presidential election was also 78 percent of registered voters compared to about 40 percent four years earlier. Voter turnout in 1996 exceeded the record for the highest turnout in Ghana—the 1969 elections in which 63 percent of registered voters went to the polls.[13]

Other remarkable features of the 1996 elections include the following. Prominent NDC parliamentarians as well as members of Rawlings's cabinet lost their seats. Among the "casualties" were Dr. Ibn Chambas, the veteran deputy foreign affairs minister and former deputy speaker of the first Parliament (under the Fourth Republic), D. S. Boateng, Ghana's longest-serving minister of labor, who lost his seat in Koforidua, and Albert Bosumtwi-Sam, the former chief whip of Parliament, who was voted out of office in Sekondi in the Western Region. On the opposition side, Rawlings's former vice president, K. N. Arkaah, who joined the

Table 7.3
Results of 1992 Presidential Election

Candidate	Party	Votes (%)
Albert Adu Boahen	New Patriotic Party (NPP)	30.4
Emmanuel Alexander Erskine	People's Heritage Party (PHP)	1.7
Hilla Limann	People's National Convention (PNC)	6.7
Kwabena Darko	National Independence Party	2.8
Jerry Rawlings	National Democratic Congress (NDC)	58.3

Source: Adapted from Haynes (1993: 462).

Table 7.4
Results of 1996 Presidential and Parliamentary Elections

Candidate	Party	Presidential Votes (%)	Parliamentary Seats
Jerry Rawlings	National Democratic Congress (NDC)	57.4	132
J. A. Kufour	Great Alliance: New Patriotic Party (NPP) and People's Convention Party (PCP)	39.6	65
Dr. Edward Mahama	People's National Convention (PNC)	3.0	1

Source: Ghana Embassy, Washington, D.C. See also *West Africa*, June 23–29, 1997: 990.

Note: The December elections left two seats vacant, so that the parliament had 198 lawmakers instead of 200. Since then, the opposition alliance has increased its seats to 66 and the NDC to 133 seats in by-elections (*West Africa*, June 23–29. 1997: 990). According to the Ghana embassy in Washington, D.C., however, as of August 18, 1997, one of the NDC seats in parliament was being contested in court by the Great Alliance. A ruling against the NDC could decrease the number of NDC parliamentarians by 1 while increasing that of the Great Alliance.

opposition's Great Alliance as its vice presidential candidate, lost his bid to become a parliamentarian in his own hometown.

As already noted, if Rawlings's popularity has waned, it has not diminished substantially (see Table 7.5). With the exception of the Asante Region (the stronghold of the opposition NPP), where he had only 33 percent of the presidential votes, in all the remaining nine regions, Rawlings garnered more than 50 percent of the votes: 55 percent in Central Region, 57 percent in Western Region, 54 percent in Greater Accra, and 53 percent in Eastern Region. In the Brong Ahafo Region, Rawlings's margin of victory was much bigger, 62 percent of the votes cast. In the Upper and Northern Regions, he fared just as well with votes of over 60 percent.[14] By contrast, the strongest opposition presidential candidate fared very well only in the region in which he was expected to do so: Ashantiland, the hotbed of opposition to Rawlings.

Why Rawlings and the NDC Have Won

A combination of factors explains the relative popularity of Rawlings and his party and their successes at the polls. The NDC's management of the transition itself has been a major advantage. Not only has it tightly regulated the processes and timetables for the entire transition, it also has concocted a series of surprises that have worked to the disadvantage of the opposition. A case in point is the 1992 elections. The lapse between the lifting of the ban on political parties and presiden-

Table 7.5
Votes Won by Rawlings in 1996 Elections by Region (%)

Region	Votes (%)
Asante	32.8
Brong Ahafo	61.7
Central	55.2
Eastern	53.8
Greater Accra	54.0
Northern	62.1
Upper East	74.6
Upper West	69.0
Western	57.3

Source: Adapted from the *Daily Graphic* (Accra, Ghana), December 9, 10, and 11, 1996; and *Ghana News* (Ghana Embassy, Washington, DC), March 1997, pp. 16–17.

tial elections was only three months. The major opposition parties barely had enough time to start canvassing for votes. The NDC strategically made decisions and announced them in a manner that could not be anticipated by the opposition parties. The opponents of Rawlings could therefore not predict and plan counter-measures to defeat him at the polls. As if politics were an uneven poker game, the NDC kept all the aces, making it practically impossible for the opposition to respond adequately. Why did the opposition accept to play on such unleveled terms? Jeffries and Thomas have speculated that the opposition might have accepted the transition on terms dictated by the NDC because it was acutely anxious to see the country's return to civilian-constitutional rule.[15]

In addition, the opposition parties have contributed to their own demise by over-estimating their strength vis-à-vis Rawlings and the NDC. They may not have gauged correctly Rawlings's popularity and staying power. Dating back to June 4, 1979, Rawlings has remained fairly popular among Ghanaians, although this varies by region. In spite of the harsh dimensions of the SAP, which has been implemented under Rawlings, Ghanaians' perception of Rawlings as a so-called man of the people or the ordinary person's ally still lingers. Even if some of his ministers are suspected to be corrupt, Rawlings as an individual leader is not deemed a typical politician interested only in his material well-being. Shillington has correctly referred to Rawlings's dominance of the Ghanaian political scene as the "Rawlings factor."[16] He has added a third dimension to the Kwame Nkrumah and Danquah-Busia traditions.[17]

Rawlings and the NDC have had overwhelming advantages of incumbency. With the exception of the first independence government headed by Kwame Nkrumah (1957–66), Rawlings and his NDC have probably done the most to improve Ghana's infrastructure. The virtually unprecedented pace of development and repair of the country's physical facilities has boosted the NDC's chances for success at the polls. A few cases support the point. Under Rawlings and the NDC, for the first time all the 110 district capitals have been linked to the national electricity grid. One outcome has been that several villages and towns, including Nkroful (Kwame Nkrumah's birthplace), which were deprived of electricity under previous regimes can now enjoy it. Between 1991 and 1996, numerous villages were supplied with mechanically operated water pumps and bore holes. This has improved access to potable water in towns and villages.

Rawlings's record in road rehabilitation and building has been even more impressive. Thanks largely to his long tenure in office and financial support from overseas, Rawlings has surpassed the record set by the Nkrumah government in boosting road transportation. Several cities, towns, and villages are linked by not only repaired but also newly constructed roads. This is especially the case in the Asante, Central, and Brong Ahafo Regions. Local and foreign travelers can now use improved facilities at the nation's premier airport, Kotoka International Airport. Safety and security have been improved to the extent that international airline companies that abandoned Ghana from the mid 1970s to the early 1980s are returning to the country. Nationals of neighboring countries increasingly prefer using Ghanaian ports for shipping because of improved security and other services. With dredging and computerization, the country's two harbors have been made more efficient. These developments—backed by financial support from the IMF, World Bank, and other Western donors—have buttressed Rawlings's popularity.[18] They have made his name virtually synonymous with one of the most highly visible infrastructure development programs not only in Ghana but in West Africa. This source of Rawlings's popularity may have been one of the numerous Achilles' heels that the opposition could not overcome.

Rawlings, with the support of Western donors, has also succeeded in shifting the base of political power in Ghana from urban to rural areas. With the SAP culminating in the loss of thousands of jobs and the withdrawal of subsidies enjoyed by urban dwellers, he and the NDC have found a new power base in the countryside. Farmers have benefited tremendously in terms of access to water, electricity, roads, and even telephones. Also, cocoa farmers are now paid one of the highest producer prices in the subregion, which induces others in neighboring countries to smuggle their crop to Ghana for sale. The appreciable reversal of the fortunes of Ghanaians has contributed to Rawlings's popularity. Compared to other Africans, Ghanaians, under Rawlings, at least in terms of political stability, personal safety, and economic security, are relatively well off.

Where electoral outcomes are concerned, strategies always matter. The opposition, especially in 1992, contributed to the PNDC-NDC's victory by failing to unite behind a single candidate in the presidential and parliamentary elections. Although on November 20, 1996, the two main opposition factions—the Nkrumah and Danquah-Busia groups—gallantly adopted a united front (in the form of the Great Alliance) to challenge Rawlings and his NDC, delays in their efforts might have made it more difficult for them to surmount the formidable organizational hurdles they confronted. Compared to the NDC, the majority of the leaders of the Great Alliance, which formed the main opposition in the 1996 elections, were largely elitist and distant from the Ghanaian masses. This is especially applicable to the Danquah-Busia elements in the Great Alliance. Much of the leadership of this opposition is derived from the remnants of the PCP and the UP. A significant number of the leaders are aging and cannot match the relative youthfulness of the NDC. Also, because of their exclusion from politics and business under the NDC for over a decade, most of the old guard have been stripped of prestige and other resources. They have had to compete with severe financial and organizational handicaps.

Last but certainly not least, the estimated billions of dollars pumped into Ghana by various Western donors have allowed the PNDC-NDC to buy the silence of previously vociferous urban middle classes. These are mostly professional and technical people who have reaped enormous financial windfalls from the SAP since 1983. For example, local consultants can now obtain lucrative contracts to provide goods and services at large profits. These consultants enjoy dramatically improved access to expensive foreign currencies, which they use in maintaining their newfound luxurious life-styles. Although they may not be overt and active backers of Rawlings, they can be deemed closet supporters because privatization and other policies implemented by the PNDC-NDC have been to their financial advantage. At the very least, they are not as vehemently opposed to Rawlings as they were to General Acheampong in the 1970s. Finally, military officers now reap the benefits of programs associated with the SAP, in the form of overseas training and scholarships which give them access to convertible currencies. This may have dampened any temptation to initiate coups.

BEYOND ELECTIONS: EVALUATING GHANA'S TRANSITION

Have consecutive national elections ended military intervention for good and inaugurated an era of stable and democratic governance in Ghana? As several commentators have correctly observed, one or two or even several back-to-back successful elections alone cannot make a democracy or insure long-term political stability.[19] One additional condition for the certification of a country's political system as democratic is the degree to which human and civil rights are constitutionally guaranteed and enforced. As a result of the enforcement of Chapter 15, Article 14, of the 1992 Constitution, the arbitrary detention of individuals by state security agents, especially the police, for extended periods of time is being curtailed. It is now common for a suspect to appear before a magistrate in less than forty-eight hours after arrest to post bail or arrange a hearing.

The establishment of a relatively autonomous media commission (headed by Professor Kofi Kumado, a lawyer, under the first term of government of the Fourth Republic), in fulfillment of Chapter 12 of the 1992 Constitution, has profoundly altered the atmosphere in which journalists operate. A new era in which they freely assert their professional rights is on the verge of being developed. This is typified by the first boom in media growth in modern Ghana. There are currently approximately twenty newspapers. Although *Graphic* and *Times*, the two national dailies, are still state owned, several new private papers are competing fiercely with them for readership and advertisement. In addition, for the first time, Radio Ghana, operated by the state-owned Ghana Broadcasting Corporation, no longer has a monopoly over the national airwaves. As of June 1996, several private FM stations had licenses to broadcast in Accra, Kumasi, and other cities.

Another harbinger of improved civil rights in Ghana may be found in the labor sphere. According to the Ghana Trade Union Congress (the country's main workers' federation), the 1992 Constitution has led to a "new air of freedom" conducive to the exercise of workers' rights, such as collective bargaining. This era contrasts sharply with the last decade in which SAP contributed to the stifling of collective bargaining.[20] One hallmark of this new wave of workers' freedoms is that currently by law, even the state (as an employer) is not exempted from bargaining directly with civil servants. Even more important, for the first time in the history of Ghana, provisions on freedom of association and expression by workers are incorporated into the Constitution (Chapter 5, Article 21, Sections 1d and 1e). Workers can bargain with employers and express their views on national issues without fear of incurring the wrath of state security agencies. This was clearly in evidence in 1995 during the anti-Value Added Tax (VAT) demonstrations. Ghanaians in several major urban centers expressed their newfound freedoms and right to challenge unpopular government policies through mammoth protests and marches. Such antigovernment demonstrations (or demos, as they are called) could not have been conceivable under the regimes that preceded the Fourth Republic.

Democracy may also be measured by the degree to which contestants for power accept the rules of the game and their outcome. Unlike the controversy-ridden 1992 elections, the 1996 polls reflected what, for lack of appropriate terminology, may be deemed mature behavior on the part of both the government and the opposition. There was little of the bitterness that characterized the first transition elections. Before the results were made official, Dr. Mahama and Kurfour conceded defeat and offered sincere congratulations to Rawlings. They then urged their supporters to accept the results of the polls. Instead of basking in his victory, Rawlings cordially reciprocated by reminding Ghanaians that the results were not a win for his party but a victory for all Ghanaians. He immediately alluded to the gigantic tasks of nation-building that lay ahead of the Fourth Republic.[21] In part, this was due to the fact that the opposition had participated in the preparations for the elections, as had wide segments of Ghanaian civil society (e.g., NEDECO). Voter turnout was also higher in the second transition elections than in the first (80 percent in 1996 versus only 40 percent in 1992). Nationals of Ghana may be said to be exhibiting growing tolerance and even political maturity, which constitute significant improvements on past political behaviors and patterns.

PROSPECTS FOR AND CHALLENGES TO DEMOCRACY IN GHANA

In order for Ghanaians to reap the benefits of their relative success at the polls fully, some considerable hurdles have to be overcome on the path to political stability and good governance. One of these challenges will emerge in the year 2000 when, due to constitutional provisions, Rawlings cannot run again for president. The viability of Ghana's new democracy will be tested severely by how Rawlings's party, the NDC, manages the issue of succession. Because Rawlings has so dominated Ghanaian politics in the last fifteen years and because the NDC is an assortment of political groups, how it replaces Rawlings could impinge on not only how it fares at the polls, but also on whether the Fourth Republic is preserved. How would the NDC react to losing the presidency and its majority in Parliament in the year 2000? Indeed, will Rawlings accept the strictures of the Constitution and step aside, or will he attempt to do what has been done in Peru and Argentina (i.e., push for changes in the constitution that would prolong his rule)? The succession question will serve as a barometer of the ruling party's and Rawlings's commitment to democracy.

The state of the economy, especially living and working conditions, should play a prominent role in the future of democracy in Ghana. If the costs of social services (education, health, water, and transportation) and food keep rising, and the local currency continues its free-fall in value while joblessness and hopelessness rise, then the new democracy might be imperiled. Thus the outcome of Ghana's economic programs will have political ramifications. For how long will the international community be willing to bankroll Ghana's economic reform efforts? The institutional performance of governmental bodies under the Fourth Republic needs addressing. Due to the long absence of a Parliament in Ghana, there is a dearth of technical skills in crafting legislation. Furthermore, to make democracy truly meaningful, the public needs information from a well-informed, responsible, and independent media. If the media engages in self-censorship and unbridled sycophancy (as it did under previous regimes), then it will have failed to provide the public and lawmakers with the information necessary to make intelligent public policy decisions. All of this points to the urgent need to inculcate into parliamentarians, media personnel, party operatives, lawyers, judges, government bureaucrats, private human rights groups, trade unions, and other bodies the kinds of values and attitudes that are supportive of the democracy Ghanaians hoped to live under when they voted overwhelmingly for the 1992 Constitution.

Based on the above, Ghana may not have as yet turned the democracy corner but it may be in sight. Ghana may be on the verge of breaking the coup jinx, which has thwarted the constitutional and predictable transfer of power and engendered political instability. However, much will hinge on the behavior of the party (NDC) and government in power and the opposition parties inside and outside Parliament. They need to convince the majority of Ghanaians that they are genuinely committed to democracy by firmly upholding the principles embedded in the Constitution. This is the formidable task ahead for Ghanaian politicians who seek to rule, as well as for a public that has given them such a mandate through the ballot box.

NOTES

1. For contrasting views of the 1992 Ghanaian elections, see Richard Jeffries and Clare Thomas, "The Ghanaian Elections of 1992," *African Affairs* 92, no. 92 (1993), pp. 331–366; Kwame Ninsin, "Some Problems in Ghana's Transition to Democratic Governance,*" Africa Development* 18, no. 2 (1993), pp. 5–22; Michael Oquaye, "The Ghanaian Elections of 1992—A Dissenting View," *African Affairs* 94 (1995), pp. 259–275.

2. Kojo Yankah, *The Trial of J. J. Rawlings: Echoes of the 31st December Revolution* (Tema, Ghana: Ghana Publishing Corporation, 1986).

3. E. Gyimah-Boadi, "Notes of Ghana's Current Transition to Constitutional Rule," *Africa Today* (4th quarter, 1991), pp. 5–17.

4. See John Wiseman, *Democracy in Black Africa: Survival and Revival* (New York: Paragon House Publishers, 1990). See also John Wiseman, *The New Struggle for Democracy in Africa* (Brookfield, VT: Aldershot, 1996).

5. The PNDC attempted to replace the country's legal institutions with revolutionary ones such as so-called people's courts and public tribunals to unleash justice by ordinary Ghanaians. The PNDC initially viewed the courts, as it did most pre-December 31st institutions, as corrupt and responsible for the society's numerous ills and the absence of justice. See Michael Oquaye, "Human Rights and the Transition to Democracy under the PNDC in Ghana," *Human Rights Quarterly* 17, no. 13 (August 1995), pp. 556–573.

6. From 1978 to 1979, a coalition of students, workers, and professional bodies (mostly lawyers and doctors) challenged the Supreme Military Council to return the country to civilian rule. The challenge was responsible for the Unigov fiasco through which the SMC had sought to retain power; it led to Rawlings's First Coming and the formation of the AFRC.

7. Michael Oquaye, "The Ghanaian Elections of 1992," p. 261.

8. Author interview with PNDC operative, summer 1991.

9. John Clark, "Reform or Democratization for Africa?: Troubling Constraints and Partial Solutions," *TransAfrica Forum* (Spring 1996), pp. 3–19.

10. Kwamina Panford, "Structural Adjustment, the State, and Workers in Ghana," *Africa Development* 29, no. 2 (1994), pp. 71–95. See also Eboe Hutchful, "From Revolution to Monetarism: The Economics and Politics of Adjustment Programme in Ghana," in Bonnie Campbell and John Loxley, eds., *Structural Adjustment in Africa* (New York: St. Martin's Press, 1989), pp. 92–131.

11. The strong interests vested in Rawlings and the PNDC by the international community were expressed by the *Financial Times* of London, which contended that a loss by Rawlings would have resulted in the opposition abandoning the SAP. See *Financial Times*, 3 November 1992.

12. This innovation was abolished, and both presidential and parliamentary polls were held on 7 December 1996.

13. *Daily Graphic* (Accra, Ghana), 11 December 1996.

14. This could be attributed to two causes. First, the Brong Ahafos never aligned with the Danquah-Busia factions. Second, they have benefited tremendously from the boost in infrastructure under the PNDC-NDC.

15. Richard Jeffries and Clare Thomas, op. cit., p. 340.

16. Kevin Shillington, *Ghana and the Rawlings Factor* (New York: St. Martin's Press, 1992).

17. Prior to the rise of Rawlings, Ghanaian politics was dominated by two political camps—the Nkrumah and Danquah-Busia factions. The former formed the first post-independence government of the Convention people's Party (PCP) and the latter, the opposition called the United Party (UP).

18. It is estimated that the IMF and World Bank have pumped $8 billion into the Ghanaian economy in the last decade. Economist Intelligence Unit. *Country Report: Ghana*, 1 October 1995.

19. See Ann Seidman and Robert Seidman, *State and Law in the Development Process: Problem Solving and Institutional Change in the Third World* (New York: St. Martin's Press, 1994).

20. Kwamina Panford, "IMF/World Bank's Structural Adjustment Policies, Labour and Industrial Relations and Employment in Ghana," *African Development Perspectives Yearbook 1994/95.* Vol. 4 (New Brunswick, NJ: Transaction Publishers, 1996), pp. 193–205.

21. *Daily Graphic* (Accra, Ghana), 9 December 1996.

8
The Irony of Wealth: Democratization in Gabon

Nelson N. Messone and Jean-Germain Gros

INTRODUCTION

Gabon was not spared by the tidal wave of mass protests, demonstrations, and riots which forced many African autocratic regimes to bow to popular demands for political reform in 1990. Although Omar Bongo, Gabon's long-time president, initially tried to trivialize opposition demands, he was among the first African incumbents to convene a democratic National Conference in April 1990 and subsequently organize multiparty legislative and presidential elections in 1993. However, in Gabon the path to democratic reform has been fraught with roadblocks and frustrations. This chapter focuses on some key questions pertaining to democratization in Gabon. How was Omar Bongo able to remain in power when it appeared in the early 1990s that he would be one of democratization's African victims? In other words, what combination of factors are critical in determining whether African incumbents such as Bongo retain or lose power as a result of political reform? What are the prospects for democracy in Gabon? Going beyond Gabon, how important is national wealth to democratization outcomes, and how critical is the role of external actors—especially that of former colonial powers such as France—in Africa's ongoing political transformation?

The chapter is divided into sections. The first section lays out the theoretical framework, which combines rational choice theory, New Institutionalism, and international relations; the second section uses Gabon as an empirical case to "test" the theory (or theories). Why rational choice, New Institutionalism, and international relations? In the first instance, politics is about individual actors making decisions in the public sphere; acting at particular historical junctures, they can either be agents of change or stagnation. Furthermore, while we recognize that individuals sometimes participate in politics because they are moved by selflessness, we posit that it is more often the case that they are motivated by a desire to optimize their own political utility (hereby defined as the capture or preservation of power).

Following this line of reasoning, we have adopted a profile of political actors, based on Peter Ekeh's and Robert Bates's works. However, because rational choice theory, which Bates' work certainly typifies, does not take into account the role of institutions in shaping behavior, we use the insights of New Institutionalism to strengthen the model. In pursuing their political utility, political actors face various constraints stemming from their own "bounded rationality" and the institutional environment, which includes that of domestic politics. Thus, the outcomes of political decisions are determined by the interpersonal qualities of the actors who make them and macrosocial circumstances. Finally, we use international relations theory of dependency to draw attention to the connection between neocolonialism and democratization in Gabon and in sub-Saharan Africa.

THEORETICAL FUSION

In "Colonialism and the Two Publics in Africa," Peter Ekeh explains that in postcolonial Africa, political actors are tied to two public realms.[1] On the one hand, they are part of a civic public from which they gain materially but fail to honor the duties of a "good citizen." On the other hand, they belong to a primordial public (e.g., an extended family, a whole ethnic group) from which they derive the intangible gains of identity and psychological security. The urgent need for security and identity stems from the cost associated with the psychic turbulence of advances in education, urbanization, and other aspects of postcolonial Africa. Political actors, operating simultaneously in these realms, are subjected to the "unwritten law of the dialectics that it is legitimate to rob the civic public in order to strengthen the primordial public."[2] Thus they use the spoils of state power not only to achieve psychological security in the primordial public, but also for strategic political reasons, that is, to build a base within which to anchor their rule.

The "two publics" produced civil-service-based regimes prone to corruption, as elites came to rely on government patronage to maintain the allegiance of constituents back home and the rising population of urbanites. The social basis of postcolonial regimes was therefore the civil service. In the absence of the kind of legitimacy that is usually conferred by popular mandate, regimes, especially in the oil-rich African states of Gabon, Congo-Brazzaville, and Cameroon, found it necessary to promote parasitic and ostentatious consumerism, fueled by employment in the bureaucracy and government-owned enterprises and access to cheap imported goods (the latter made possible by a deliberate policy of overvalued currencies.) This type of consumerism fostered a culture in which opportunistic, strategically-based urbanites (or *parvenus*) reaped the largest benefits, but it also spilled into the countryside, thanks to Ekeh's two-publics dichotomy.[3] The distribution of spoils took place within the ambit of the one-party state led by leaders who had unlimited access to state resources and who could reward and punish allies at will. With the demise of one-partyism, the formal rules of the political game have changed, but not political behavior, which, for reasons to be discussed momentarily, is more resistant to change.

Transitions to multiparty politics (or democratization phase one) constitute "end-game bargaining between retreating despots and insurgent democrats."[4] But the bargaining takes place on quite uneven terms, thanks to what might be called the organic advantages of incumbency. Resource imbalance is perhaps the most significant advantage that incumbents have over insurgents in Africa. State resources, whose evaporation need not be explained to the general public, because of the absence of accountable government, enhance incumbents' ability to respond to pressures to unseat them. With economic power, they may preempt the military's temptation to trade them for a rival or to initiate a coup. Resources also allow incumbents to buy off their civilian opponents by offering them cabinet posts and cash. (In Gabon, this practice is known as the passing of the envelope.) In the period immediately preceding elections, resources allow incumbents to atomize the opposition by providing financial support to new political parties, which are often little more than appendages of ruling parties. Incumbents, who are able to maintain control over resources as well as control over the terms upon which political change is introduced, have a much better chance at optimizing utility (i.e., staying in office) than those who are not.

The rational choice approach helps to explain political behavior at the individual level. Africans were not irrational when they set up the one-party state and used their newfound state power in ways that Westerners may find hard to comprehend. Corruption, mismanagement, graft, and favoritism were logical by-products of the two-publics world. Rational choice theory, however, remains an incomplete framework as long as the impact of institutions on individual behavior is not seriously assessed. Here institutions are defined as "obligations and duties, rules of behavior, norms, roles."[5] During the transition to democratic rule, the influence of authoritarian institutions does not completely disappear, even as new ones are being established. This is what institutionalists call institutional persistence. Established institutional structures tend to maintain themselves or channel future change. New Institutionalism recognizes that institutions can socialize and select their personnel; they can give rise to networks of personal ties which influence utility-optimizing behavior with negative consequences (shirking, cheating, and dissimulation). Finally, institutions can produce rules and routines resistant to change. A similar phenomenon observed by psychologists is called cognitive consistency, wherein individuals respond to change using old referents and methods.

The tendency for multiparty elections in Africa to be less than free and fair can be explained in terms of the enduring nature of institutions. Molded, shaped, and socialized by institutions developed under the one-party state, incumbents—and many of the politicians who aspire to unseat them—are not likely to adapt immediately to the new rules and constraints imposed by democratization. They accept formal political change only grudgingly and with the expectation that they can shape the process to insure a favorable outcome. Referring to the incumbent party in Gabon, an observer cogently pointed out that it "was not conceived to face competition, let alone engage in debate. By its very nature, it can only accommodate monopoly. Hence its incapacity to internalize the democratic logic."[6] Opportunism, including cheating, shirking, and dissimulation, become common as actors attempt to optimize their gains.

The final piece of the democratization puzzle is the international environment. Any serious study of political reform in contemporary Africa cannot fail to ignore the continent's place within the international division of labor and the consequences that this has on its economies and politics. Sub-Saharan Africa is the one area of the world where colonialism has arguably left its deepest scars. Thus, African democratization must be anchored, in part, in the logic of dependency and neocolonialism. Conceptual clarity is necessary here. Dependency is a special kind of relationship involving two or more partners of unequal endowments; it is, therefore, different from the more clichéd interdependency, which suggests equality and mutuality. In the realm of economic relations between states, dependency manifests itself in various ways, unequal commodity exchange and foreign aid being perhaps the most common in the late twentieth century. Colonialism, the direct political control of a territory by outsiders, was intended to solidify dependency relationships; neocolonialism does the same, except that rather than exerting direct political control over dependent states, outside powers, acting through local elites, exercise influence.[7] In sum, both dependency and neocolonialism are power-relation concepts.

Most African countries today are dependent and neocolonial, rather than simply interdependent and postcolonial (the latter is merely a temporal concept). That is to say, they can barely manage their economic affairs without external help, which, therefore, render local elites susceptible to accepting the desiderata of various foreign benefactors. Dependency and neocolonialism need not have the negative stigma that they have had ever since they were coined in the late 1960s and early 1970s. Indeed, economic dependency may actually facilitate democratization, in that countries dependent on foreign aid are unlikely to be able to resist the strings, including political conditionalities, that come with such aid. By contrast, those that are well-endowed in natural resources and less dependent on the alleged benevolence of the international community may have a greater capacity to resist domestic and foreign pressure for change. It may not be an accident that the African states that have made the greatest strides toward democratization have tended to be among Africa's poorest; Malawi, Benin, and Mali are three examples. Poverty and aid dependency by no means guarantee political progress, however. For one thing, poor countries may evade the proverbial radar screen of the international community; their failure to implement political reform may be outweighed by humanitarian considerations or simply international indifference. Democratization failures in Niger, the Central African Republic, Sierra Leone, and Burkina Faso may be attributed to the fact that even though these countries are extremely aid dependent, the international community—meaning the West—simply do not seem to care about them.

The above suggests that both dependency and neocolonialism are relativist concepts; some countries are more dependent than others. The behavior of neocolonial elites toward democratization, as well as that of the international community, will be shaped by this factor. How countries like Gabon deal with democratization pressure will be different from how poorer sister countries cope with the same. Rich in oil, timber, and other resources, Gabon can ignore international pleas for political change (that is, when such pleas are even forthcoming and sincere). President Bongo, in other words, enjoys relative autonomy vis-à-vis the international community, because he can bring resources to bear in his dealing with outsiders. The late Sani Abacha of Nigeria, or for that matter leaders of the rentier states of the Middle East, could also do the same.

In the post-Cold War era, geopolitical and ideological considerations are no longer the *pièce maîtresse* (centerpiece) of interstate relations. Trade, however, is. Representing less than 3 percent of world industrial output, Africa, in the age of globalization, is virgin territory. African countries with oil, precious metals, large consumer markets, and middle classes with significant disposable incomes cannot be ignored by international investors for long, regardless of their political systems. Some African leaders are thus in a position to play one potential trading partner against another. Omar Bongo has been very skillful in using oil contracts to receive economic and political support from France. He has deflected international criticism with French backing, especially since the ascension to power of the Gaullists.

The irony of wealth, in the age of globalization, is that rich states, especially those that are not major players on the world scene, à la mainland China, are less likely to come under serious international pressure to democratize as long as authoritarianism does not interfere with "good governance" (meaning market-friendly macroeconomic policies and a relatively clean public administration). Of course, the same factors that allow elites in well-endowed countries a measure of autonomy vis-à-vis the international community also play well at home and may delay democratization. Elites with money can pay soldiers and civil servants on time, build new roads in politically important provinces, and buy off opposition politicians. In sum, democratization is shaped by the nexus of three factors: leadership, the domestic institutional compact, and the international environment. Of the three, leadership may be the most important since politics, if a reminder is necessary, is ultimately about self-interest-seeking actors making decisions of a public nature under conditions of constraints and uncertainty. How well the Gabon case fits the framework just outlined is the focus of the next section of this chapter.

GABON: BRIEF HISTORY AND BACKGROUND TO POLITICAL CHANGE

Described by one author as a "neo-colonial enclave" of France, Gabon has been firmly in the Western camp since independence.[8] The phases of decolonization in Gabon were similar to those experienced by other francophone African states; they included the abolition of forced labor, overseas territory status during the Fourth Republic in France, adult suffrage in 1956, autonomy in March 1959 after the 1958 Referendum, and independence on August 17, 1960. From 1944 to inde-

pendence, competitive politics was vibrant but with much vicissitudes. Three political figures emerged at independence: Paul Indjenjet Gondjout, Leon M'ba, and
Jean-Hilaire Aubame. They led the main parties of that period: the *Bloc Démocratique Gabonais*, the *Union Démocratique et Socialiste Gabonaise*, and the *Parti
du Regroupement Africain*. At independence, Mba became president but soon ran
into irreconcilable differences with Jean-Hilaire Aubame in the coalition government that was formed.

Mba was about to call for new elections to defuse an incipient political crisis
with his coalition partners when a group of four young officers staged a coup in
1964. He was forced to resign, while Aubame was made head of a provisional government. France led its first military intervention in Gabon to restore Mba to power
without an official request from Gabon, setting a precedent. The intervention
caused protests throughout Africa and the world. After Mba was restored he faced
more opposition, which he sought to silence. In March 1964, he arrested 150 opponents, the military mutinied, and members of the provisional government were
given long jail sentences or banned from politics. A cycle of opposition-repression
continued until Leon M'ba was admitted to Claude Bernard Hospital and died on
November 27, 1967. The Constitution was amended to make Bongo his successor
as president in February 1967.

The one-party state came to Gabon in 1968 when Omar Bongo declared in a
speech: "Gabonese Women, Gabonese Men . . . I have made the great decision to
create a political party, which, hereafter will be called the *Parti Démocratique Gabonais* [PDG]. From now on, there will be one and single party, the *Parti
Démocratique Gabonais*."[9] Shortly thereafter, an ordinance established the *Parti
Démocratique Gabonais* as the sole legal party in the country. The rationales for
this change were common to other single-party states: to fight underdevelopment
"in giant steps"; to create a stable environment for attracting foreign investment,
which required that old social cleavages be tamed; to rally all active forces in the
country, especially the youth, in mobilization efforts; and to achieve national
unity, with the party acting as the crucible. Needless to say, the record on these
promises was poor in the eyes of most of the Gabonese who protested in 1990.

Indeed, the underlying causes of popular protests in Gabon, as elsewhere in Africa, can be attributed to the failure of single-party rule to fulfill its promises. Its
proponents claimed it would bring about national unity and foster development;
yet its legitimacy and security relied on existing socioethnic cleavages. Instead of
political development, the single party constrained political choice and freedom,
with gross abuses of human rights. Omar Bongo has been described as "an autocrat: a non-ideological pragmatist, a statist, a mercantilist, an economic nationalist."[10] For others, Bongo is a "benign autocrat," different from "venal dictators"
such as Mobutu of Zaire. He rhetorically advocated national unity, but his regime,
to borrow from Uwazurike, "degenerated into a form of oligarchic patrimonial-
ism" whereby Bongo has ruled primarily with members of his ethnic group, family
relatives and other cronies.[11]

A turning point for the worst for Bongo was the socialist victory in France in
1981. An opposition movement, *Mouvement de Redressement National*

(MORENA), soon emerged. Its first action was to circulate a seventeen-page so-called white paper on the Bongo regime's mismanagement of the Gabonese economy, its corruption, and violence. Soon tracts began to circulate at Omar Bongo University, denouncing Bongo and calling for the reestablishment of multiparty democracy. On December 1, 1981, MORENA staged the *gare routière* (bus station) demonstration, the first of its kind that Gabon had experienced since the 1964 coup.[12] In August 1985, it formed a provisional government in France headed by Max Anicet Koumba, and supported by the *Parti National Gabonais*, created in March 1982 by Father Paul Mba Abessolo, who was to become Bongo's leading challenger in the 1993 presidential election, the *Front Révolutionnaire d'Action Populaire* led by Parfait Anotho Edowisa, the *Association des Etudiants Gabonais* led by André Mba Obame, and *Solidarité Gabonaise*. Bongo also survived two attempted coups in 1985 and 1987.

Bongo responded harshly to these events. He ordered the arrest of MORENA leaders in Libreville, among whom were people who had previously participated in his regime.[13] In the trials that followed, MORENA activists were sentenced to fifteen to twenty years of prison. The key plotter of the 1985 attempted coup, Flight Lieutenant Mandja, was not imprisoned but executed. Nevertheless, these events planted seeds of protests that would soon be harvested. Specifically, in 1989 tracts began to surface in Libreville openly criticizing the Bongo regime. Communication technology played an important role. Pierre Mamboundou, leader of the *Union du Peuple Gabonais* (UPG), an arch-rival of Bongo and architect of the 1987 failed coup, flooded Libreville with faxed messages to just about anybody who owned a fax machine. On July 4 Bongo delivered the so-called Bitam Declaration in which he made it clear that "there will not be multipartyism, neither today or tomorrow."[14] Protests against Bongo, however, continued, intensified now by student demands for higher stipends and civil servants clamoring for higher wages. It was the combination of popular demands for political change and demands for the satisfaction of more parochial concerns that forced Bongo to back down in 1990. However, the way he responded attests to the enduring effects of established norms and rules, as the New Institutionalism school asserts. But first, how did economic issues come to mix with the lack of political freedom to generate pressure for change in Gabon?

At independence in 1960, Gabon possessed one of the greatest economic potentials in sub-Saharan Africa and was until 1986 presented to international investors as an acceptable investment risk.[15] Gabon's small population of about one million or less, allowed the country to boast the highest per capita GNP of the region in the 1970s at $4,250. Gabon's prosperity was made possible by the oil boom of the 1970s, considerable mineral wealth in uranium and manganese deposits, and a forest rich in various hardwoods. Yet, the country was not spared the wasteful management characteristic of single-party rule. Public wealth was poorly spent and unevenly reallocated. During the 1977 OAU Summit, Bongo spent $800 million to build a fortified palace which required marble flown from Italy, and a $28 million conference palace.[16] The state spent about three-quarters of the 1977 budget to host the summit. When inflation soared in 1978, the International Monetary Fund

(IMF) and the World Bank imposed a stabilization program on Gabon. Another resource-absorbing project was the Transgabonais railroad, which started in 1974 against the advice of the World Bank. It came to account for most of Gabon's external debt.

In the 1970s, 63 percent of state revenues were allocated to the main centers of Libreville, Port-Gentil, and Franceville-Moanda-Mounana. The income of a Librevillois was about twenty-two times that of peasant farmers.[17] In 1990, it was estimated that 80 percent of GNP was in the hands of 2 percent of the population.[18] Gabon's balance of payments had been in deficits since 1986, and living standards were on the decline because of the austerity measures imposed by the IMF and the World Bank.[19] This situation generated frustrations that could not easily be contained when student protests began. In November 1989 students at Omar Bongo University's department of economics decided to go on strike. An uncontrollable dynamic was thus set in motion. In January 1990 student protests, mainly motivated by corporate interests, gathered momentum, and soon students from the entire university and the *lycées* (high schools) took to the streets. They were reacting against the shortage of teachers and poor conditions on campuses.[20] In January 1991, health care workers led a strike to protest against poor working conditions and a breach in the promise made to them by Omar Bongo to improve their situation before December 1990.

In the initial responses of the regime, past institutional patterns of behavior were apparent. Before 1990 political conflicts in Gabon were resolved in a patrimonial manner, with violence or cooptation as the operating methods. When co-optation was chosen, Omar Bongo would call the contesting parties to his palace, allow them to express their demands, and offer money, or the "envelope," as such money became known. Going to the presidential palace became synonymous with walking out with a so-called envelope. Thus the Bongo regime at first tried to manage protests with piecemeal concessions to satisfy corporate demands. Students received a financial envelope of about 230 million CFA francs. A new salary scale for the public sector and reforms in welfare benefits were also announced. In order to preempt discontent within the security forces, the regime took steps to address their concerns; specifically, it pledged to improve housing for soldiers. Six billion CFA francs for housing renovation and a construction program were subsequently allocated.[21]

The responses to corporate demands just mentioned were accompanied by timid attempts at political liberalization. During the PDG congress of 1990, the party's youth faction, led by Bongo's son, Ali Ben Bongo, and his associate, Mba Obame, created an internal current known as *les rénovateurs* (the reformers). The main objective was to renew party elites and curb the power of the senior elites known as *les caciques* (the old guards). In other words, cracks were emerging in the edifice of Bongoism. According to one person interviewed for this study, a senior special adviser then suggested to Bongo that he engineer the return of "*le petit*," Father Paul Mba, Bongo's leading challenger, which would help him buy time to defuse protests. Bongo soon followed this advice, and Father Mba's return ushered in the era of the national conference. Bongo had at first tried to reinvent one-party rule by calling opposition leaders to join in a national unity movement, which he called *Union pour la Majorité Présidentielle* (Union for the Presidential Majority) in February 1990. When this failed, another attempt was made, which Bongo called the *Rassemblement Social Démocrate Gabonais* (Gabonese Social Democrat Assembly). He failed again and subsequently realized that calls for the reestablishment of multipartyism was what the opposition was looking for.

Protests which had started with diffused corporate demands were soon channeled and articulated by political parties and other organized groups. Issues were cast in terms of the failure of the regime to bring about development, its waste and mismanagement of the country's wealth, and gross abuses of human rights. Protests culminated after Rejambe, the general secretary of the *Parti Gabonais du Progrès* (PGP), a leading challenger to Bongo, was found dead. The PGP stronghold is Port-Gentil, the economic capital of Gabon, and the place where riots reached their climax. An important phase of these riots was when workers of Elf-Gabon, the subsidiary of France's Elf-Aquitaine, went on strike and forced the closing down of oil platforms. This decision was misinterpreted both by the regime and the opposition. The regime saw the disruption as a sign of French backing of the opposition; for its part, the opposition believed this. It was under the pressure of what appeared as an uncontrollable wave of popular protests, demonstrations, strikes, and riots that the national conference was called. The initiation of the national conference can be considered the terminal phase of a period of institutional stasis fostered by the single party.

THE NATIONAL CONFERENCE: NO GUARANTEE OF SUCCESS

Writers have emphasized the utility of national conferences in bringing about meaningful political reforms throughout Africa in the 1990s.[22] In Francophone Africa in particular, national conferences were instrumental in ending, in retrospect temporarily, the careers of long-time strongmen such as Mathieu Kerekou of Benin and Denis Sassou Nguesso of Congo. The Gabon case shows that it is not national conferences per se that lead to regime change, but the juridical terms upon which such events are held. Specifically, the efficacy of national conferences in wrestling power from autocrats largely depends on whether the decisions made by their participants are legally binding or constitute mere recommendations. Bongo was one of the first African rulers to call for a national conference in March 1990. Seventy-five political parties and groups attended the conference. Its decisions were accepted in principle by all, even though some raised questions as to Gabon's readiness for competitive politics.[23]

Following the national conference and prior to the National Assembly elections of September 1990, key political reforms, as defined by Bratton and Van de Walle, were adopted.[24] A constitutional ordinance legally reestablished multipartyism in Gabon on March 22, 1990. An interim constitution was adopted shortly thereafter, with a final constitution drafted by the Interior Ministry and approved on March 1991. Restrictions on the press and on activities by intellectuals and opposition leaders were lifted. An unprecedented amount of press activity came to light for a country of Gabon's population size, with more than ten newspapers. Both presidential and National Assembly terms were limited to five years. At the closing of the national conference, opposition parties were confident that they would seize control of the new multiparty National Assembly and were moving toward defeating Bongo in the 1993 presidential elections.

For his part, Bongo had succeeded in buying time. He would soon begin to maneuver in order to reestablish control. Significantly, Bongo maintained ambiguity over his interpretation of the landmark decisions of the conference, which permitted him to make convenient changes later on. The conference was a much needed forum for discussing Gabon's political transformation and releasing long-suppressed frustrations, but it was not made sovereign. As Bongo himself stated: "The acts of the national conference are not injunctions, but recommendations."[25] A politically intoxicated opposition, blinded by the prospect of entering the State House, failed to read the meaning of this message. The fact that the conference allowed Bongo to retain control of the electoral process would soon come back to haunt the opposition. Unlike national conferences in Benin and Mali, Gabon's national conference simply did not result in an equalization of power between the incumbent and insurgents by stripping the former of its privileged access to state funds. The relative success of the transition in Benin, for example, was due to the sovereign nature of the national conference, which was itself a reflection of the organizational strength of civil society. In Gabon, on the other hand, the national conference was held when opposition to Omar Bongo was still in its formative stage. The incumbent also had money, which he used, as seen earlier, to keep the security forces behind him.

Because of good timing and control of state resources, Bongo was able to turn the national conference to his advantage. He skillfully transformed the event into a "domesticated and tamed conference which had become a structure of national concord and thus lost the aggressiveness that characterized conferences in other countries."[26] The entire process of the conference caught the opposition by surprise. In fact, it seemed to have been convened hastily to produce precisely this result. It allowed opponents to vent their frustrations but did not permit them to organize for a democratic takeover. President Bongo divided and co-opted opponents by holding in effect two national conferences, an official one and a secret one.[27] Before reforms were made public and multipartyism declared, key decisions were already made during the secret conference in which key opponents partook. The result was a division. For example, while some opponents ardently called for Bongo's departure, even a forced one, others argued that this would create a pretext for French intervention as happened in 1964. Amidst confusion mixed with excitement and uncertainty, presidential elections were set for December 5, 1993.

1993 PRESIDENTIAL ELECTIONS

The 1993 presidential elections represented an important gauge of Gabon's democratization. Although a plethora of political parties were formed following the reestablishment of multipartyism, only a few had a truly national stature. The opposition forces included the *Rassemblement National des Bûcherons* (RNB), led by Father Paul Mba and Bongo's principal opponent during the election; the *Parti Gabonais du Progrès* (PGP), led by law professor and attorney Pierre Agondjo; the *Mouvement de Redressement National* (MORENA) from which the *Bûcherons* broke away. On the other side, Bongo's *Parti Démocratique Gabonais* (PDG) and satellite parties formed the *Majorité Présidentielle*. During the campaign and prior to election day, mechanisms and procedures were put in place to insure transparency. Rules and norms were defined for media appearances and campaign advertising. Each candidate had television time to present his platform. An electoral commission was established to ensure an accurate and transparent count of the vote, with representatives of both the opposition and the incumbent majority. The catch, however, was that all electoral documents and procedures were to be validated by the Interior Ministry, then headed by a key Bongo loyalist, Antoine Mboumboou-Miyakou.

During the campaign, the opposition constantly sought to unite its forces into an electoral coalition. At the closing of the national conference, it created the *Front Uni des Associations et Partis de l'Opposition* (FUAPO). This organization generated a strong sense of unity within the opposition, yet it remained weak in its overall operation. Prior to the presidential election, the opposition regrouped again into the *Coordination de l'Opposition Démocratique* (COD), in an effort to present a single candidate as the best strategy to unseat the incumbent. In speeches and pronouncements, the electorate was instructed that Father Paul Mba would be the single opposition candidate. While the climate in the country remained generally tense, the opposition was optimistic that the presidential election would put an end to Bongo's long autocratic rule. Both the incumbent and opposition candidate campaigned throughout Gabon. Minor outbreaks of violence were reported in various parts of the country including Libreville, the capital of Gabon.

Following the December 5 vote, as ballots were being counted, the opposition was buoyant. Results after results showed that it was well on the way to victory. The electoral commission had not yet completed the count in Libreville, which accounts for nearly half of the country's population, when the minister of interior, Antoine Mboumboou-Miyakou, appeared on government television to announce that Omar Bongo had been reelected with 51 percent of the vote. These "official results" were soon validated by the Constitutional Court, headed by a woman judge thought to be Bongo's mistress. To demonstrate her disapproval of this electoral fraud and protest infringement on her authority, Pauline Nyingone, the Governor of Estuaire Province with jurisdiction over Libreville, resigned. Protest statements were also issued by international organizations, such as Belgium-based Education International.

The 1993 legislative ballot also led to controversy. They resembled the 1990 legislative elections in their irregularities. Electoral lists were inflated and ballots rigged. Foreigners were said to have been given identity cards so that they could vote; some were apparently smuggled into the country through neighboring countries. One repented insider later revealed how he participated in the rigging of electoral lists.[28] Election desks were installed in the presidential palace and the private residences of key members of the government. It must also be said, however, that the opposition committed some of the same abuses. Private militias from the opposition intimidated supporters of the government and even each other's supporters. Judging from the outcomes of the first multiparty presidential and legislative elections in Gabon, one is tempted to share the assessment that the changes initiated since 1990 are cosmetic and quite possibly temporary.[29]

EXPLAINING BONGO'S RESILIENCY

How was Omar Bongo able to pull what amounts to electoral coups, outmaneuvering his opponents and undermining democratization in Gabon? Rational choice theory is useful in explaining the denouement of political events in Gabon, in so far as electoral outcomes are largely the products of the kinds of bargaining decisions made by elites during the period preceding the first transition election. The factors that shape election outcomes can be identified in the form of specific questions. First of all, how committed are incumbent elites to free and fair elections and democratization in general? Who is in charge of election administration from beginning to end? Is it an independent electoral commission, composed of members trusted by incumbents and insurgents, or, as is common in the Francophone world, the Ministry of the Interior, which may not be beyond partiality? How strong is the organized opposition? Is it united or fragmented; in other words, are opposition leaders able to line up behind a single contestant or do they engage in internecine political warfare? Political choices clearly matter here, and those are usually made by individuals based on self-interest considerations Programmatically, does the opposition constitute a viable alternative to the ruling group, or does it merely want power for its own sake? How large is the opposition's electoral base? Is it limited to a handful of urban centers of discontent, or does it reach the countryside, where most Africans live? Do the leaders of the opposition, who are often outcasts of the ruling elite, make a serious effort to mobilize beyond their ethnic and regional base? On whose side is the army as an institution?

In 1993 the Gabonese opposition missed a historic opportunity, because of its failure to overcome some fundamental weaknesses and because of key decisions made.[30] The Coordination of Democratic Opposition established by the opposition parties to present a united front to Bongo in the 1993 elections suffered from deep divisions masked by a façade of unity. Contrary to their statements, opposition leaders appeared in multiple candidacies, speaking with discordant voices and taking aim at each other. The leading opposition figures, Father Mba and Louis Agondjo constantly criticized each other in the media. As a result, voters who yearned for unity among opposition leaders were confused. The division of the opposition was further exacerbated by the ethnic or tribal factor. Like the incumbent regime, many opponents agitated the so-called Fang "bogeyman." Non-Fang politicians have all feared the return to power of a member of the Fang group since Bongo came to power.

The Gabonese opposition lacked both financial and human resources to match those that President Bongo could mobilize. Because the national conference had called for state financing of parties, most opposition parties did not seek independent sources of financing. However, Bongo was the state; he could use public funds as political manna to undermine his strongest opponents and keep the weakest ones afloat. Here again institutional persistence was evident. In spite of a new environment of democratization, which the national conference had sought to create, old methods survived. During the 1993 legislative vote each party was to receive 20 million CFA Francs. As a result, opposition parties were created only to vanish soon after state checks were cashed. In the presidential ballot, Omar Bongo and his government attempted to restrain state largesse by initially refusing to continue financing parties. Later, Bongo indicated that he would examine requests on a case-by-case basis, considering the importance of each party. The lack of private resources forced parties and their leaders to enter compromising agreements with President Bongo, thereby weakening the opposition. So pervasive was the opposition's opportunism that one observer sarcastically concluded that, democracy would not emerge in Gabon until the country gets poorer.[31]

In our view, the balance between resources at the disposal of incumbents and opponents is a key variable in explaining electoral outcomes. The more resources a country has and the greater the access that incumbents have to those resources, the more they can engage in "creative" pre-election activities. Omar Bongo controls a special fund known as *les Fonds de Souveraineté* (sovereignty funds) the use of which is at his sole discretion. He has used these funds to coopt and weaken the opposition, to insure continued support from loyalists who might have defected, and to finance his propaganda campaign, which an opposition leader aptly called "the politics of turkey wings aimed at buying out sympathy from a population that has already rejected him for good."[32]

The security forces in particular played a significant role in Bongo's victory. One of the demands of the national conference was that the presidential guard should be dissolved. President Bongo refused to disband the presidential guard but agreed to change its name only, thereby maintaining the military "hostage" to the regime. He bought the military's support with the resources at his disposal. When co-optation of the opposition failed, Bongo's control over the security forces enabled him to use the strong-arm tactics that had been used before the transition. Thus when the opposition mobilized to protest the 1993 election results, the regime responded violently. Opposition radio stations were destroyed, journalists and leading opposition figures were detained, protesters were beaten, and a curfew was imposed. Bongo's presidential guard carried out most of these operations.[33]

The electoral misfortune of the Gabonese opposition can also be linked to its character. The Gabonese opposition parties were a mixture of new and old actors who were direct participants in the regime. As a result, they all found it difficult to play by the new rules of the game in their internal organization. As one observer put it: "Parties which advocated democracy were not practicing democracy inside."[34] Their strategies were fraught with improvisation and amateurism. In their campaigns the messages of most party leaders failed to go beyond Bongo-bashing and did not present a vision for the future; consequently, an image of competent and responsible alternative leadership was wanting. This lack of skills and vision was exacerbated by ideological poverty and a lack of critical articulation of policy. Most parties remained locked in the logic of cold war ideologies, in the form of either simplistic socialism or naive liberalism, both utterly unrelated to the daily travails of the average Gabonese.

Bongo's resiliency has external roots as well. International relations theory has identified external validation as a means that states use to assert legitimacy. In periods of domestic crisis, it is not rare that authoritarian regimes attempt to rely on external legitimacy to compensate for weakening internal legitimacy. In the case of Francophone Africa, this is where France plays a key role. France acts as a provider of legitimacy to its former colonies. Both incumbents and their opponents in French-speaking Africa factor in this variable in their political calculus, and most take their cues from Paris. French politicians on the left[35] and the right[36] see Africa as important to France's claim to world power status; this consensus has produced inertia in French policy toward Africa.[37] It has also made legitimacy a two-edged sword: France gets as much political legitimacy from the willingness of French-speaking elites to remain in the *pré carré* as it gives to them.

In Gabon, French policy also is shaped by considerable economic, political, and strategic interests. Its dependence on Gabon's raw materials such as timber and oil is significant.[38] To secure these interests, France has forged various asymmetrical commercial arrangements, and President Omar Bongo has used his position as the local overlord to build his international stature and further his domestic political objectives. Addressing the European Parliament in 1993, he stated that the "sick" Gabonese economy had to rely on the friends of Africa.[39] Shortly thereafter, the Gabonese government received 2.5 billion CFA Francs from the French Ministry of Cooperation for an environmental project. The opposition was not in a position to conduct such actions and reassure its followers that better times were ahead. In Africa, an unpopular incumbent can placate the opposition at home, if he can achieve legitimacy abroad, and, more importantly, show that he still has the capacity to bring home the proverbial bacon.

Franco-Gabonese relations are conducted through formal and informal institutions, with neither de jure nor de facto separation between private and public realms. A personalized network, known as *le Clan des Gabonais*, which includes Gabonese officials, French intelligence agents, former members of the *Service d'Action Civique* (SAC), mercenaries, money launderers, and legitimate businessmen, ensures that business is conducted in a secretive way.[40] At one point, the personal staff of the president was entirely French, and French ambassadors attended cabinet meetings dealing with matters of importance to France and Gabon. Such structures and relations have fostered various types of opportunistic behavior by French governments of all ideological stripes. To wit, the first military intervention occurred under De Gaulle to restore Léon Mba to power; the second took place under the socialist government of Mitterrand in 1990, much to the chagrin of opposition forces.

In the era of democratization, France faces a dilemma in its relations with neocolonial Francophone states. Until recently, French policy in Africa revolved around various autocrats (better the devil one knows). But these regimes, which are very corrupt, are now under pressure from a civil society that France is unfamiliar with, or in some cases, very suspicious of. Under such circumstances, inconsistencies are bound to appear. For example, France's Africa policy seemed to have shifted in 1990 at the La Baule Summit. President Mitterrand then timidly indicated that French aid would be reserved for countries that are firmly committed to democratization. French bureaucrats clearly presented the new policy as one that was forced by the European Community. In Gabon the fickleness of the policy shift soon became clear in the December 1990 elections. Bongo was able to maneuver around whatever French pressure was being applied because France was faced with a situation where important economic interests were at stake (i.e., oil) in a regime that had served these interests relatively well. The key questions, as put in *Le Monde*, were "How to bring reform without destabilizing? How much time can one allow to convince Bongo that he needs to play by power sharing?"[41]

The above confirms the veracity of the assertion made earlier, namely, the more resources a country has that the international community needs, the more leverage that its leaders have. Neocolonialism does beget dependency, but the latter is not absolute in all circumstances. Depending on the level and quality of the national resources at their disposal, leaders of neocolonial states are not entirely at the mercy of the international community. President Bongo clearly understood this when he ordered Elf-Gabon to shutdown operations in Port-Gentil in 1990 (Elf-Gabon is the local subsidiary of the French oil company, Elf-Aquitaine). Thereafter, Bongo threatened to replace the French company with an American one, which then led to a flurry of negotiations between Libreville and Paris, culminating eventually in the reopening of the oil fields under French control. Thus, in spite of his client position vis-à-vis France, Bongo could use Gabon's relatively abundant oil reserves as a bargaining chip in a way that, for example, Kerekou of Benin could not. The perverse ways in which resources work to undermine democratization in Africa should once again be noted: Resources allow incumbents to co-opt their domestic opponents and maintain their supporters' loyalty; they also permit incumbents to play off segments of the international community against each other, thereby limiting the latter's willingness to apply pressure for change.

CONCLUSION

The future of democracy in Gabon is in doubt as long as Omar Bongo is at the helm, for he is not a democrat but one of Africa's remaining autocrats. It would be a mistake, however, to suggest that Bongo's passing is by itself sufficient to bring about democracy in Gabon. Authoritarianism always transcends individuals. It is a

by-product of a neopatrimonial state in which loyalty and identify are split between two publics and in which ideologies of legitimation, so necessary for a nascent political class hungry to rule, produced democracy-averse institutions such as
the single-party state, economic mismanagement, and dependence. The lingering
effects of these factors are likely to retard Gabon's march toward political modernity. Moreover, as long as oil wealth in Gabon continues to be held hostage to executive power, it is likely to be used to ends that are antithetical to
democratization. It is in this sense that wealth may be a hindrance to, rather than a
facilitator of, democratic transition.

EPILOGUE

After the 1993 electoral coups, Bongo, his presidential majority and the opposition, rallied in the *Haut Conseil de la Résistance*, reached a stalemate over election
results. The country was virtually paralyzed by riots and demonstrations. The social climate was tense with both government and private sector activity disrupted.
For months, both sides engaged in brinkmanship. An agreement was later
brokered between the Bongo regime and the opposition known as *Les Accords de
Paris*. The main goal stated in the preamble was to "put an end, through the virtues
of democratic dialogue, to this climate of latent confrontation."[42] Other key decisions included the revision of the electoral code and the establishment of an independent National Electoral Commission. There also were provisions to reinforce
the rule of law, the rights of political parties, and freedom of the press. Finally, a
national coalition government, the *Gouvernement pour la Démocratie*, responsible for implementing the measures just mentioned and administrative decentralization, was formed. Following these agreements, Bongo successfully integrated
key opponents into this national coalition government. The question remains
whether future elections will consolidate Gabon's transition to democracy or will
act as subterfuges for continued autocratic rule.

NOTES

1. Peter P. Ekeh, "Colonialism and the Two Publics in Africa: A Theoretical Statement,"
Comparative Studies in Society and History 17, no 1 (January 1975), pp. 91–112.
    2. Ibid., pp. 109–110.
    3. For an excellent study of how the postcolonial African state has consistently favored
urban over rural interests, see Robert H. Bates, *Markets and States in Tropical Africa: The
Political Bases of Agricultural Policies* (Berkeley, CA: University of California Press,
1981).
    4. Robert H. Bates, "The Economics of Transitions to Democracy," *PS: Political Sci-
ence & Politics* (March 1991), p. 24.
    5. James March and J. P. Olsen, "The New Institutionalism: Organizational Factors in
Political Life," *American Political Science Review* 78, p. 741.
    6. Claude d'Anuibi, "Le PDG, une Machine à Tricher," *Le Bûcheron* (Libreville, Gabon)
6–12 Décembre 1995, p. 8.

7. Joseph Weatherby, "The Old and New: Colonialism, Neocolonialism and Nationalism," in Joseph Weatherby et al., eds., *The Other World* (White Plains, NY: Longman, 1994).

8. Michael C. Reed, "Gabon: A Neo-Colonial Enclave of Enduring French Interest," *Journal of Modern African Studies* 25, no. 2 (1987), p. 285.

9. *Mémorial du Gabon, 1964–1969*, (Libreville, Gabon, 1970), p. 70.

10. Robert H. Jackson and Carl G. Rosberg, *Personal Rule in Black Africa: Prince, Prophet, Autocrat, Tyrant* (Berkeley, CA: University of California Press, 1982), pp. 143–145, 156–159. See also Reed, op. cit., p. 286.

11. P. Chudi Uwazurike, "Confronting Potential Breakdown in Africa: The Nigerian Re-Democratization Process in Critical Perspective," *Journal of Modern African Studies* 28, (1990), p. 67.

12. One of the authors of this chapter was then a student and participated in a demonstration that took place on the Omar Bongo University campus, which security forces had encircled. Students were protesting the arrest of then rector, Jean-Pierre Nzoghé-Nguema.

13. "Gabon: Bongo's Woes," *Africa Confidential*, 28 April 1982, pp. 7–8.

14. Bitam is a small city in the Northern Province of Woleu Ntem where the ethnic majority of the Fang lives. It is a key electoral and political ground for any aspiring national politician. Bongo was obviously exploiting internal division between the Fang in Bitam and those in Oyem, the capital city of the Woleu Ntem. See "La Déclaration de Bitam du président Omar Bongo," *L'Union*, 7 Juillet 1989, p. 8.

15. François Misser, " Risk: the Game of International Investment," *African Business*, London, November 1986, pp. 57, 59. The North-South Export Consultants used a 7 point scale, where in the Financial Risk category Cameroon ranked first at 4.5, followed by Gabon, South Africa, Kenya, and Zimbabwe at 3.5. In the Business Environment Risk category, Gabon ranked first with 5. It also came first in the category Risk of Expropriation and Nationalization.

16. David Lamb, *The Africans* (New York: Vintage Books, 1984), p. 99.

17. Pierre Péan, "Le Gabon à l'heure du pétrole," *Jeune Afrique*, 27 Juin 1975, p. 22.

18. George Berton, "Afrique de l'Ouest: Diagnostic d'une Crise," *Croissance*, Mai 1990, p. 18.

19. République Gabonaise, *Tableau de Bord de l'Economie: Situation 1994, Perspectives 1995* (Libreville, Gabon: Direction Générale de l'Economie, 1995), p. 109.

20. Otimbo Ndjogou, "Les Raisons d'une Grève," *Le Bûcheron*, 29 Janvier 1991, p. 3.

21. Daniel Bouchard, "Améliorer la Politique Sociale dans nos Armées," *L'Union*, 28–29 Juillet, p. 6.

22. For analyses of national conferences, see John Heilbrunn, "Social Origins of National Conferences in Benin and Togo," *Journal of Modern African Studies* 31, 2 (1993), p. 279; and Jacques Mariel Nzouankeu, "The Role of the National Conference in the Transition to Democracy in Africa: The Cases of Benin and Mali," *Issue* 21 (1993): pp. 45–47.

23. Samuel Ntoutoume Ndzeng, *Le Procès du Conflits des Lois et des Vides Juridiques en Afrique Francophone après l'Instauration du Multipartisme: Gabon—Loi No. 4/91 du 3 avril 1991 Relative aux Partis Politiques* (Libreville, Gabon: Collection Gabonaise ANZAL, Avril 1991). The author is also the leader of a political organization called ANZAL, and he argues that the 1990 constitutional reforms contained flaws that favored Bongo's Parti Démocratique Gabonais.

24. Michael Bratton and Nicholas Van de Walle, "Popular Protest and Political Reform in Africa," *Comparative Politics* (July 1992), p. 442.

25. *L'Union*, 28–29 Juillet 1990, p. 1.

26. Jacques Mariel Nzouankeu, op. cit.

27. This type of information is not factually and readily available; it is based on accounts by insiders of the Bongo regime revealed to one of the authors.

28. See *Le Bûcheron*, "J'ai participé au gonflage de la population de la rive droite à Fougamou," 6–12 Décembre 1995, p. 8. In an interview, Placide Nzigou-Nzamba, leader of the *Rassemblement pour la République* (modeled after the French RPR) confesses how he and other close associates of Bongo rigged electoral lists in the town of Fougamou, which is located in the Ngounié province, a key contested ground for both the ruling regime and the opposition. He was prosecuted, allegedly because he knew too much. See also his letter to Bongo published in the same issue of *Le Bûcheron*.

29. Samuel Decalo, "The Process, Prospects and Constraints of Democratization in Africa," *African Affairs* 91 (1992).

30. Fortunat Obiang Essono, "Faiblesses et Errements de l'Opposition," *L'Union*, 25 Février 1993, p. 2.

31. Ibid.

32. Turkey wings are one of the favorite food delicacies of the average Gabonese, mainly because they are cheap. The link between turkey wings and politics was made by General Simon Mengome Atome, an opposition member of the National Assembly. See *Le Bûcheron*, 6–12 Décembre 1995, p. 4.

33. Amnesty International, "Crainte de Mauvais Traitement en Détention," statement issued on 26 February 1994.

34. Fortuna Obiang Essono, op. cit.

35. François Mitterrand, "Présence française et abandon," *Tribune Libre* 12 (1957), p. 59.

36. Michel Aurillac, *L'Afrique à Cœur* (Paris: Berger-Levrault, 1987), p. 237. The author was minister of economic cooperation under the Chirac Government in 1986–87.

37. Tony Chafer, "French African Policy: Towards Change," *African Affairs* 91 (1991), pp. 39–40.

38. This dependence is 100 percent for cobalt, 87–100 percent for uranium, 83 percent for phosphates, 35 percent for manganese from Gabon. See "La France et l'Afrique," *Marchés Tropicaux*, 2041, 21 Décembre 1984, p. 3169.

39. See *L'Union*, "Omar Bongo vante la démocracie gabonaise et séduit le Parlement Européen," 25 Février 1993.

40. See Michael Reed, op. cit. See also Guy Martin, "The Historical, Economic, and Political Bases of France's African Policy," *Journal of Modern African Studies* 23, no. 2 (1985), pp. 192–194. An insider's account of the intimate network of groups and personalities that shape French policy toward Africa under Charles de Gaulles, remnant of which probably still exists, can be found in the biography of Jacques Foccart, de Gaulle's right-hand man in Africa. See Philippe Gaillard, *Foccart Parle*, (Paris: Fayart/ Jeune Afrique, 1995). Foccart tells of how Bongo was flown to Paris to be "tested," before receiving French support as successor to Leon M'Ba.

41. Jacques Almaric, "Plaies d'Afrique, v. La France embourbée," *Le Monde*, 14 Juillet 1990, p. 2.

42. *Accords de Paris: Négociations Politiques entre L'Exécutif et sa Majorité et l'Opposition Regroupée au Sein du Haut Conseil de la Résistance* (HCR), Libreville, 7 Octobre 1994, p. 1.

Bibliography

Abbink, John. "Breaking and Making the State: The Dynamics of Ethnic Democracy in Ethiopia." *Journal of Contemporary African Studies* 13, no. 2 (1995).

Adewale, Ademoyega. *Why We Struck: The Story of the First Nigerian Coup* (Ibadan, Nigeria: Evans Brothers, 1981).

Adjei, Michael. *Death and Pain: Rawlings' Ghana: The Inside Story* (London, UK: Black Line, 1993).

Africa Watch Report. *Academic Freedom and Human Rights Abuses in Africa* (New York: Human Rights Watch, 1991)

——. *Where Silence Rules: The Suppression of Dissent in Malawi* (New York: Human Rights Watch, 1990).

Ajayi, Ola Rotimi, and Julius Ihonvbere. "Democratic Impasse: Remilitarization in Nigeria." *Third World Quarterly* 15, no. 4 (1994).

Akpan, Ntieyong. *The Struggle for Secession 1966–1970: A Personal Account of the Nigerian Civil War* (London: Frank Cass, 1971).

Almond, Gabriel, and Sidney Verba. *The Civic Culture* (Princeton, NJ: Princeton University Press, 1963).

Almond, Gabriel, and James Coleman, eds. *The Politics of the Developing Areas* (Princeton, NJ: Princeton University Press, 1960).

Amnesty International. "Crainte de Mauvais Traitement en Détention." Statement issued on 26 February 1994, Libreville, Gabon, and London, UK.

Anglin, Daniel. "Southern African Responses to Eastern European Development." *Journal of Modern African Studies* 28, no. 3 (1990).

Ansah-Koi, Kumi. "The Socio-Cultural Matrix and Multi-Party Politics in Ghana: Observations and Prospects." Kwame A. Ninsin and F.K. Drah, eds. *Political Parties and Democracy in Ghana's Fourth's Republic* (Accra, Ghana: Woeli Publishing Services, 1993).

Araya, Mesfin. "The Eritrean Referendum: Political and Social Implications." *Ethiopian Review* (November 1992).

Aurillac, Michel. *L'Afrique à Cœur* (Paris: Berger-Levrault, 1987).

Babangida, Ibrahim. "Laying the Foundation of a Viable Democracy and the Path of Honour." *Newswatch*, 5 July 1993.

Balsvic, Randi. *Haile Selassie's Students: The Intellectual and Social Background To Revolution, 1952–1977* (East Lansing: Michigan State University African Studies Center, 1985).

Baregu, Mwesiga. "The Rise and Fall of the One-Party State in Tanzania." Jennifer Widener, ed. *Economic Change and Political Liberalization in Sub-Saharan Africa* (Baltimore, MD: Johns Hopkins University Press, 1994).

Bates, Robert. "The Economics of Transitions to Democracy." *Political Science and Politics* 24 (March 1991).

——. *Markets and States in Tropical Africa: The Political Bases of Agricultural Policies* (Berkeley, CA: University of California Press, 1981).

Berhanu, Kassahun. "Ethiopia Elects a Constituent Assembly." *Review of African Political Economy* 22, no. 63 (1995).

Berton, George. "Afrique de l'Ouest: Diagnostic d'une Crise." *Croissance* 327 (Mai 1990).

Blangden, Ralph. "The Bill of Rights Today." A. N. Christensen and E. M. Kirkpatrick, eds. *The People, Politics and the Politician* (New York: Henry Holt, 1941).

Bratton, Michael, and Nicholas van de Walle. "Neopatrimonialism and Political Transitions in Sub-Saharan Africa." *World Politics* 46, no. 1 (July 1994).

——. "Popular Protest and Political Reform in Africa." *Comparative Politics* 24, no. 24 (July 1992).

Le Bûcheron (Libreville, Gabon), 6–12 Décembre 1995.

Bulcha, M. *Flight and Integration: Causes of Mass Exodus From Ethiopia and Problems of Integration in the Sudan* (Uppsala, Sweden: Scandinavian Institute of African Studies, 1988).

Bulletin of Tanzanian Affairs (Dar es Saalam, Tanzania) no. 12 (March 1981).

Busia, Kofi. "The Ingredients of Democracy." G. C. Mutiso and S. W. Rohio, eds. *Readings in African Political Thought* (London, UK: Heineman Educational Books, 1986).

Cameroon Tribune (Yaoundé, Cameroon) 11 October 1995.

Carter Center. *African Governance in the 1990s* (Atlanta, GA: Emory University, 1995).

——. *Beyond Autocracy in Africa* (Atlanta, GA: Emory University, 1989).

Chafer, Tony. "French African Policy: Towards Change." *African Affairs* 91 (1991).

Chazan, Naomi, Robert Mortimer, John Ravenhill and Donald Rothchild. *Politics and Society in Contemporary Africa* (Boulder, CO: Lynne Rienner, 1992).

Chipasula, Frank. *When My Brothers Come Home* (Middletown, CT: Wesleyan University Press, 1985).

Chirwa, Chijere. "Regionalism, Ethnicity and the National Question in Malawi." *Sapem* (December 1994–January 1995).

Chole, Eshetu. "Ethiopia's Balance of Payments: 1975–1985." *Journal of Ethiopian Studies* 22 (November 1989).

Clark, John. "Reform or Democratization for Africa?: Troubling Constraints and Partial Solutions." *TransAfrica Forum* 10 no. 1 (Spring 1996).

Cliffe, Lionel. "Democracy in a One-Party State: The Tanzanian Experience." Lionel Cliffe and John S. Saul, eds. *Socialism in Tanzania* (Nairobi: East African Publishing House, 1972).

——. *One-Party Democracy in Tanzania* (Dar es Salaam: East African Publishing House, 1967).

Cohen, James. *Agrarian Reform in Ethiopia: The Situation on the Eve of the Revolution's Tenth Anniversary: Development Discussion Paper No. 164* (Cambridge, MA: Harvard Institute for International Development, 1984).

Committee for Academic Freedom in Africa Newsletter, no. 8 (Spring 1995)

Cullen, Trevor. *Malawi: A Turning Point* (Edinburgh, UK: Pentland Press, 1994).

Dahl, Robert. *Polyarchy* (New Haven, CT: Yale University Press, 1971).

Daily Champion (Lagos, Nigeria), 7 October 1993.

Daily Graphic (Accra, Ghana), 11 December 1996.

——. 9 December 1996.

Daily News of Tanzania (Dar es Salaam), 14 July 1995.

——. 18 July 1990.

——. 22 February 1990.

Daily Times of Malawi, 14 February 1989.

——. 10 February 1989.

Danopoulos, Constantine. *Civilian Rule in the Developing World* (Boulder, CO: Westview Press, 1992).

Decalo, Samuel. "The Process, Prospects and Constraints of Democratization in Africa." *African Affairs* 91 (1992).

Donham, Donald, ed. *The Southern Marches of Imperial Ethiopia: Essays in History and Social Anthropology* (Cambridge, UK: Cambridge University Press, 1986).

Dudley, Billy. *Instability and Political Order: Politics and Crisis in Nigeria* (Ibadan, Nigeria: Ibadan University Press, 1973).

Economist Intelligence Unit. *Country Report: Ghana* (October 1995).

Ekeh, Peter. "Colonialism and the Two Publics in Africa: A Theoretical Statement." *Comparative Studies in Society and History* 17 no. 1 (January 1975).

Ethiopian Herald (Addis Ababa, Ethiopia), 20 May 1995.

Falola, Toyin, ed. *Britain and Nigeria: Exploitation or Development?* (London, UK: Zed Books, 1987).

Fatton, Robert. *The State and Civil Society in Africa* (Boulder, CO: Lynne Rienner, 1992).

Financial Times (London, UK), 24 July 1995.

——. 3 November 1992.

Fortman, Bas de Gaay. "Conceptualizing Democracy in an African Context." *Quest* 8, no. 1 (1994).

Fukuyama, Francis. *The End of History and the Last Man* (New York: Free Press, 1992).

Girard, Michel. *Les Individus dans la Politique Internationale* (Paris: Economica, 1994).

Gros, Jean-Germain. "The Hard Lessons of Cameroon." *Journal of Democracy* 6, no. 3 (July 1995).

Guardian (Dar es Saalam, Tanzania), 11 February 1995.

Guardian (Lagos, Nigeria), 14 September 1995.

——. 18 December 1993.

Gyimah-Boadi, E. "Notes of Ghana's Current Transition to Constitutional Rule." *Africa Today* 38, no. 4 (winter 1991).

Harbeson, John. *The Ethiopian Transformation: The Quest for the Post Imperial State* (Boulder, CO: Westview Press, 1988).

Haynes, Jeff. "The State, Governance and Democracy in Sub Saharan Africa." *Journal of Modern African Studies* 31 no. 3 (1993).

Heilbrunn, John. "Social Origins of National Conferences in Benin and Togo." *Journal of Modern African Studies* 31, no. 2 (1993).

Herald (London, UK), 9 October 1995.

Herbst, Jeffrey. *The Politics of Reform in Ghana, 1982–1991* (Berkeley: University of California Press, 1993).

Hess, Robert. *Ethiopia: The Modernization of Autocracy* (Ithaca, NY: Cornell University Press, 1970)

Hiwot, Addis. "Ethiopia: From Autocracy to Revolution." *Review of African Political Economy* 1 (1975).

Holcomb, Bonnie, and Sisai Ibssa. *The Invention of Ethiopia: The Making of a Dependent Colonial State in North-East Africa* (Trenton, NJ: The Red Sea Press, 1990).

Hutchful, Eboe. "From Revolution to Monetarism: The Economics and Politics of Adjustment Programme in Ghana." Bonnie Campbell and John Loxley, eds. *Structural Adjustment in Africa* (New York: St. Martin's Press, 1989).

Hyden, Goran. "Governance and the Study of Politics." Goran Hyden and Michael Bratton, eds. *Government and Politics in Africa* (Boulder, CO: Lynne Rienner, 1991).

——. *No Shortcuts to Progress* (Berkeley, CA: University of California Press, 1980).

Iane, Peter. *The State of the Tanzanian Economy* (Dar es Salaam, Tanzania: University of Dar es Salaam, Economic Research Bureau, 1984).

Ihonvbere, Julius. "The Military and Political Engineering Under Structural Adjustment: The Nigerian Experience Since 1985." *Journal of Political and Military Sociology* 20 (Summer 1991).

Ihonvbere, Julius, and Toyin Falola. "The Illusion of Economic Development" and "Colonialism and Exploitation." Toyin Falola, ed. *Britain and Nigeria: Exploitation or Development?* (London, UK: Zed Books, 1987).

——. *The Rise and Fall of Nigeria's Second Republic: 1979–1984* (London: Zed Books, 1985).

International Institute for Strategic Studies (IISS). *Military Balance: 1976/77–1982* (Washington, DC, 1982).

Inter Press Service (IPS), 15 October 1995.

Jackson, Robert, and Carl Rosberg. *Personal Rule in Black Africa: Prince, Prophet, Autocrat, Tyrant* (Berkeley, CA: University of California Press, 1982).

Jeffries, Richard, and Clare Thomas. "The Ghanaian Elections of 1992." *African Affairs* 92, no. 92 (July 1993).

Joseph, Richard, "Affluence and Underdevelopment: The Nigerian Experience." *Journal of Modern African Studies* 16, no. 2 (1978).

——. ed. *Gaullist Africa: Cameroon Under Ahmadu Ahidjo* (Emegu, Nigeria: Fourth Dimension Publishers, 1978).

Kegley, Charles, and Eugene Wittkopf. *World Politics* (New York: St. Martin's Press, 1997).

Keller, Edward. "Drought, War and the Politics of Famine in Ethiopia and Eritrea." *Journal of Modern African Studies* 30, no. 4 (1992).

——. *Revolutionary Ethiopia: From Empire to People's Republic* (Bloomington and Indianapolis, IN: Indiana University Press, 1988).

Kendie, Daniel. "Which Way the Horn of Africa: Disintegration or Confederation?" Paper presented at the Sixth Michigan State University Conference on North-East Africa, East Lansing, April 1993.

Kishindo, Pascal. "The Impact of a National Language on Minority Languages: The Case of Malawi." *Journal of Contemporary African Studies* 12, no. 2 (1994).

Kuhlman, Thomas. *Asylum or Aid? The Economic Integration of Ethiopian Refugees in the Sudan* (Leiden, Netherlands: African Studies Center, 1994).

Kurian, George Thomas. *Encyclopedia of the Third World.* 3rd ed. Vol. 1 (New York: Facts on File, 1987).

Lamb, David. *The Africans* (New York: Vintage Books, 1983).

Lefebvre, Jeffrey. *Arms for the Horn: US Security Policy In Ethiopia and Somalia, 1953–1991* (Pittsburgh, PA: University of Pittsburgh Press, 1992).

Legum, Colin, and Geoffrey Mmari, eds. *Mwalimu: The Influence of Nyerere* (Trenton, NJ: Africa World Press, 1995).

LeMarchand, René. "Managing Transition Anarchies." *Journal of Modern African Studies* 32, no. 4 (1994).

Levine, Donald. *Wax and Gold: Tradition and Innovation in Ethiopian Culture* (Chicago, IL: University of Chicago Press, 1965).

Lewis, Arthur. *Politics in West Africa* (London, UK: George Allen and Unwin, 1985).

Macfie, A. L., and D. D. Raphael, eds. *The Theory of Moral Sentiments*, by Adam Smith (Indianapolis, IN: Liberty Fund Inc., 1984).

Mackintosh, John. *Nigerian Government and Politics* (London: Longman, 1985).

Malawi Broadcasting Corporation (MBC), 19 October 1992.

Mapanje, Jack. *The Chattering Wagtails of Mikuyu Prison* (London: Heinemann,1985).

March, James, and Johan Olsen. "The New Institutionalism: Organizational Factors in Political Life." *American Political Science Review* 78 (1984).

Marchés Tropicaux, 2355, 28 Décembre, 1990.

———. 2041, 21 Décembre 1984.

Marcus, Harold. *A History of Ethiopia* (Berkeley: University of California Press, 1994).

Markakis, John. "Ethnic Conflict and the State in the Horn of Africa." K. Fuki and John Markakis, eds. *Ethnicity and Conflict In the Horn of Africa* (London,UK: James Currey, 1994).

———. "Ethnicity and Conflict with Reference to Ethiopia and the Sudan." *Proceedings of the International Conference on the Role of the Social Sciences in Conflict Resolution*, Helsinki, Finland, 1992.

———. *National and Class Conflict in the Horn of Africa* (Cambridge, UK: Cambridge University Press, 1987).

———. *Ethiopia: Anatomy of Traditional Polity* (Oxford, UK: Oxford University Press, 1974).

Markakis, John, and Asmelash Beyene. "Representative Institutions in Ethiopia." *Journal of Modern African Studies* 5, no. 2 (1967).

Marx, Karl. "The Eighteenth Brumaire of Louis Bonaparte." Robert C. Tucker, ed. *The Marx-Engels Reader* (New York: W.W. Norton, 1972).

Mazrui, Ali. *Soldiers and Kinsmen in Uganda: The Making of Military Ethnocracy* (Beverly Hills, CA: Sage, 1975).

Mbarga, Ndi. *Ruptures et Continuité au Cameroon* (Paris: l'Harmattan, 1993).

Mbuyinga, Elenga. *Tribalisme et Problème National en Afrique Noire: Le Cas du Kamerun* (Paris: l'Harmattan, 1989).

McHenry, Dean. *Limited Choices* (Boulder, CO: Lynne Rienner, 1994).

McMahon, Edward. "African Elections." *The Democratic Challenge in Africa, Working Papers Series* (Atlanta, GA: The Carter Center of Emory University, 13–14 May 1994).

McMaster, Carolyn. *Malawi: Foreign Policy and Development* (London, UK: Julian Friedman, 1974).

Mentan, Tatah. "Press and National Liberation: Historical and Contemporary Cameroon Perspectives." Unpublished, 1993. Send inquiries to Tatah Mentan, P. O. Box 1328, Yaoundé, Cameroon, Central Africa.

Merera, Gudina. "The Ethiopian Transition From Military Autocracy to Popular Democracy: Some Major Issues for Consideration in Crossing the Crossroads." *UFAHAMU* 22, nos. 1 and 2 (1995).

Le Messager (Yaoundé, Cameroon), 12 June 1992.

Mhone, Guy. "The Political Economy of Malawi: An Overview." Guy Mhone, ed. *Malawi at the Crossroads: The Post-Colonial Political Economy* (Harare, Zimbabwe: SAPES Books, 1992).

Mitterrand, François. "Présence française et abandon." *Tribune Libre* 12 (1957).

Monga, Célestin. *The Anthropology of Anger: Civil Society and Democracy in Africa* (Boulder, CO: Lynne Rienner, 1996).

Mukong, Albert. *Prisoner Without a Crime* (Limbe, Cameroon: Alfresco, 1985).

Naanen, Ben. "Oil Producing Minorities and the Restructuring of Nigerian Federalism: The Case of the Ogoni People." *Journal of Commonwealth and Comparative Politics* 33, no. 1 (1995).

National Democratic Institute for International Affairs. *Democratization in Cameroon International Delegation Report* (Washington, DC: National Democratic Institute for International Affairs, 1991).

National Electoral Commission. *Parliamentary Election Official Results, and Presidential Election Official Results* (Dar es Salaam, Tanzania: NEC HQ, 1995).

Ndzeng, Samuel Ntoutoume. *Le Procés du Conflit des Lois et des Vides Juridiques en Afrique Francophone après l'Instauration du Multipartisme: Gabon-Loi N¼ 4/91 du 3 avril 1991 Relative aux Partis Politiques* (Libreville, Gabon: Collection Gabonaise ANZAL, 1991).

New Nigerian, 8 January 1993.

New York Times, 11 January 1997.

——. 2 March 1996.

——. 1 December 1995.

Ngniman, Z. *Cameroun: La Démocratie Emballée* (Yaoundé, Cameroon: Clé, 1993).

Ninsin, Kwam. "Some Problems in Ghana's Transition to Democratic Governance." *African Development* 18, no. 2 (1993).

Nnoli, Okwundiba. *Introduction to Politics* (Essex, UK: Longman Group, 1986).

Nolutshungu, Sam. "Fragments of a Democracy: Reflections on Class and Politics in Nigeria." *Third World Quarterly* 12, no. 1 (1990).

Ntalaja, N. "The National Question and the Crisis of Instability in Africa." Emmanuel Hansen, ed. *Africa Perspectives on Peace and Development* (London, UK and Atlantic Highlands, NJ: Zed Books, 1987).

Nweta, Nimi. "Cracks Emerge as CCM Presidential Nomination Nears." *The East African*, 7–23 July 1 1995.

Nyerere, Julius K. *Freedom and Development: A Selection from Writings and Speeches 1968–1978* (Oxford, UK: Oxford University Press, 1973).

——. "The Arusha Declaration." In *Freedom and Socialism* (Oxford, UK and Dar es Salaam, Tanzania: Oxford University Press, 1968).

——. "Democracy and the Party System." In *Freedom and Unity: Uhuru na Umoja* (Oxford, UK: Oxford University Press, 1967).

Nzouankeu, Jacques Mariel. "The Role of the National Conference in the Transition to Democracy in Africa: The Cases of Benin and Mali." *Issue* 21 (1993).

O'Donnell, Guillermo, Philippe Schmitter, and Lawrence Whitehead, eds. *Transitions from Authoritarian Rule: Prospects for Democracy* (Baltimore, MD: Johns Hopkins University Press, 1986).

Ofori, Ruby. "Rawling's Challenge." *Africa Report* 39, no. 3 (May–June 1994).

Oquaye, Michael. "The Ghanaian Elections of 1992—A Dissenting View." *African Affairs* 94 (1995).

——. "Human Rights and the Transition to Democracy under the PNDC in Ghana." *Human Rights Quarterly* 17, no. 3 (August 1995).

Panford, Kwamina. "IMF/World Bank's Structural Adjustment Policies, Labour and Industrial Relations and Employment in Ghana." *African Development Perspectives Yearbook 1994/95.* Vol. 4 (New Brunswick, NJ: Transaction Publishers,1996).

——. "Structural Adjustment, the State and Workers in Ghana." *Africa Development* 19, no. 2 (1994).

Panter-Brick, Samuel, *Soldiers and Oil: The Political Transformation of Nigeria* (London, UK: Frank Cass, 1978).

——. ed. *Nigerian Politics and Military Rule* (London, UK: Athlone, 1970).

Péan, Pierre. "Le Gabon à l'heure du pétrole." *Jeune Afrique*, 27 Juin 1975.

Picket, J. "The Ethiopian Economy." In *Africa South of the Sahara*, 24th ed. (London: European Publishers, 1995).

Pratt, Cranford. *The Critical Phase in Tanzania, 1945–1968* (Cambridge, UK: Cambridge University Press, 1976).

Przeworski, Adam. "Some Problems in the Study of the Transition to Democracy." Guillermo O'Donnell, Phillippe Schmitter, and Laurence Whitehead, eds. *Transitions from Authoritarian Rule: Comparative Perspectives* (Baltimore, MD: Johns Hopkins University Press, 1986).

Pye, Lucian. "Communications and Political Articulation." Lucian Pye, ed. *Communications and Political Development* (Princeton, NJ: Princeton University Press, 1963).

Reed, Michael. "Gabon: A Neo-Colonial Enclave of Enduring French Interest." *Journal of Modern African Studies* 25, no. 2 (1987).

Relief and Rehabilitation Commission (PMAC). *Regional Vulnerability Profile Report to Donors' Meeting* (Addis Ababa: Ethiopia, 1985).

République Gabonaise. *Tableau de Bord de l'Economie: Situation 1994, Perspectives 1995* (Libreville, Gabon: Direction Générale de l'Economie, 1995).

Research and Action Group For Peace in Ethiopia and the Horn of Africa (RAGPEHA). *ADDIS DIGEST,* nos. 6–7 (September–October 1995).

Robinson, Pearl. "Democratization: Understanding the Relationship between Regime Change and the Culture of Politics." *African Studies Review* 37, no. 1 (April 1994).

Rotimi, Ola Ajayi, and Julius Ihonvbere. "Democratic Impasse: Remilitarization in Nigeria." *Third World Quarterly* 15, no. 4 (1994).

Rovinski, Samuel. *Cultural Policy in Costa Rica* (Paris: UNESCO, 1991).

Rueschemeyer, Dietrich et al. *Capitalist Development and Democracy* (Chicago, IL: University of Chicago Press, 1992).

Rustow, Dankwart. "Transition to Democracy." *Comparative Politics* 2, no. 3 (1970).

Samoff, Joel. "Single-Party Competitive Elections in Tanzania." Fred Hayward, ed. *Elections in Independent Africa* (Boulder, CO: Westview Press, 1987).

Saro-Wiwa, Ken. *Genocide in Nigeria* (London, UK and Port Harcourt, Nigeria: Saros International, 1994).

Schmitter, Philippe. "Society." *The Transition to Democracy: Proceedings of a Workshop.* Commission on Behavioral and Social Sciences and Education, National Research Council (Washington, DC: National Academy Press, 1991).

Seidman, Ann, and Robert Seidman. *State and Law in the Development Process: Problem Solving and Institutional Change in the Third World* (New York: St. Martin's Press, 1994).

Seymour, Martin Lipset. "Some Social Requisites of Democracies." *American Political Science Review,* 53 (1994).

Shillington, Kevin. *Ghana and the Rawlings Factor* (New York: St. Martin's Press, 1992).

Shivji, Issa. *Class Struggles in Tanzania* (Dar es Salaam, Tanzania: Tanzania Publishing House, 1976).

Short, Philip. *Banda* (London: Routledge and Kegan Paul, 1974).

Sorensen, Georg. *Democracy and Democratization* (Boulder, CO: Westview Press, 1993).

Susungi, Nfor N. *The Crisis of Unity and Democracy in Cameroon* (Abidjan, Ivory Coast: 1991).

Tadesse, Kiflu. *The Generation* (Silver Spring, MD: Independent Publishers, 1993).

Tamrat, Tadesse. *Church and State in Ethiopia: 1270–1527* (Oxford, UK: Oxford University Press, 1972).

Tareke, Gebru. *Ethiopia: Power and Protest: Peasant Revolts in the Twentieth Century* (Cambridge, UK: Cambridge University Press, 1991).

Taylor, Charles. *Hegel and Modern Society* (Cambridge, UK: Cambridge University Press, 1979).

Tegegn, Melakou. "Eritrea: Evolution Towards Independence and Beyond." Abebe Zegeye and Siegfried Pausewang, eds. *Ethiopia in Change* (London: British Academic Press, 1994).

Teka, Tegegne. "Cooperatives and National Development: The Ethiopian Experience." *Institute of Development Research Working Paper,* no. 18 (Addis Ababa, Ethiopia: Institute of Development Research, 1984).

Tekle, Amare. "The New Constitution of Ethiopia." *Journal of African Studies* 15, nos. 3–4 (1988).

Tell (Lagos, Nigeria), 18 December 1995.

———. 13 November 1995.

———. 6 December 1993.

TEMCO. *Report of Tanzania Election Monitoring Committee on the October 1995 Legislative and Presidential Elections* (Dar es Salaam, Tanzania: University of Dar es Salaam, 1995).

Thomson, Blair. *Ethiopia: The Country That Cut Off Its Head* (London, UK: Robson Books, 1975).

Tibebu, Teshale. *The Making of Modern Ethiopia* (Lawrenceville, NJ: The Red Sea Press, 1995).

Tiruneh, Fentahun. *The Ethiopian Students: The Struggle to Articulate the Ethiopian Revolution* (Chicago, IL: Nyala Type, 1990).

Tocqueville, Alexis de. *Democracy in America* (New York: Knoph, 1945).

Turner, Jonathan. *The Structure of Sociological Theory* (Homewood, IL: Dorsey Press, 1974).

Turner, Terisa. "Nigeria." John Dunn, ed. *West African States: Failure and Promise* (Cambridge, UK: Cambridge University Press, 1978).

Turok, Benjamen. "What Does the World Bank Mean by Empowering Ordinary People?" *The African Response: Adjustment or Transformation.* Proceeding of the Institute for African Alternatives, Addis Ababa, Ethiopia, 1992.

Udogu, Emmanuel Ike. "The Allurement of Ethnonationalism in Nigerian Politics: The Contemporary Debate." *Journal of Asian and African Studies* 29, no. 34 (1994).

——. "National Integration Attempts in Nigerian Politics." *Canadian Review of Studies in Nationalism* 27 (1990).

Ullendorf, Edward. *The Ethiopians: An Introduction to Country and People* (Oxford, UK: Oxford University Press, 1973).

Underrepresented Nations and Peoples Organization (UNPO). *Ogoni* (The Hague, Netherlands: UNPO, 1995).

Union (Libreville, Gabon). 25 Février 1993.

——. 28–29 Juillet, 1992.

United Republic of Tanzazania. *Report and Recommendations of the Commission on the Democratic System Tanzania.* Vol. 1 (Dar es Salaam, Tanzania: Dar es Salaam University Press, 1991).

United States Agency for International Development (USAID). *The Transition to Democratic Governance in Tanzania: An Assessment and Guidelines for Near-Term Action.* Contract No. AFR-0542-Q-00-1109-00. ARD and MSI for USAID, 1994.

Uwazurike, P. Chudi. "Confronting Potential Breakdown in Africa: The Nigerian Re-Democratization Process in Critical Perspective. " *Journal of Modern African Studies* 28, no. 1 (1990).

Vail, Leroy, and Lan White. "Tribalism in the Political History of Malawi." Leroy Vail, ed. *The Creation of Tribalism in Southern Africa* (London, UK: James Curry, 1989).

Van de Walle, Nicolas. "Political Liberalization and Economic Reform in Africa." *World Development* 22, no. 4 (April 1994).

Wall Street Journal, 10 December 1996.

Weatherby, Joseph. "The Old and New: Colonialism, Neocolonialism and Nationalism." Joseph Weatherby et al., eds. *The Other World* (White Plains, NY: Longman, 1994).

West Africa, 1–7 February 1993.

Widener, Jennifer, ed. *Political Liberalization in Africa* (Baltimore, MD: Johns Hopkins University Press, 1991).

Williams, Gavin, ed. *Nigeria: Economy and Society* (London, UK: Rex Collings, 1976).

Wiseman, John. *The New Struggle for Democracy in Africa* (Brookfield, VT: Aldershot, 1996).

——. *Democracy in Black Africa* (New York: Paragon Publishers, 1990).

Wittkopf, Eugene. *Trend and Transformation.* 6th ed. (New York: St. Martin's Press, 1997).

World Bank. *World Development Report* (Washington, DC: World Bank, 1993).

——. *Sub-Saharan Africa: From Crisis to Sustainable Growth* (Washington, DC: World Bank, 1989).

Yankah, Kojo. *The Trial of J. J. Rawlings: Echoes of the 31st December Revolution* (Accra, Ghana: Ghana Publishing Corporation, Tema, 1986).

Yembe, Omer. "Ethnic Diversity and Administration." *Ethnie et Développement* (Yaoundé, Cameroon: CRAC, 1994).

Zewde, Bahru. "Haile Selassie: From Progressive to Reactionary." Paper presented at the Sixth Michigan State University Conference on North-East Africa, East Lansing, Michigan, 23–25 April 1992.

Index

Abacha, Sani, 16, 59, 66–68, 71, 73
Abessolo, Paul Mba, 135, 136–37, 139
Abiola, Alhaja Kudirat, 67
Abiola, Moshood, 62, 64, 67
Abubakar, Abdulsalam, 73
Acheampong, I. K., 116
ADMARC. *See* Agricultural Development and Marketing Council
AFORD. *See* Alliance for Democracy
AFRC. *See* Armed Forces Ruling Council
African Fabian socialism, 18
Agricultural Development and Marketing Council, 25
Ajasin, Michael, 66
Akerele, Kofoworola, 66
Akinyemi, Bolaii, 66
Akirinade, Alani, 67
Alliance for Change in Cameroon through a Sovereign National Conference, 46
Alliance for Democracy, 32, 36–37
Almond, Gabriel A., 42, 48
Amour, Salmin, 105
Angola, 7
ARC-CNS. *See* Alliance for Change in Cameroon through a Sovereign National Conference
Arkaah, K. N., 119–20
Armed Forces Ruling Council, 64

Aubame, Jean-Hilaire, 134
Authoritarianism, 43
Autocracy, 9, 17

Babangida, Ibrahim, 63, 64–65, 66, 74 n.18
Badey, Albert, 70
Bahru, Zewde, 90–91
Banda, Hastings Kamuzu: and the army, 10; Bandastan, 1, 38 n.1; collapse of regime, 31–36, 37; education, 22–23; ideology, 17; leadership type, 23–24; and the media, 31; opposition to, 29; personal collapse, 39; and women, 38 n.7
Baregu, Mwesiga, 102
Basil, Emah, 44–45
Bates, Robert H., 130
Bédié, Henri Konan, 8
Berhanu, Kassahun, 17
Biya, Paul: brand of democracy, 42–43; and civil administrators, 52–53; and constitutional rights, 48–49; and economy, 8; and ethnic and regional differences, 47, 50–51; French support, 53–54; and international community, 13; military force, 51; resistance to reform, 44–46; as successor to Ahidjo, 41
Black, Yondo, 11, 44

Blangden, Ralph, 49
Boahen, Adu, 113, 116
Boateng, D. S., 119
Boesak, Alan, 28
Bongo, Ali Ben, 136
Bongo, Omar, 5, 16; and communication
   technology, 135; and international
   community, 13; leadership type, 5, 7,
   16; military control, 141; and multi-
   party election, 139–41; and national
   conference, 138; as oligarchic patri-
   monialist, 143–44; opposition against,
   134–37
Bongoism, 11, 136
Bosumtwi-Sam, Albert, 119
Bratton, Michael, 19, 137
Bulcha, Mark, 79
Bwanausi, Augustine, 23
Bwezani, operation, 35–36

Cameroon: ARC-CNS, 46; citizenship,
   47–48; CPDM, 11, 43, 44–45, 49, 51;
   economics, 43, 49–50; generals, 52
   (table); multiparty legalization, 44–45;
   NCOPA, 45; patrimonial administra-
   tion, 51–52; transition to democratiza-
   tion, 42–44, 47, 54–56; UNDP, 46
Cameroon People's Democratic Move-
   ment, 11, 43, 44–45, 49, 51
Campaign for Democracy, 65, 74 n.20
Catholic Church, 14, 30
CCM, 101, 102–10, 112 n.30
CD. *See* Campaign for Democracy
Chakuamba, Gwanda, 34, 35
Chama Cha Mapinduzi. See CCM
Chambas, Ibn, 119
Chihana, Chakufwa, 32, 36, 37
Chilembwe, John, 21
Chiluba, Frederick, 6, 19
Chipembere, Henry, 32
Chirac, Jacques, 13
Chirwa, Orton, 23, 27
Chirwa, Robson, 35
Chisiza, Yatuta, 26
Chiume, Kanyama, 23
Chiwanga, David, 29
Chokani, Willie, 23
Chomsky, Noam, 39 n.11
Churches, 14, 29–31
Civic United Front, 104

Civil society: definition, 10; influence,
   14, 16, 37–38; institutions, 11–12,
   38
Cold War, 3, 13, 20 n.19, 116–17, 133
Coleman, James, 42
Constitutional Review Committee, 63
Consumerism, 130
CPDM. *See* Cameroon People's Demo-
   cratic Movement
CRC. *See* Constitutional Review Com-
   mittee
CUF. *See* Civic United Front

Democracy: definition, 19 n.2; development, 2; ideological debates, 41–42;
   taxonomy, 19–20 n.7; transition to,
   113; universalization and conventionalization, 42
Democratization: and multiparty politics,
   131; and national wealth, 129; perspectives, 4, 19–20 n.7
Democratizers, 4–7
Derg, 83, 84
Diffusionists, 20 n.19
Djam, Oumarou, 45
Dos Santos, José Eduardo, 6, 7

Economics, 8, 9, 132–33
Ekey, Peter P., 130
Enahoro, Anthony, 66, 67
Eritrean separatist movements, 84
Ethiopia: Bonapartism in, 84; civil society purges, 84–85; civil war, 87–88;
   economics, 86–87; elite politics, 80;
   ethnic self-government, 90–92; fam-
   ine, 82, 87; history, 78–79; and
   Marxist-Leninist ideology, 6–7, 17,
   83; Mengistu regime, 87–88; peasant
   agriculture, 85–86; PMAC, 83; post-
   revolution accomplishments, 83; revolution, 82; Selassie reign, 80–82. *See
   also* Ethiopian Student Movement;
   Mariam, Mengistu Haile; Transitional
   Government of Ethiopia
Ethiopian People's Revolutionary Democratic Front, 17, 77, 88–90
Ethiopian Student Movement, 81–82
Ethnic federalism, 7, 18, 90–92
Ethnicity, 14, 17, 18, 26. *See also* Ogoni
   crisis

Falana, Femi, 63
Farmers associations, 11
Fochive, Jean, 45
Francophone Africa, 12, 43, 142–43
Free-market ideology, 24
Front Uni des Associations et Partis de l'Opposition, 139
Fru Ndi, John, 44, 51
FUAPO. See *Front Uni des Associations et Partis de l'Opposition*
Funding, external, 12, 13–14, 116–17, 122, 127 n.18

Gabon: Franco-Gabonese relations, 142; history, 133–34; multipartyism, 137, 139–40. *See also* Bongo, Omar
Gadama, Aaron, 29
Ghana: chronology of events, 118 (table); chronology of governments, 115 (table); civil rights, 123–24; economics, 125; election results, 119 (table), 120 (table), 121 (table); multipartyism, 114–18; Western influence on, 116–17. *See also* Rawlings, Jerry
Globalization, 15, 20 n.19, 133
Goudjout, Paul Indjenjet, 134
Groupe Spécial d'Opération (GSO), 51

Habre, Hussein, 43
Habyarimana, Juvénal, 7
Haile Selassie I, 80–82
Haman, Garga, 51
Harbeson, John, 80
Hiwot, Addis, 79–80
Hyden, Goran, 19, 101

ICDA. *See* Interim Committee for Democratic Alliance
Ihonvbere, Julius O., 16
Individual leadership, 4, 112 n.28
Institutionalism, 131, 135
Institutions: and civil society, 11–12, 14; importance of, 8; professional, 11; religious, 11; resistance to change, 16
Interim Committee for Democratic Alliance, 32
International community: and democratization, 9, 14–15, 17, 116–17; and multipartyism, 12; and neocolonialism, 132, 143; and political reform, 13; provision of funding, 13–14; resources of, 16

Jehovah's Witnesses, 28
John Paul II, 31
Joseph, Richard, 54
Journalism, 27

Kadzamira, Cecilia Tamanda, 21
Kamuzu Academy, 25, 39 n.9
Kamuzuism, 34
KANU. *See* Kenya African National Union
Kaunda, Kenneth, 5, 9, 18
Kenya African National Union, 13
Kenyatta, Jomo, 23
Kerekou, Mathieu, 6, 9
Khama, Seretse, 5
Kobani, Edward, 70

Land Reform Act of 1975, 83
Land Use Decree, 68
Leadership, 4, 16
LESOMA. *See* Socialist League of Malawi
Levels of analysis, 15, 16
Lewis, W. Arthur, 41
Liberalization, 2, 3, 5, 18
Limann, Hilla, 114
Lipset, Seymour Martin, 8
Lissouba, Pascal, 5–6, 19
Litumbe, Njoh, 51
Living Our Faith, 30

MAFREMO. *See* Malawi Freedom Movement
Malawi: agriculture, 25; and bordering countries, 26–27; and the church, 29–31; ethnic diversity, 26, 32, 36–37; government suppression, 24, 27–31; Kamuzu Academy, 25, 39 n.9; neopatrimonial administration, 24; post-World War II, 22; pro-Western policies, 25; and regional polarization, 36–37; SAMACO, 29; University of, 28; youth league, 24. *See also* Alliance for Democracy; Banda, Hastings Kamuzu; Interim Committee for Democratic Alliance
Malawi Congress Party, 23

Malawi Freedom Movement, 27
Malawi Women's League, 24
Malawi Youth Pioneers, 24, 34, 35
Mamboundou, Pierre, 135
Mandela, Nelson, 5, 71
Mandja, Flight Lieutenant, 135
Mapanje, Jack, 29
Marcel, Mbow Zanga, 52
Marcus, Harold, 82
Mariam, Mengistu Haile, 77, 84–85
Markakis, John, 78, 79–80
Matenje, Dick, 29
Matrilineal system, 24
M'ba, Leon, 134
Mbida, Andre-Marie, 50
Mboumboou-Miyakou, Antoine, 139
Mbuyinga, Elenga, 55
MCP. *See* Malawi Congress Party
Menelik II, 79, 80
Mentan, Tatah, 10
Merera, Gudina, 88
Mhone, Guy, 38 nn. 2, 8
Mikuyu Detention Camp, 29
Military, 9, 16, 134
Mitterand, François, 12, 43, 143
Mkapa, Benjamin, 105, 106
Modernization theory school, 8
Moi, Daniel Arap, 7, 11, 13, 18
MORENA, 134
MOSOP. *See* Movement for the Survival of Ogoni People
Mourides, 11
Mouvement de Redressement National (MORENA), 134–35
Movement for the Survival of Ogoni People, 69–71, 75 n.24
Mozambique, 17
Mpakati, Attati, 27
MPLA. *See* Popular Movement for the Liberation of Angola
Msuya, Cleopa, 105
Mukong, Albert, 48
Multiparty elections, 4, 6, 107, 131–32, 140
Multipartyism, 3, 5, 18
Muluzi, Bakili, 33, 36, 37
Munthali, Suzgo, 28
Muzorewa, Abel, 28
Mwini, Ali Hassan, 8, 104, 105
MYF. *See* Malawi Youth Pioneers

NAC. *See* Nyasaland African Congress
NADECO. *See* National Democratic Coalition
National Coordination of Opposition Parties and Associations, 45
National Democratic Coalition, 66–67
National Democratic Institute of America, 46
National Union for Democracy and Progress, 46, 49
National Union for the Total Liberation of Angola, 7, 25
National Youth Council of Ogoni People, 69–72
NCOPA. *See* National Coordination of Opposition Parties and Associations
Ndi, John Fru. *See* Fru Ndi, John
Negative campaigning, 36–37
Neoautocrats, 6
Neopatrimonialists, 3, 8, 24
Ngniman, Z., 55
Nguesso, Denis Sassou, 9
Niger, 15
Nigeria: AFRC, 64; CD, 65, 74; and civil society, 65–66, 72; elite political parties, 62–64; and foreign sanctions, 71; history, 59–60; interim national government, 65, 74 n.18; military role, 59–62, 64–65, 66, 73; NADECO, 66; political development, 61–62; SDP, 64; Third Republic, 62–63. *See also* Abacha, Sani
Ninsin, Kwame, 113
Nkomo, Joshua, 28
Nkrumah, Kwame, 23
Nyasaland African Congress, 23
NYCOP. *See* National Youth Council of Ogoni People
Nyerere, Julius K.: and multipartyism, 18, 99, 102–5; political and personal success, 16, 109–10; political philosophy, 97–100
Nyingone, Pauline, 139

OAU. *See* Organization of African Unity
Obame, Mba, 136
Obasanjo, Olasegun, 73
Obiorah, Ralph, 66, 67
Ogoni crisis, 68–71, 75 n.24
Okuntimo, Paul, 70

Okwudiba, Nnoli, 47
Olorunomi, Dapo, 67
Olympio, S., 47
Onagoruwa, Olu, 67
One-partyism, 5, 18
Operation Bwezani, 35–36
Opportunistic democratizers, 5–6. *See also* Neoautocrats
Oquaye, Michael, 113, 116, 126
Orage, Samuel, 70
Orage, Theophilus, 70
Organization of African Unity, 25

Panford, Kwamina, 126
Pasqua, Charles, 45
Patassé, Ange Félix, 5, 19
Paul VI, 30
Peasant and Urban Dwellers' Associations, 83
Perot, Ross, 74 n.11
Pluralism, 3
PMAC. *See* Provisional Military Administrative Council
PNDC, 114, 116, 122, 126 n.5
Political compact, 8
Political culture, 2
Political liberalization, 2, 3, 5, 18
Political society, 16
Popular Movement for the Liberation of Angola, 7, 25
Power alternation, 2
Provisional Military Administrative Council, 83, 84
Provisional National Defense Council (PNDC), 114, 116, 122, 126 n.5

Rational choice theory, 131
Rawlings, Jerry: and AFRC, 114; as born-again democratizer, 6; and farmers, 11; influence on politics in Ghana, 116–18; and international community, 16, 117, 126 n.11; and PNDC, 114; "Rawlings Factor," 121–22
Reagan, Ronald, 31
Rejambe, 137
Religion, 29–31
Resource endowments, 17
Resources, 14, 17, 131, 141
Rewane, Alfred, 67

Rovinski, Samuel, 44
Rule of law, 2
Rustow, Dankwart, 48
Rwanda, 7, 14

SAMACO. *See* Save Malawi Council
Sangala, Twaibu, 29
Saro-Wiwa, Ken, 68–69, 70–71
SATUCC, Southern Africa Trade Union Coordination Council
Save Malawi Council, 29
Savimbi, Jonas, 7, 25
SDF. *See* Social Democratic Front
SDP. *See* Social Democratic Party
Seko, Mobutu Sese, 7, 104
Selassie. *See* Haile Selassie I
Senegal, 5, 11, 18
Senghor, Leopold, 5
Shell Oil, 68
Shivji, Issa, 101
Shonekan, Ernest, 65
Sierra Leone, 15, 17
Sithole, Ndabaningi, 28
Smith, Adam, 10
Social Democratic Front, 44, 46, 55
Social Democratic Party, 64
Socialist League of Malawi, 27
Societal pressure, 4, 11, 15
Socioeconomic compact, 8
Somalia, 11
South Africa, 3, 8
Southern Africa Trade Union Coordination Council, 32
Soyinka, Wole, 47, 67
State of rights, 3
State-society relations, 2, 3
Structural Adjustment Programs, 15
Suleiman, Dan, 66
Sunjo, Nganso, 45
Susungi, N. N., 55

Talib, Abou, 106
Tanganyika African National Union, 98–101, 103
TANU. *See* Tanganyika African National Union
Tanzania: election results, 107 (table), 108 (table); and familyhood, 101–2; multipartyism, 102, 111 n.21; and socialism, 18, 97–100. *See also* Nyerere,

Julius K.; Tanganyika African Na-
    tional Union
Tembo, John, 21, 29, 34–35
TGE. *See* Transitional Government of
    Ethiopia
Tocqueville, Alexis de, 10
Tofa, Bashir, 62, 64
Togo, 7
Transitional Government of Ethiopia,
    88–89
Tunubu, Bola, 66
Tutu, Desmond, 28

UDF. *See* United Democratic Front
Ujamaa vijijini, 101
Ukiwe, Ebitu, 66
UNDP. *See* National Union for Democ-
    racy and Progress
Union Progressiste Sénégalais, 5
UNITA. *See* National Union for the To-
    tal Liberation of Angola

United Democratic Front, 32–33, 36–37
United States, 13, 74 n.11
UPS. *See Union Progressiste Séné-
    galais*

Valentine, Ndi Mbarga, 55
Van de Walle, Nicholas, 137
Verba, S., 48

Williams, Gavin, 54
World Bank, 12, 27, 116, 117
World War II, 21

Yar'Adua, Sheu, 65
Yembe, Omer, 44
Youmba, Jean-René, 45

Zaire, 7, 8
Zambia, 5, 6, 9, 18, 19
Zenawi, Meles, 6
Zimbabwe, 26

About the Contributors

KASSAHUN BERHANU is a lecturer in political science at Addis Ababa University, Ethiopia.

JEAN-GERMAIN GROS is assistant professor of political science and public policy administration and Center for International Studies fellow at the University of Missouri in St. Louis.

JULIUS O. IHONVBERE joined the Ford Foundation in 1997. Prior to that he was associate professor of government at the University of Texas in Austin.

SAM A. MCHOMBO is associate professor of linguistics at the University of California at Berkeley.

TATAH MENTAN teaches at the Advanced School of Mass Communications, University of Yaoundé, Cameroon. He was at Radio Cameroon (now Cameroon Radio and Television, CRTV) from 1968 to 1972 and 1975 to 1979.

NELSON N. MESSONE is at Omar Bongo University and the Gabon Institute of Economics and Finance. Both institutions are in Libreville, Gabon.

KWAMINA PANFORD is interim chair of the African-American studies department at Northeastern University in Boston, Massachusetts.

ISBN 0-313-30793-8

90000>

EAN

9 780313 307935

HARDCOVER BAR CODE